MW00813793

"Like so many writers, especially theorists, Judith Butler's early work has created a disproportionate sort of gravitational pull—a force that exceeds not only Butler's early intentions but also, perhaps, her later wishes. Since at least the late 90s Butler has been writing about so much more than gender, and yet her increasing fame still remains tethered to notions such as performativity and drag. Schippers may be the first author to take Butler's later writings seriously *on their own terms. The Political Philosophy of Judith Butler* reads Butler as a widely-ranging political philosopher and as a public intellectual and it mines Butler's later writings for their concepts of livability and relationality, thereby showing the significance of Butler's broader project to debates in global politics and international ethics. In so doing, Schippers makes a crucial contribution not just to Butler scholarship but to international political theory."

—Samuel A. Chambers, *Johns Hopkins University*

"This fresh and insightful study of Judith Butler focuses on her writings from 2001 onwards. Centered on an exploration of the ideas of relationally, ekstasis, dispossession and liveability, *The Political Philosophy of Judith Butler* seeks to assess Butler's contribution to international political philosophy and post-9/11 public discourse. Lucidly written, precise, and original in scope, this engaging and timely book will be of interest not only to readers new to Butler's writings but also to Butler scholars as well."

—Moya Lloyd, *Loughborough University*

"Schippers tackles Butler post-*Gender Trouble* and post-9/11, linking performativity to liveability, and to the other ethical concepts through which Butler actively engages the global politics of violent conflict and military intervention. *The Political Philosophy of Judith Butler* presents her as a brave and controversial public intellectual, unafraid of character smears and partisan outrage, giving the lie to Nussbaum's charge that her philosophy made her the 'professor of parody'. This book presents Butler as a key reference point for the scholarly study of global politics."

—Terrell Carver, *University of Bristol*

The Political Philosophy of Judith Butler

Judith Butler can justifiably be described as one of the major critical thinkers of our time. While she is best known for her interventions in feminist debates on gender, sexuality, and feminist politics, her focus in recent years has broadened to encompass some of the most pertinent topics of interest to contemporary political philosophy.

Drawing on Butler's deconstructive reading of the key categories and concepts of political thought, Birgit Schippers expounds and advocates her challenge to the conceptual binaries that pervade modern political discourse. Using examples and case studies like the West's intervention in Iraq and Afghanistan and the Israeli-Palestinian conflict, Schippers demonstrates how Butler's philosophically informed engagement with pressing political issues of our time elucidates our understanding of topics such as immigration and multiculturalism, sovereignty, and the prospect for new forms of cohabitation and citizenship beyond and across national boundaries.

A detailed exposition and analysis of Butler's recent ideas, championing her efforts at articulating the possibilities for radical politics and ethical life in an era of global interdependence, this book makes an important contribution to the emerging field of international political philosophy.

Birgit Schippers is a Senior Lecturer in Politics at St Mary's University College Belfast, UK. Her areas of interest include French feminism, citizenship, identity politics, and post-structural and psychoanalytic models of politics.

Routledge Innovations in Political Theory

For a full list of titles in this series, please visit www.routledge.com

The Political Philosophy of Judith Butler

Birgit Schippers

Routledge
Taylor & Francis Group

LONDON AND NEW YORK

First published 2014 by Routledge

2 Park Square, Milton Park, Abingdon, Oxon OX14 4RN
711 Third Avenue, New York, NY 10017, USA

Routledge is an imprint of the Taylor & Francis Group, an informa business

First issued in paperback 2016

Copyright © 2014 Taylor & Francis

The right of Birgit Schippers to be identified as author of this work
has been asserted by her in accordance with sections 77 and 78 of the
Copyright, Designs and Patents Act 1988.

All rights reserved. No part of this book may be reprinted or reproduced or
utilised in any form or by any electronic, mechanical, or other means, now
known or hereafter invented, including photocopying and recording, or in
any information storage or retrieval system, without permission in writing
from the publishers.

Notice:
Product or corporate names may be trademarks or registered trademarks,
and are used only for identification and explanation without intent to infringe.

Library of Congress Cataloging-in-Publication Data

Schippers, Birgit.
The political philosophy of Judith Butler / by Birgit Schippers.
    pages cm. — (Routledge innovations in political theory ; 57)
  1. Butler, Judith, 1956– 2. Political science—Philosophy.
3. International relations—Philosophy. I. Title.
  JA71.S2794 2014
  320.01—dc23
  2013050049

ISBN 978-0-415-52212-0 (hbk)
ISBN 978-1-138-69640-2 (pbk)

Typeset in Sabon
by Apex CoVantage, LLC

For Tom

Contents

Acknowledgements

My encounter with Butler's ideas began as part of a PhD project, and I wish to express my sincere gratitude to my supervisor, Moya Lloyd, for engaging my interest in Butler's work. For their encouragement and support at various stages of this project I would like to thank Vincent Geoghegan, Ivor Hickey, Damian Knipe, Gerard McCann, Gabrielle NigUidhir, John Thompson, and Angela Vaupel. Thanks are also due to Darcy Bullock and Natalja Mortensen from Routledge. I wish to acknowledge financial support received from the Research Office at St Mary's University College Belfast, facilitating my participation at several research conferences and visits to the British Library. Staff at the British Library Humanities reading room were, as always, enormously helpful in sourcing material I needed for my research. I am continually grateful for the support I get from Sara Leopold from St Mary's University College Library; her ability to track material in the shortest time possible is second to none! Portions of this book have been presented at various conferences and seminars, and I would like to note my thanks to audiences and participants at the following events: European Conference on Politics and Gender (QUB 2009); Category of Violence Workshop (University of Aberdeen 2011); Political Studies Association Annual Conference (Ulster 2012); European Studies Research Seminar (St Mary's College 2012); Society for Women in Philosophy Ireland (UCD 2012); Political Thought Specialist Group (LSE 2012); and Society for Women in Philosophy Ireland Spring Conference (UCD 2013). I would also like to take this opportunity to express my gratitude to the two anonymous reviewers; their generous and useful suggestions have been encouraging and have helped me in improving the quality of my manuscript. It goes without saying that the sole responsibility for this book's content, including any errors or omissions, lies with me. My biggest debt, as always, is owed to my partner, Tom Hartley, who provides love, support, sustenance, and sharp political insight. It is to him that this book is dedicated.

Abbreviations

AC	*Antigone's Claim: Kinship between Life and Death*
BTM	*Bodies that Matter: On the Discursive Limits of "Sex"*
CHU	*Contingency, Hegemony, Universality: Contemporary Dialogues on the Left*
ES	*Excitable Speech: A Politics of the Performative*
FW	*Frames of War: When is Life Grievable?*
GT	*Gender Trouble: Feminism and the Subversion of Identity*
GAO	*Giving an Account of Oneself*
PL	*Precarious Life: The Powers of Mourning and Violence*
PLP	*The Psychic Life of Power: Theories in Subjection*
PW	*Parting Ways: Jewishness and the Critique of Zionism*
SD	*Subjects of Desire: Hegelian Reflections in Twentieth-Century France*
UG	*Undoing Gender*
WSNS	*Who Sings the Nation-State? Language, Politics, Belonging* —

Introduction

Who "am" I, without you?

(*Precarious Life*)

At a recent symposium dedicated to the discussion of Judith Butler's work, one of the panellists, like Butler a distinguished scholar, professed to remember the chair she sat in when she first encountered Butler's famous book *Gender Trouble: Feminism and the Subversion of Identity* (1990).[1] I cannot vouch for the veracity of this story, but I think it offers a fitting illustration of the import and impact of *Gender Trouble* on feminist scholarship. Butler's contributions to the field of gender studies and feminism are widely known, and her influence on the shape and direction of feminist theorizing for more than two decades is nothing less than impressive.[2] Since its first publication in 1990, *Gender Trouble* has been issued for a second edition, published in 1999, and has been translated into numerous languages. Although not Butler's first book,[3] *Gender Trouble's* denaturalizing account of the sexed body, its critique of the heterosexist frame in which gender is said to emerge, and its proposition of a performative constitution of gender identity has spawned an enormous critical commentary.

Like many of her readers, I first encountered Butler's ideas through *Gender Trouble*. And while I have no recollection of the chair I sat in when I first read the book, I do remember being both 'troubled' and exhilarated by this text and its ideas. For me, *Gender Trouble* pointed up the possibilities of feminism, and in doing so, it made feminism exciting: it changed my thinking about what feminism could be, what gender could mean, and what gender theory could explain. Of course, Butler's continued and still growing appeal has long surpassed her impact on feminism and gender studies. Initially trained in philosophy, her influence reaches into academic fields beyond philosophy. The response to her work has always been multi- and interdisciplinary, and she has left her mark on a whole range of academic specialisms in the humanities and social sciences, including legal studies (see Loizidou 2007), literary studies (see Salih 2002), media and cultural studies (see Brady and Schirato 2011; McRobbie 2006), sociology (see Kirby 2006), religious studies (see Armour and St. Ville 2006), moral philosophy (see Thiem 2008), and political theory (see Carver and Chambers 2008; Lloyd 2007).[4] My study acknowledges and builds on the significance of *Gender Trouble,* but my focus lies elsewhere: I am interested in Butler's political philosophy beyond *Gender Trouble,* and I explore her contribution to international theory and to post-9/11 public political discourse.

That Butler's ideas transcend the boundaries of philosophy may be emblematic of the porous nature of disciplinary confines; it also attests to the pertinence of the issues that she addresses and to the appeal and originality of her arguments. Almost twenty-five years since the publication of *Gender Trouble,* she continues to speak to those with an interest in radical theory and the radical transformation of existing conditions, and she appeals to academic and non-academic audiences alike. Rather than offering 'hip' comments (see Nussbaum 1999) on ephemeral topics, Butler's work provides her readers with sophisticated and significant analyses of some of the key problems that critical theory and public political discourse in the first part of the twenty-first century grapple with, and which may well continue to engage her readers in decades to come.

While the emphasis of and approach pursued in her work has broadened since the early 1990s, it is fair to state that some of the key theoretical claims and positions first outlined in *Gender Trouble* continue to shape Butler's political theorizing to date. For example, her critical genealogy of the subject, notwithstanding modifications and developments, plays a continuing role in her thinking (see Chapter 1). Her theorization of the abjection of subjugated groups is an enduring feature of her writings; her challenge to representational forms of politics, which she first articulated in relation to feminism, has come to inform new contexts and constellations; and her emphasis on subversive and resignificatory political practices, which seek to contest and rebut hegemonic terms of identity regulation, remain a constant thread in her work. Of course, *Gender Trouble,* as indeed Butler's wider oeuvre, is not without its critics, and the very ideas that her followers find so compelling have invited her detractors to launch stinging, and at times deeply personal, attacks on her. Her decentring of the female subject and of female agency, her performative account of gender, and her theorization of the body and its relationship to materiality have triggered many controversies and disputes within feminism.[5]

As I indicated above, my interest lies with Butler's political philosophy beyond *Gender Trouble,* and with her contribution to international theory and to post-9/11 public political discourse. To investigate this contribution, I draw mainly on her books published since 2001,[6] and I supplement my reading of these texts with an analysis of selected articles, book contributions, and interviews, again mainly from the post-9/11 period. For reasons of expediency, I sometimes refer to Butler's pre-9/11 texts as her 'early' writings, while I describe her post-9/11 work as 'recent' or 'current'. I am mindful of the challenges that such classifications may invite: for one, I do not wish to imply that this date, notwithstanding its import to many around the world, constitutes a radical break or departure in Butler's thinking and writing. Rather, I see it as a catalyst for a shift in thematic orientation, towards an increasing engagement with international or global issues such as the political fallout from the wars in Iraq and Afghanistan, US foreign policy, and the conflict in Israel-Palestine.

Furthermore, while her 'recent' writings put forward a distinctively normative approach, supported by her widely discussed turn to ethics, and her revised consideration of questions of ontology (I attend to this aspect in Chapter 1), I suggest that many of the ideas that distinguish this recent work are already presented, albeit some of them in embryonic form, in her pre-9/11 writings.[7] Hence, despite my focus on Butler's political philosophy beyond feminism, it would be impossible to cast aside her earlier work. For example, her critique of the subject and her decentred account of political agency are key themes of her work that facilitate novel conceptions of coalitional politics; they overcome the impasse of feminist identity politics, but they also have significant implications for recent work on the formation of political coalitions in the context of the war on terror (see Chapter 4). Thus, I will on occasion make reference to Butler's gender theory, but it is not my aim to provide a detailed exposition or new interpretation of this aspect of her oeuvre. Of course, it would be impossible to surgically remove Butler's feminism from her wider political philosophy; such an attempt would also ignore how her recent work articulates the significance of feminism in new contexts (see Butler 2009a). Where I acknowledge and indeed sometimes draw on the ideas associated with Butler's earlier texts, I do so selectively, insofar they illuminate her later work.

While the focus on drag and performativity has dominated the reception of Butler's ideas,[8] my analysis is to foreground two themes that constitute the parameters of her recent work and that surface, albeit under different names, in her writings: first, her emphasis on relationality, ek-stasis and dispossession, and second, the idea of liveability. These themes constitute the focus of my discussion in Chapters 1 and 2, but they also frame my overall reading of Butler's work. To briefly unpack these ideas, relationality, ek-stasis, and dispossession portend, for Butler, a conception of a subject fundamentally given over to an other. Such radical alterity construes the subject not just as relational, but also as a relation. As she argues in *Giving an Account of Oneself* (2005), her study of moral philosophy, 'in the beginning *I am my relation to you*, . . . given over to a you without whom I cannot be and upon whom I depend to survive' (*GAO*, 81; italics in original). Further, this emphasis on survival evokes Butler's interest in the concept of liveability: this is the key analytical lens through which she appraises the political conditions under which lives can be lived, and through which she critiques the frames of reference whereby some lives become recognized, and thus liveable, while other lives are marginalized and abjected. My interest lies in the connection she makes between liveability and global politics: it is my overall objective to harness Butler's political philosophy for thinking through some of the pressing issues of contemporary global politics, and to gauge her contribution to the emerging field of international political theory. I contend that her writings help us to understand some of the major issues that occupy current debates in political philosophy and in public political discourse, and that they provide a necessary critical corrective to the dominant analytical strand in international theory. As I argue throughout this book, the significance of Butler to these debates lies in the connection she makes between an existential-phenomenological account of liveability and sociological arguments about the unequal gendered and racialized geopolitical distribution of recognition and suffering; this link, furthermore, is underwritten by her ethico-political attention to conditions of plurality and heterogeneity.

The range of Butler's topics is wide: it includes war, military intervention, and, more broadly, the justification of the use of violence. Butler also engages the role of the state in the context of global interdependence; the increased significance of religion and its relationship to secularism; the rights agenda and the globalization of human rights; the conditions of multiculturalism; the prospects for progressive sexual politics; articulations of citizenship in the face of migration processes, border disputes, and globalization; and globalized political responses to the economic crisis. These pursuits, as I already intimated, are borne out of her philosophical reflections on liveability and recognition, and these, in turn, explain both the focus and the omissions in Butler's work. For example, while she articulates some of the concerns of the global democracy movements, specifically as they respond to the current economic crisis, she does not offer a detailed assessment of this crisis.[9] Similarly, while she remarks upon the destruction of sentient life in the wake of the military invasion of Iraq, she does not provide a wider commentary on environmental destruction or energy policy. Likewise, although she is acutely aware of the global AIDS crisis, she does not offer an account of global public health. Each of these topics could justifiably be described as pressing global issues, but, as Carver and Chambers (2008) argue, 'she has her eye on some things at the expense of others' (163). Her focus is a selective one, derived, overall, from her interest in questions of liveability, (state) violence and the responses to war, and the formation of global political practices under conditions of plurality and heterogeneity.

Another facet of Butler's work is worth stressing here. For a writer whose critics have accused her of engaging in obtuse, inaccessible, and politically paralysing theorizing (see Nussbaum 1999), Butler engages in a wide range of public activities. Thus, to fully appreciate the extent and reach of her contribution to contemporary radical thought, it is crucial to recognize her engagement with public political discourse beyond academia. This engagement has shaped her work, both in terms of the issues that occupy her and with respect to the dissemination of her ideas.[10] As I have already indicated, Butler's focus on global issues such as the war on terror, the conflict in the Middle East, or the relationship between secularism, multiculturalism, and sexual politics, are of huge public interest. Such a 'turn' to public engagement has also influenced her style of writing and her willingness to address personal issues, such as her upbringing as a Jew and the influence of Jewish ethics on the development of her thinking. If anything, it has made her ideas more accessible to a wider audience, beyond the confines of scholarly debate. She is a sought-after speaker and interviewee who participates regularly in public events and debates,[11] and she contributes to a multiplicity of political causes, ranging from rights for sexual minorities, to movements for (global) democracy, to the situation in Israel-Palestine.[12]

Thus, while Butler's recent writings remain philosophically ambitious, they put their philosophical discourse in the service of understanding and critiquing the world. In doing so, they straddle the often lamented gap between academia and 'real life', between theory and practice. As Butler (2011a) counsels, 'theory only registers what is already happening in a social movement. . . . I put into theoretical language what was already being impressed upon me from elsewhere' (206). It is significant to highlight this facet, because it challenges perceptions of Butler as belonging to a group of scholars engaging in forms of 'high theory' that bear no resemblance to 'real-life' concerns. In what follows, I provide a 'broad-brush' approach to the questions and topics that are addressed in more detail in the following chapters. I begin by outlining Butler's reception in political philosophy, before turning to the international or global dimension of her work. I also provide a critical reflection on Butler's sources, influences, and approaches. I conclude with a brief map of the chapter structures, themes, and arguments of my book. The reception of Butler's ideas in the political philosophy scholarship will be outlined in the next section, where I also sketch some of the arguments pursued in this book.

BUTLER AND POLITICAL PHILOSOPHY

As I have already intimated before, much of Butler's reception in feminism and gender theory turns on her use of the notion of performativity, which articulates the idea that gender is not the externalization of an inner core or identity; neither is gender the embodied and visible outworking of a fixed or determinate bodily morphology. Rather, gender is a practice requiring repetition, conducted under the constraints of existing regimes of gender intelligibility that can be changed and subverted in new and unexpected directions. Although I am both mindful of and sympathetic to Butler's influence on feminism, women's and gender studies, and queer theory, and to her multi- and interdisciplinary reach and appeal, I have located my investigation in a more narrowly demarcated field, that of political theory and philosophy.[13] Aided by the reception and consolidation of ideas and approaches that are commonly subsumed under the label of post-structuralism, Butler's critique of the subject, of identity and identity politics, and of the representational claims of feminism has been put to use for critical reflections on politics and the subject beyond gender and feminism. Likewise, her account of politics as contingent and her stress on coalitional practices and on a politics of resignification, which aims to redeploy the terms of political discourse in new and unexpected ways, has also informed recent political theory. The growing number of publications that seek to explore and utilize Butler's thinking for political theory is indicative of the impact she is making in this field, and there is much interest in Butler as a political philosopher of and beyond gender. Some of this work uses the trope of trouble to configure Butler's relations with political theory (see for example Carver and Chambers 2008). Lloyd (2007) considers Butler's conception of the subject in relation to norms and power. Other political theory receptions attend to her treatment of sovereignty (Dean 2008) and rights (Zivi 2008), and to the existential-phenomenological foundations of Butler's political philosophising (see Coole 2008; Lloyd 2007). There is also work published on Butler's contribution to debates on radical democracy (Lloyd 2009; Schippers 2009), on the state (Lloyd 2005, 2007; Passavant and Dean 2001), on recognition (see Ferrarese 2011; see also Allen 2006), on mourning (McIvor 2012) and on the relationship between ethics and politics (Rushing 2010).[14] Moreover, studies on Butler's treatment of law, ethics, and moral philosophy (see for example Loizidou 2007, 2008; Thiem 2008), while not emanating from within political studies departments, are also of interest to political theorists and philosophers. Taken together, these readings of Butler offer a rich texture of interpretations that draws on, develops, and critiques Butler's own radical account of politics.

My study builds on this work: as I already have indicated, I draw on Butler's post-9/11 texts in order to read her as an international theorist and global public intellectual, whose ideas and writings make a significant contribution to (international) political philosophy and to public political discourse, and who has much to offer to the critical analysis of our current global constellation. For me, the key questions to be asked of Butler are as follows: how can the scholarly attention appropriate Butler as a political philosopher? More specifically, what do Butler's responses to the challenges of global interdependence contribute to the emerging field of international political philosophy? And finally, how do Butler's political-philosophical reflections inform her interventions into post-9/11 public political discourse? I respond to these questions in the chapters that follow, but at this point it is helpful to sketch Butler's key contribution to political philosophy. This contribution, I suggest, revolves around the following themes: (1) her theory of the subject, of subjectivity, and of power; (2) her critique of the state and of sovereignty; (3) her critique of violence; (4) the novel emphasis on universal obligations, including the emphasis on rights and on ethics; (5) and her conception of citizenship and bi-nationalism. To briefly map the approach and arguments to be pursued in the ensuing chapters, I suggest that the significance of Butler's contribution, derived from her phenomenological reading of global politics, centres on her deployment of the notion of liveability; it articulates how lived experiences are framed in the context of global politics, and how these experiences are undergone unequally, structured along gendered and racialized lines. Further, such approach to global politics is underpinned by her conception of the subject, understood as ek-static, dispossessed, and relational.

I suggest that her recent work provides answers to the normative conditions of political life. The alleged poverty regarding all things normative, of which post-structuralist thinkers have sometimes been accused, is addressed significantly in Butler's recent writings. Although, as I will argue, this move in her work is not without problems, Butler's phenomenological analysis connects with her recent explicit commitment to ethics, and this linkage, often perceived as problematic, should be read through the lens of her recent explicit consideration of Jewish philosophy. Finally, as I intimated above, my focus lies with an exploration of Butler's 'new' themes, such as her analysis of religion and secularism, her discussion of Israel- Palestine, or her critique of US foreign policy—which, I believe, speak to pressing global political issues of our time. Thus, I read Butler as an international theorist, and I locate her contribution in those strands of international theory that challenge a statist focus and that emphasize instead the interconnection between various domains of social and political life, between the local and the global.

I develop these arguments at various junctions throughout my book, but before I outline the broad parameters of what I consider to be the Butler's contribution to international theory, I want to clarify my use of the terminological distinctions within this field. International political theory, broadly construed, articulates the key concerns and concepts of normative political theory and philosophy, such as justice, equality, or rights, in an international context.[15] Its key premise is that political-philosophical analysis can no longer be contained within the nation state, the traditional unit of enquiry for such analysis,[16] and that the key concepts of political philosophy are applied in an international or global context. Typical areas of inquiry include the study of global justice and distribution; the justification of violence, war, and military intervention, and the rules of conduct during war; self-determination and the configuration of citizenship in an era of global migration; and, more widely, questions of global governance. One feature of international political theory is the fact that it does not posit the state as a privileged unit of analysis. Such an approach chimes strongly with Butler's own critical distance to the state (see Chapter 5). In this respect, my use of the term international political theory bears close resemblance to the way Simon Caney (2005) describes 'global political theory', which he understands as a form of theorizing that includes reflection on nonsovereign forms of political organization. He distinguishes global political theory from 'international political theory', conceived as the way states treat each other, and from 'global ethics', said to focus on moral obligations owed by individuals. I hold on to the term international political theory, mainly to follow convention and to align my focus with the wider discourse community that has established itself around the term international political theory and a set of ensuing questions and methodologies. Further, in contrast to Caney, I include the concerns of global ethics and the exploration of non-sovereign forms of politics under the label of 'international political theory'.

How, though, should we distinguish international political theory from international relations theory? Such distinction could be described as one of emphasis: while international political theory foregrounds political theory, international relations theory foregrounds international relations. Others conceive of international political theory as an effort to bridge the divide between international relations and political theory: international political theory is said to theorize the international and to internationalize political theory issues and concepts.[17] While some of the well-known theoretical approaches in international relations theory, such as realism, constructivism, or idealism, exert influence on international political theory scholarship, its key concerns are not primarily framed through the lens of international relations theory. Most significantly, international political theory's focus, as deployed in this study, lies first and foremost with normative political theorizing in a global context, and it engages normative thought to theorize the various intersections of local and global concerns, rather than through a focus on relations between nation states. I wish to issue a note of caution, though: the boundaries between international political theory and international relations theory are porous and indeed arbitrary. For example, it would be misleading to suggest that international political theory scholars disregard the state as an object of inquiry; neither do they dismiss the normative value of the state. It would be equally misleading to suggest that all international relations theorists are uncritical of the state, or that they regard the state as the only, or most significant, unit of analysis. To further explore the fault lines, differences, and commonalities between international political theory, international relations theory, and indeed global political theory would require a separate investigation that would lead beyond the scope of my study. Instead, I want to proceed to an overview of Butler's reception in international theory, broadly conceived, and to offer a provisional sketch of my own reading of her contribution to this field.

Many of the themes that structure Butler's reception in political theory, such as her account of the decentred subject, her emphasis on contestability, or her writings on mourning, also surface in international theory. That Butler is regarded as a scholar of weight in international thought is acknowledged in her inclusion in a recent collection on critical theorists in international relations (see Masters 2009). Her ideas have been utilized in scholarly writings on the performativity of the state (see Weber 1998), 9/11, the 'war on terror', security and biopolitics (see Neal 2008), the representation of US hegemony and masculine values in popular visual culture (see Lacy 2007), the global politics of melancholia and grieving (see Zehfuss 2007), and cosmopolitanism (see Brassett 2008, 2010; Jenkins 2011; McRobbie 2006). It is my claim that Butler has just as much to say on pressing global issues as on the topics of gender, sexuality, and identity, for which she is justifiably well known. Yet despite this engagement with Butler's writings in the wider field of international studies, and notwithstanding the international orientation of her recent work, it is important to acknowledge that she does not feature prominently in significant texts in the field,[18] and that her prominence within the discourse community of international theory does not mirror her standing in gender studies and feminism. Although her work is read by scholars of international relations, international relations theory, and international political theory, she has not yet become a key reference point for the study of global politics or international political theory. The relative neglect of Butler cannot be explained with reference to her association with 'high theory', or a potential bias against post-structuralist theorizing. The considerable interest in post-structuralism within the wider international theory community should provide fertile soil for the reception of Butler's work (see Zehfuss 2009; Edkins 1999; Edkins, Pin-Fat, and Shapiro 2004).[19]

As I have suggested, there is some engagement with the concept of performativity, imported into international political theory via feminist international relations, but a more detailed engagement does not take place until after 9/11, thus coinciding with Butler's turn towards international issues. It should also be stated that Butler's own work does not engage significantly with relevant texts and approaches in the contemporary international political theory scholarship. To put it bluntly, there exists, as yet, no international political theory equivalent to *Gender Trouble*. This limited engagement with some of the key authors is not just due to Butler's resistance to disciplinary boundaries. Although she explicitly frames her recent work in a global context, her own references come predominantly from the field of modern and contemporary political thought and philosophy (see my discussion in the next section).

My aim is to make Butler's contribution to international political theory more explicit. What portends this contribution is Butler's attachment to a philosophy of alterity, which she articulates in relation to her discussion of dispossession, to ek-stasis, to exile and diaspora, to scattering and displacement. To harness this focus on negativity, Butler subscribes to a framework of ethics and relationality. It is within this context that her international theory, introduced systematically in *Precarious Life: The Powers of Mourning and Violence* (2004b), takes shape, and it centres on four issues. These are (1) the constitution of the subject in a global context of war, violence, and material inequality; (2) the displacement of state sovereignty, and the articulation of new, post-sovereign forms of cohabitation; (3) the relationship between religion, secularism, and multiculturalism; and (4) the revision of the significance of human rights and international law. I wish to propose that it is around the existential-phenomenological framing of global politics, focussed on the notion of liveability, that Butler's most significant contribution to international political theory lies, and in the remainder of my book I seek to develop this reading of Butler's international theory further.

Butler's discussion of vulnerability, grievability, and ethical responsibilities within global context connects with her critique of US foreign policy in the wake of 9/11 (and with considerations of global ethics and international political philosophy), but also, crucially, with the genealogy and constitution of the individual. Hence, the subject, or self (not to be understood as the autonomous actor of liberal political thought), and his/her agency and ethical obligations are constituted in a global context that comes to frame the emergence of agency and responsibility. For one, Butler's recent writings are acutely aware of the criss-crossing of global, international, and national issues. Some of the most pressing political problems of our time, such as the organization of citizenship across and beyond national borders, the role of sovereignty, the deployment of violence and strategies of non-violence have found a forceful articulation in Butler's recent work. Second, Butler's discussion of these global problems is underpinned by her attention to the question of ethics, contributing to ongoing debates in the field of global ethics. This ethical undercurrent in Butler's recent thought is accompanied by a strong normative orientation of her recent work (see below). Finally, key to my argument is Butler's commitment to the idea of human vulnerability and (inter-)dependence. Such commitment, I want to suggest, further strengthens her contribution to global ethics, and to a search for a more just and liveable world. Specifically, this contribution centres around her philosophy of the subject and her ethico-politics. Moreover, I wish to contend that Butler's treatment of a series of topics that are significant to international political theory is in fact more plausible and attractive than many positions put forward by international theorists who argue in an analytical vein. Whilst her philosophical reflections underpin her current thinking on global politics, she is now examining the post-9/11 world, including the conduct of war, the mourning of violent losses, the role of religion in public life, and the function and operation of state and nation under conditions of globalization and plurality. To gain further purchase on Butler's location within political philosophy, it is prudent to identify the sources that inform her thinking. This aspect of Butler's work, as I demonstrate in the next section, is not without controversy, and it has led her critics to charge her with eclecticism and theoretical inconsistency.

PROTAGONISTS, ANTAGONISTS, AND INTERLOCUTORS: BUTLER'S 'UNFAITHFUL READINGS'

As is well known, Butler's philosophical home is Continental thought, but the space she occupies there is perplexingly wide and eclectic. Although often associated with 'French theory', especially with the writings of Michel Foucault, it is worth remembering that her initial philosophical training in the academy was in German idealism, phenomenology, and the Frankfurt School.[20] As she states, it was only after she left her doctoral studies at Yale University that she became 'open to French theory' (*SD*, viii). Clearly, her most famous texts, especially *Gender Trouble*, are steeped in Foucauldian ideas and terminology, but this dominance should not cloud the fact that other (French) influences, including those of existential phenomenology, play an important role in her writings, both in her earliest published essays (see for example 1986; 1987; 1988), as well as in her more recent work. Diana Coole (2008), in a perceptive analysis that stresses the existential phenomenological themes at work in *Gender Trouble*, highlights the continued persistence of this strand of Butler's work (see also Lloyd 2007). Butler's occupation with the idea of liveability, as well as her account of the ek-static structure of the subject and its implications for politics, should be counted amongst the existential heritage of her philosophical thought, and as I have already indicated, it is this debt to existential phenomenology and some of its key themes that inform my own interpretation of her writings.

The idea of ek-stasis, which plays an important role in existentialist thought, also provides the link back to Hegel's philosophy, to which Butler remains strongly attached (see my discussion in Chapter 1), and which also connects her engagement with the ideas of Simone de Beauvoir and, to a lesser extent, Sartre. Psychoanalytic ideas, including those of Freud, Melanie Klein, and Jean Laplanche, continue to influence her writings, as do the work of Derrida, Merleau-Ponty, Spinoza, and Nietzsche. Of particular significance to Butler's recent work are the ideas of Walter Benjamin, Hannah Arendt, and Theodor Adorno (I discuss these throughout my book), while Butler's ethics is increasingly informed by her reading of Emmanuel Levinas.[21]

Such dazzling array of influences could plausibly be regarded as testament to the intellectual capacity and range of Butler's own philosophical thinking. However, it has also puzzled many of her readers, who struggle to reconcile seemingly incompatible philosophical positions. Although Butler is mindful of her own eclecticism, she is unperturbed by it. Synthesis, as she declares in *Giving an Account of Oneself*, is not her aim (2005, 21). Rather, as she continues, each philosopher and theorist considered by her offers an important contribution that allows her to think through the problems that occupy her work. Yet there is no easy way to rebut the charge of eclecticism, or even the stronger charge of theoretical incoherence (Coole 2008, 12). Clearly, philosophical traditions are not closed off or rigidly demarcated entities, and it is plausible enough to construe points of convergence or to establish connections, for example, between an account of the subject derived from Foucault, from Hegel, and from Freud (see *The Psychic Life of Power* (1997a)). However, it has been argued that such connections are often purchased at the price of a selective engagement with the traditions or with individual thinkers (see Lloyd 2007), and this charge of a selective reading, including a lack of attention and close reading, is difficult to shake off.[22] Still, one of the most compelling elements of Butler's work is her continued deployment of the existential-phenomenological tradition, coupled with her continued reliance on Foucauldian conceptions of power and her psychoanalytically informed conception of the subject. How this informs her political philosophy will be discussed in the following chapters.

Butler's eclecticism is not the only cause of unease amongst some of her readers. Her choice of sources has also invited criticism. Some of this criticism, by now well documented, centres on her deployment of Foucauldian ideas (see Benhabib 1995), while much of the discomfort of those who are broadly sympathetic towards her ideas crystallizes around Butler's reliance on the work Derrida and, more recently, on her alleged neglect of genealogical investigations at the expense of (Levinasian) ethics (see Coole 2008; Lloyd 2008; Dean 2008). For example, both Lloyd (2008) and Coole (2008) fault Butler for her adherence to a textual post-structuralism, which they associate with the work of Derrida, with Lloyd favouring a stronger emphasis on Nietzschean and Foucauldian theory, and Coole advocating a return to the focus on existential themes that characterized some of Butler's earlier work prior to the publication of *Gender Trouble* (1990). Such stress on textual theory is said to underplay the significance of historical and social factors at the expense of abstract theorizing. Butler's recent use of Levinas could be challenged in the same vein, although I want to suggest that her deployment of the concept of precarity, that is, the unequal global distribution of liveability, goes some way towards redressing these concerns (see my discussion in Chapters 1 and 2). Admittedly, Butler's eclecticism and her choice of sources present difficulties and challenges, but they also, I believe, provide new opportunities: although her approach may not appeal to those readers who seek close readings and interpretations of primary texts, it allows her to deploy her political-philosophical reflections, albeit selectively, in the service of thinking through the political condition. It is this approach that also guides my investigation into Butler's work. I want to conclude this introduction with a brief sketch of the chapter structure and the topics and arguments that I will pursue.

STRUCTURE OF THE BOOK

The first two chapters of my book survey and assess the constituent elements of what I refer to as Butler's political philosophy of the human. Chapter 1 deals with the politics of subject formation. Although commonly read as a theorist of performativity, I approach Butler's political philosophy through the framework of ek-stasis, relationality, and dispossession. With this approach, I seek to foreground the existential-phenomenological elements of Butler's work, which have obtained renewed significance in her recent writings. Three themes occupy my discussion in this chapter: (1) Butler's emphasis on ecstatic relationality; (2) her discussion of recognition; and (3) the wider significance of her so-called turn to ontology and ethics. I develop Butler's conception of ecstatic subjectivity, which I read in the context of her turn to ethics and ontology. To illustrate Butler's argument further, I draw from her writings on intersex, transgender and racialized modes of recognition in the context of the war on terror.

Chapter 2 assesses a semantic shift in Butler's recent writings, which increasingly references 'the human'. This shift, I suggest, is closely related to her discussion of the concept of liveability and its differential application in public political discourse. I illustrate this discussion with reference to recent debates on marriage equality. Developing this discussion, I compare Butler's work with the capabilities approach, and I harness her writings to develop a discursive account of the human arising from human rights discourses. As I will argue, at the heart of her work sits her claim that life is precarious; she concludes that we are connected with others on whom we depend for our survival, and for whom we are responsible.

Chapter 3 engages with Butler's recent writings on violence, specifically her topical response to the so-called war on terror, to the racialized and gendered discourse on terrorism, and to the—equally racialized and gendered—framing of bodily vulnerability, loss, and grieving. Of importance to my discussion is the consideration of Butler's underlying political-philosophical perspective, which, I demonstrate, frames her engagement with questions of ethics and violence and with the recognition of life and of loss. Two aspects will be pursued further: first, by asking whether an understanding of violence as disruptive could be put in the service of radical politics, I discuss Butler's account of violence as constitutive of subjects and communities, and I assess her account against other conceptions of violence associated with modern political thought. Second, I outline her work on the political regulation of grieving, which she has pursued in relation to sexual politics on the one hand (such as the losses from AIDS and from sexual violence), and in the context of the so-called war on terror on the other hand. Developing my discussion from the previous chapter, and drawing further on Butler's discussion of recognition, life, and bodily vulnerability, I am interested in the relationship she construes between violence and non-violence, and I examine her suggestions for an ethics of non-violence and for the prospects of articulating non-violent political relationships with others.

Chapter 4 introduces Butler's recent reflections on religion and secularism and their respective relation to progressive sexual politics. I am particularly interested in her claim that a critique of the secular constitutes the necessary frame for any progressive politics that also draws on the demands of race and gender. This assertion, I suggest, offers a persuasive contribution to recent work on multiculturalism, and I interpret Butler's account as a key challenge to those positions, especially within feminism, that posit the demands of progressive sexual politics and the demands of minority ethnic and religious cultures as mutually exclusive. I want to demonstrate how depictions of progress and civilization come to regulate the prevailing understanding of the relationship between progressive sexual politics on the one hand (embodied, for example, in policies of gender equality and the rights of sexual minorities), and recent positions on multiculturalism on the other, embodied in a conceptualization of Muslim communities as antithetical to progressive politics. Further, this chapter sketches what I call Butler's political theology, and it maps her politics of cultural heterogeneity, both of which I construe out of Butler's ek-static conception of the subject. Tracking Butler's recent engagement with Jewish philosophy, I suggest, further underwrites her conception of the subject as relational and dispossessed.

Chapter 5 considers Butler's treatment of the concept of sovereignty, which I discuss in the context of international political philosophy. One of my aims is to clear up an ambivalence at the heart of her writings (this is also reflected in the critical commentary), which seems to adhere to a belief in the sovereign power of the state on the one hand, while advocating a post-sovereign radical account of politics on the other. Building upon my discussion of coalitional politics from previous chapters, I return to the question of political alliances, which I now consider under conditions of global conflict. Of key importance to my discussion is an assessment of Butler's call for 'non-nationalist modes of belonging', which she ponders in the context of diaspora and cohabitation and, more specifically, in relation to the conflict in Israel-Palestine. Drawing on Butler's reflections on the situation in the Middle East and her appropriation of Jewish conceptions of diaspora and non-violence, I want to think through diasporic and cohabitative forms of statehood and nationhood and consider, furthermore, the prospects for critical forms of cosmopolitanism (she refers to this as 'new internationalism'). The focal point of this chapter is Butler's conception of the state and, with it, her treatment of sovereignty. I offer a re-reading of Butler's engagement with the law and with human rights, which constitutes a development in her work and provides a more clearly defined connection between her ethics and politics than is expressed in other facets of her work.

My conclusion foregrounds Butler's status as a public intellectual by engaging with her emphasis on critique. I reflect on Butler's conception of critique, which, I suggest, constitutes the thread of her philosophical project. I delineate her unsettling of the boundaries of scholarly and public political engagement. As I demonstrate, the concept of 'the public' lies at the heart of this enterprise.

NOTES

1. Butler is Maxine Elliot Professor in the Departments of Rhetoric and Comparative Literature and the Co-director of the Program of Critical Theory at the University of California, Berkeley. She also holds the Hannah Arendt Chair of Philosophy at the European Graduate School. She is recipient of the Adorno Prize, awarded by the city of Frankfurt (see Chapter 4) and is named as one of '25 Visionaries Who Are Changing Your World' by *Utne Reader*. Butler's reach

has long surpassed academia and has seeped into popular culture: the expression 'Don't Judith Butler me' is said to feature in a scene in the Israeli movie *Ha-Buah* (*The Bubble* 2006) (see Butler 2011a, 205).

2. Apart from *Gender Trouble,* Butler's most significant books on gender theory to date are *Bodies that Matter: On the Discursive Limit of "Sex"* (1993) and *Undoing Gender* (2004a). Her attention to questions of gender also permeates the discussion in some of her other books, especially in *The Psychic Life of Power: Theories in Subjection* (1997b) and in *Antigone's Claim: Kinship between Life and Death* (2000a). In addition to these books, Butler has also published numerous journal articles and contributions to special issues and edited collections that deal with gender.

3. Butler's first book is *Subjects of Desire: Hegelian Reflections in Twentieth Century France* ([1987] 1999). I engage with some of the themes of this book in Chapter 1.

4. These references are not a complete list of all engagements with Butler; they are merely indicative of some of the better-known texts in the field.

5. The reception of Butler's feminist ideas, and especially of *Gender Trouble,* are too numerous to list here. A useful overview of the controversies that captured feminist theory in the 1990s is Butler's exchange with Seyla Benhabib, Nancy Fraser, and Drucilla Cornell in *Feminist Contentions: A Philosophical Exchange* (1995). For a hostile reading of Butler, see Nussbaum (1999). Analyses of Butler's relationship with feminism can be found in Carver and Chambers (2008), Kirby (2006), Lloyd (2007).

6. These include: *Undoing Gender* (2004a); *Precarious Life: The Powers of Mourning and Violence* (2004b); *Giving an Account of Oneself* (2005); her conversation with Gayatri Spivak in *Who Sings the Nation-State? Language, Politics, Belonging* (2007a); *Frames of War: When is Life Grievable?* (2009a); *Parting Ways: Jewishness and the Critique of Zionism* (2012a). Butler's most recent book, *Dispossession: The Performative in the Political* (2013a), published jointly with Athena Athanasiou, consists of a series of interviews and conversations between the two scholars. Given its late publication in my own writing process, I could not engage extensively with the ideas developed in this book.

7. See for example her discussion of universalism (Butler 1996; 2000b), her formulation of an ek-static conception of the subject (Butler [1987] 1999), or her attention to the idea of vulnerability (Butler 1997a). To elucidate the context of emergence, I draw, where necessary, on ideas developed in some of her earlier work. See also Carver and Chambers (2008), who dispute the idea of a 'turn' in Butler's work towards ethics, and who stress instead the persistence and continuity of Butler's engagements.

8. Butler borrows the notion of performativity from the work of the language philosopher J. L. Austin (1962), and from Derrida's reading of Austin (1991).

9. Butler is regularly criticized for her alleged lack of attention to questions of distribution and to economic issues more widely. I engage with some of these criticisms in Chapter 1.

10. See for example her involvement with the International Gay & Lesbian Human Rights Commission (*UG*, 34).

11. For some of her recent interviews see 2007c; 2009c; 2010; 2011a; 2011e; 2012b; 2013b. Although too numerous to list here, many of Butler's public speaking engagements can now be accessed on YouTube.

12. Butler is an advocate of the BDS movement. BDS (Boycott, Divestment, Sanctions) is a rights-based, global campaign that originated in Palestine, and that has three aims: (1) to end the occupation of Palestine; (2) to recognize full citizenship of Arab-Palestinian citizens of Israel; (3) and to uphold the right of

Palestinian refugees to return to their homes. See my discussion in Chapter 4; on BDS see www.bdsmovement.net/.

13. For the purpose of this study I use the terms 'political theory' and 'political philosophy' interchangeably.

14. The contributions to Carver and Chambers (2008) provide a very useful insight into the breadth of Butler's reception within political theory and political philosophy, broadly construed, ranging from sympathetic readings to highly critical interpretations.

15. For some of the key texts see for example Chris Brown (2002); Brown, Nardin and Rengger (2002); Browning (2011); Caney (2005); Edkins (1999); Edkins, Pin-Fat and Shapiro (2004); Hutchings (1999); and Walker (1993).

16. For example, the *Journal of International Political Theory*, in its mission statement, refers to the 'international dimension of contemporary life' which has driven 'political inquiry beyond its traditional boundaries' (see www.uk.sagepub.com/journals/Journal202228?productType=Journals&subject=J00&sortBy=sortTitle+asc&pager.offset=20&fs=1).

17. See the International Political Theory series published by Palgrave MacMillan (www.palgrave.com/products/SearchResults.aspx?s=IPoT&fid=3062).

18. See for example Chris Brown (2002); Daddow (2009); Hutchings (1999); and Weber (2005).

19. Several other critical theorists working in the same broad tradition as Butler, such as Foucault, Agamben, Connolly, Derrida, or Hardt and Negri, have each spawned a considerable following in international political theory.

20. In her recent work, Butler frequently refers to the exposure to philosophical texts in the home, as well as to her engagement with ethical problems in the context of her synagogue (see 2000d, 2006e, 2011a).

21. The various interlocutors in her 'feminist' work include not only Monique Wittig but also Julia Kristeva and feminist scholars working within/beyond the tradition of structural anthropology.

22. I would suggest that her treatment of the state is emblematic for this lack of close reading. See for example Passavant and Dean (2001) as well as my discussion in Chapter 5.

1 The Politics of Subject Formation

> There is, as it were, a sociality at the basis of the "I" and its infinitude from which one cannot—and ought not to escape.
>
> (*Giving an Account of Oneself*)

Considering the import of *Gender Trouble* to the reception of Butler's oeuvre, it is not surprising that the concept of performativity, which features so prominently in her book, is the idea most widely associated with her writings. Clearly, it is not possible to get past the notion of performativity if we want to make sense of Butler's ideas.[1] However, in this chapter, I approach Butler's contribution to political philosophy from a different angle: I want to suggest that her ideas and concepts furnish us with an account that conceives of the subject as ek-static, dispossessed, and relational.[2] Given the wide range of sources that inform Butler's account of the subject, such foregrounding of the concepts of ek-stasis, relationality, and dispossession require some justification. As is well known, Butler offers her readers a complex narrative of subject constitution, of how the subject might come 'to be'. She draws on existential-phenomenological narratives of becoming and doing; on accounts of subjection that, in turn, develop Foucauldian accounts of power and norms, Freudian concepts of internalization, identification, and melancholia, and Althusser's concept of interpellation. Equally significant are Hegel's discussion of sociality; Spinoza's insistence on persistence; and Levinas's concept of alterity. These sources should not be read as distinct strands or elements of Butler's political philosophy of the subject; rather, they form complex relationships that contribute to her distinctive account of the subject.

For Butler, 'being' remains an unruly category, troublesome in the present and always comported towards the future and thus towards new possibilities of being. This renewed attention to the notion of ek-stasis[3] and to conceptions of relationality, dispossession, dependency, and liveability (see also Chapter 2), carries existential weight: it puts forward a conception of the subject-human that anchors sheer physical survival and material bodily needs in a complex relationship to alterity. It also reformulates the idea of autonomy by undercutting those conceptions of the self that deny a fundamental dependency on alterity; in their place, Butler articulates autonomy in the context of relationality and ethico-political obligations towards others.

My aim in this chapter is to outline the steps of this development. To gain purchase on Butler's political philosophy, I begin by considering the relationship between desire and ek-stasis; helping me to unpack this relationship further is Butler's deployment of Spinoza and the development of his ideas in the work of Hegel. However, my concern in this chapter is not with the plausibility or originality of Butler's respective readings of either Spinoza or Hegel; rather, my interest lies with the way that she deploys their ideas to develop her account of the subject-human. The consideration of ek-stasis and desire will be followed by an analysis of Butler's contribution to contemporary discourses on recognition. As I already have suggested, aiding Butler's overall undertaking into the question of the subject-human and of recognition are the ideas of the German philosopher Hegel, whose writings have significantly influenced her work. I want to explore the following question: if, as Butler asserts in *Subjects of Desire* ([1987] 1999), Hegel speaks to twentieth-century French philosophy, how does Butler speak to contemporary political philosophy? In other words, how does her philosophy relate to the political conditions and problems of this century?[4] My discussion makes two moves: working through her account of desire, ek-stasis, and recognition, I present Butler's conception of the subject as grounded in relationality. How such ecstatic relationality connects with her conception of ethics and ontology occupies me in the second part of this chapter. This latter aspect has been the subject of considerable discontent in sections of the critical commentary, pertaining to the question of whether Butler's analysis privileges transcendental conceptions over social and historical discussion. I want to suggest that her account of subject formation is simultaneously anchored in existential questions as well as in contingent structures of power.

DESIRE, ECSTASY, RELATIONALITY

Much recent attention has been given to the significance of power and norms in Butler's account of the subject and in her treatment of violence (see my discussion in Chapter 3; see also Chambers 2007; Lloyd 2007). In brief, norms are said to provide a structure of intelligibility that allows the emerging subject to assume a recognized and recognizable position within a given cultural framework. Crucially, if norms facilitate the emergence of the subject, they also, paradoxically, generate what Chambers (2007) calls 'normative violence'. That is, norms simultaneously engender and impede possibilities of living one's life differently, outside, or beside existing structures of intelligibility.[5] In doing so, they subject those who do not comply with or conform to existing standards of intelligibility to violence. Butler famously illustrates such normative operation of violence in the constitution of the subject with respect to gender, specifically transgender and intersex (see Butler 1990; see also Butler 2004a), while her more recent work stresses the operation of violence in the constitution and regulation of religious and racialized subjectivities (see Butler 2004b, 2009a, 2012a). I attend to this aspect of her work in the next chapter. Here I am concerned with a different route into the problematic of the subject, which has obtained renewed weight in her recent texts: this is the route travelled, though never completed, along desire and ek-stasis. I should highlight that this is not a new problematic for Butler. In fact, some of her earliest published work draws on the ek-static structure, or reality of human beings, which Butler derives from her reading of Sartre, and which she deploys within the context of providing a phenomenological account of corporeal existence (see Butler 1986, 1987). What interests me here, and what I regard as worthy of attention, is the emphasis she places on the role of alterity and relationality in the generation of the subject. It is this facet of her account of subjectification that I want to unravel.

Although desire evokes notions of physical or sensual appetite, of craving and longing, even of sexual lust, such a formula does not fully capture how philosophy has conceived of desire. Always more than physical passion, it denotes the idea that human beings engage with the world around them, with the objects they find and create, but also with other human beings and their desires. In doing so, desire underpins an integral element of philosophical enquiry, serving the pursuit of knowledge. It is also construed as philosophy's other: as Butler suggests, '[b]ecause philosophers cannot obliterate desire, they must formulate strategies to silence or control it' (*SD*, 2). As I indicate in the next section, there is some debate regarding the ontological status of desire: following Foucault, desire is formed by power, and our desires are shaped and regulated in distinctive ways, in conformity with hegemonic ideas of subjectivity. For now, I want to remain with Butler's pursuit of her discussion of desire within the context of her engagement with Hegel and Hegelian ideas. Although she is, rightly, regarded as a philosopher in the tradition of Hegel, it is essential to stress the import of the seventeenth century Dutch philosopher Spinoza to her (and indeed Hegel's) thinking on desire, and it is to this aspect that I turn now.

As I already intimated, while the Hegelian, and indeed Foucauldian, Derridean, and Freudian roots of Butler's political thought are well documented, less notice has been paid to her use of Spinoza.[6] Yet her reading of Spinoza underpins key aspects of her current work. As she claims in *Undoing Gender*, 'the Spinozan *conatus* remains at the core of my own work' (*UG*, 198; italics in original). Attention to Spinoza already surfaces in *Subjects of Desire: Hegelian Reflections in Twentieth-Century France* ([1987] 1999), and it informs her discussion in *The Psychic Life of Power: Theories in Subjection* (1997b), but I want to draw on a recent essay that engages directly with aspects of Spinoza's ethics and that puts forward key themes of Butler's work, leading to an articulation of the idea of relationality. In 'The Desire to Live: Spinoza's *Ethics* under Pressure' (2006c), Butler ponders

Spinoza's claim that the desire to live or persist is the desire to persevere in one's being, regarded as the foundation of all desire. On the surface, such assertion invites readings that stress one's individualistic stake in one's own self-preservation. Butler, however, is at pains to read Spinoza for what she terms 'possibilities for social ethics' (111). These, according to Butler, draw on the social dimension of the desire to live, and they anchor desire in our responsibility for others. Two elements lie at the heart of this interpretation: her insistence on the plural dimensions of desire and life, and her claim, undeveloped in this essay, of the ek-static structure of subjectivity.

The assertion of sociality is central to Butler's reading of Spinoza. With this claim she challenges not just accusations of Spinoza's alleged individualistic streak, but, rather, she develops a theme that is key to her own work: the thesis that sociality sits at the heart of being, in fact, that sociality precedes being and the emerging sense of self.[7] This theme underpins her discussions in *Undoing Gender* (2004a) and in *Giving an Account of Oneself* (2005), where Butler attends to questions of ethics, but for now I want to remain with the discussion of desire. As Butler (2006c) argues, although desire presupposes an 'I', this 'I' is dependent upon others who facilitate the 'I's' desire in the first place. Thus, if desire, and with it, life, depend upon sociality, then desire can only ever occur under conditions of sociality and plurality, producing a 'deconstitution of singularity' (126) that comports the 'I' beyond itself. Here we have arrived at the notion of ek-stasis, which she borrows from Hegel and the existential-phenomenological tradition (see Butler 1986, 1987), and which is one of Butler's most significant ways of capturing the concept of the subject as dispossessed yet relational.[8] Reflecting on the role of the body in its engagement with the world, Butler (1986) contends that 'the body is a mode of desire . . . a being comported beyond itself, sustaining a necessary reference to the world'; further, building on Sartre, because humans strive after possibilities not realized or not realizable, they are '"beyond" themselves. This *ek-static* reality of human beings is . . . a corporeal experience' (38; italics in original).

As I intimated, Butler introduces the concept of ek-stasis into her discussion as early as 1986, but here I want to draw on one of her books from 2004, *Undoing Gender*, where Butler gives this concept renewed attention. Pondering the question of whose lives matter, whose lives are recognized as having been lived, and whose lives are grievable (see also Chapters 2 and 3), Butler positions the subject as relational, thereby undercutting any claims to autonomy that the subject may express. In radicalized fashion, Butler suggests that the language of autonomy is misleading, since what lies at the heart of the subject is a mode of dispossession, or being beside oneself. This 'ethical enmeshment' (*UG*, 25) has consequences for the life of the subject, because it makes us vulnerable to the actions of others, including those actions that are violent (see my discussion below and Chapter 3). The language Butler uses to articulate such vulnerability is indicative of her claim regarding the openness of the subject: she talks about 'being dispossessed', 'being undone', 'being beside oneself', 'given over to the other', 'being a porous boundary', and 'being outside myself'. Such modes of dispossession, however, do not ring the death of the subject; rather, as Butler suggests, '*the ec-static character of our existence is essential to the possibility of persisting as human*' (*UG*, 33; italics in original). With the notion of ek-stasis, which emerges initially via her theory of the subject, Butler formulates a notion of the subject as dependent upon, or given over to an other. In *Undoing Gender* (2004a), this idea is captured with her expression of 'being undone': this means that the connection, or ties, we have with others constitutes our sense of self (*UG*, 18). And while, as I want to suggest, this concept has intrinsic value as the foundation for a conception of ethics, it can be put to use in the formulation of an international political theory that challenges conceptions of sovereignty, that is orientated, both ethically and politically, towards conditions of otherness, and that can begin to conceive of community as a project of cohabitation, responsibility, and liveability. Moreover, it is grounded in conceptions of grievability and precariousness that add force to the ethico-political ambition of Butler's wider political thought. Dispossession further underwrites the paradoxical nature of the subject. But while this paradox was initially formulated exclusively in relation to subjection to norms (see Butler 1997b), it is now developed in relation to the existence of the other.

The subject's relationality and sociality portend its vulnerability to the actions of known and unknown others. This claim implies that ethical obligations towards the other occur 'under pressure' (Butler 2006c, 127): I am comported towards the other, possibly against my wishes. In fact, such comportment constitutes the 'I', it deconstitutes singularity and disorientates the subject. This is a central theme in Butler's recent work that deserves separate attention in a later section of this chapter (see also Chapter 2). Yet sociality also enables forms of community that sustain the subject. Crucially, Butler is at pains to stress two aspects: first, community does not presuppose communitarian forms of collective life, understood as the unity or singularity of the group. Second, modes of dispossession and ethical obligation transcend national boundaries, and must therefore consider international or global conditions of relationality and interdependence, including the creation of global communities and global forms of solidarity (see Chapters 4 and 5). This claim is central to her overall argument, and it is worth quoting her at length (see also Chapter 3):

> [I]f my survivability depends on a relation . . . to a "you" . . . without whom I cannot exist, then my existence is not mine alone, but is to be found outside myself, in this set of relations that precede and exceed the boundaries of who I am. If I seek to preserve my life, it is not only because I seek to preserve my own, but because who "I" am is nothing without your life, and life itself has to be rethought as this complex, passionate, antagonistic and necessary set of relations to others. . . . If I

survive, it is only because my life is nothing without the life that exceeds me, that refers to some indexical you, without whom I cannot be.

(*FW*, 44)

By insisting on an account of ek-static subjectivity, Butler further foregrounds the idea of the decentred subject. Under what conditions such ek-static subject obtains recognition will be explored in the next section, but before I do so, I want to identify a key question that should be put to Butler's account of ek-static subjectivity: what kind of norms, or what operation of power is at play in the constitution of the ek-static subject? This question, I suggest, is indeed central to the appraisal of Butler's political philosophy.

THE POLITICS OF RECOGNITION

While we may all experience, or rather undergo, desire, we do not do so in isolation; rather, following Hegel, our desire clashes with the desire of an other, culminating in a struggle for recognition that, potentially, provides us with a sense of self. Thus, the significance of the concept of desire for modern philosophy is at least twofold: for one, it brings corporeality, antagonism, and passion into politics, while it also establishes sociality as a fundamental feature of politics. Importantly, though, desire is more than a private embrace of two desiring individuals who come to recognize one another. Rather, it has ramifications for our understanding of rights, citizenship, and identity. In other words, what appear on the surface as existential needs, as physical or emotional cravings, have profound implications for politics, law, and the state. There is a caveat, though, and this point (essentially a Foucauldian insight) is stressed by Butler repeatedly: having one's desire recognized does not release desire from regulation and normalization. As some scholars have pointed out, desire, recognition, and identity do not unfold outside time and space; they are not abstract categories. Rather, they obtain their meaning in concrete contexts, framed by norms, by dominant views that determine who deserves recognition and who doesn't, and whose desires are considered to be legitimate, and whose aren't. As I intimated above, desire is formed by normative power. Put simply, we are socialized into displaying acceptable desires, and the norms that govern our desire also normalize our behaviour. Thus, desire does not lie outside or beyond power. In fact, as Butler discusses in *The Psychic Life of Power* (1997b), norms produce desire (see also *CHU*, 151). Thus, the desires of the recognized female citizen or gay spouse do not lie outside or beyond power. Rather, they become regulated within a newly expanded or reformulated framework of citizenship and marriage respectively. What, then, is the linkage from desire to recognition?

In any given society, we find individuals and groups who are denied recognition of their identities, their rights, and their desires. What's more, we penalize those whose desires we consider to be wrong or dangerous.

Desires can be denounced as unnatural, abominations, destructive, disloyal. Sexuality and family life are two important instances that illustrate the regulation of desire; they can be charged with undermining the family, the community, religion, or even the state (see Chapter 2). The struggles of women to be recognized as equal citizens also demonstrates how masculine conception of what it means to be a citizen can be subverted. Thus, what we might want to call identity politics contains implicit assumptions about desire and its recognition.

If desire opens towards ek-stasis, a route travelled via relationality, it also raises the spectre of recognition, a concept that sits at the heart of Butler's political philosophy. To unpack its significance further, I return to *Subjects of Desire* ([1987] 1999)—this time, however, not to its Spinozan presuppositions, but rather to consider Butler's appropriation of the towering figure of modern Continental philosophy, Hegel. In *Subjects of Desire*, Butler argues that the French reception of Hegel's *Phenomenology* responds to a challenge in French intellectual life and society, such as the question of human action and the role of history. Animating Butler's reading of Hegel and eliciting her French Hegelian insights is the challenge of her own time. As she acknowledges in her preface to the paperback edition of *Subjects of Desire*, published in 1999, 'all of my work remains within the orbit of a certain set of Hegelian questions: What is the relation between desire and recognition, and how is it that the constitution of the subject entails a radical and constitutive relation to alterity?' (*SD*, xiv). More than two decades since the first publication of *Subjects of Desire*, Butler's questions may be reformulated in the following way: how can alterity be lived under global conditions of violence and inequality? What forms of global community are possible? And what are my ethical obligations towards distant and unknown others? In fact, one could argue that Butler tackles the challenge of becoming and temporality itself, that is, the operation of a narrative on time and progress that comes to frame the Western subject (see *Frames of War* (2009a) and my discussion in Chapter 4). It is the engagement with the subject, travelling towards but never fully reaching consciousness, which underpins her ongoing commitment to exploring questions of otherness.

Hegel's philosophy constitutes a key reference point for current work in this field. To develop his import further, I shall briefly unpack the unfolding of recognition in Hegel's philosophy before alluding to its deployment in post-Hegelian critical political thought. Within Hegel's wider oeuvre, recognition is traced back to two separate sources: his Jenaer writings, which have influenced Axel Honneth's work on recognition (see Honneth 1995), and his famous *Phenomenology* from 1803, which constitutes the reference for the development of Butler's thinking. To remain within the framework of the *Phenomenology*, Hegel's philosophy of recognition entails three key elements: (1) an emphasis on the constitutive role of struggle and conflict in the emergence of the self; (2) the necessity of an intersubjective dimension to identity, in other words, the necessity of the existence of an other to the emergence of the self; and (3) a stress on the equal nature of recognition. In the *Phenomenology*, Hegel demystifies those philosophies that posit the self as an independent, autonomous being. To develop his account, he imagines two consciousnesses who have not yet acquired a sense of self. When they meet, a struggle for sheer physical survival commences, with each consciousness wanting to impose its will upon the other. However, instead of one eventually killing the other, the weaker consciousness submits to the strength and superiority of the winner. The life and death struggle transforms into a relationship between lord and bondsman. Because he has lost, the bondsman is condemned to serving the master's need. While on the face of it the master occupies the more enviable position, he becomes increasingly dependent upon his bondsman. Because they are both rational creatures, lord and bondsman recognize their mutual dependence on one another, and start to recognize each other as equals.

The significance of Hegel's rendering of recognition to the development of modern and contemporary political thought, and to the formulation of revolutionary and liberation struggles, cannot be underestimated.[9] I already have alluded to the reception of Hegel in twentieth-century French philosophy in the previous section; notwithstanding differences in reception and interpretation, his philosophy of recognition is of similar import to sections of contemporary political philosophy, where recognition has become one of the most widely discussed ideas over the last two decades. Most contemporary students of Hegel share a fundamental commitment to recognition's centrality to the constitution of the self and to the generation of collective identity. Significantly, though, many contemporary thinkers focus less on recognition than on misrecognition, that is, the absence or refusal of recognition. It is the absence or, following Lacan, rather the constitutive failure of recognition that lies at the heart of struggles for recognition. Recall that Hegel stresses the importance of equality in the process of recognition, that is, of the imperative of both master and slave to recognize each other as equals. As contemporary readers of Hegel have observed, this cannot always be presumed. For example, Canadian philosopher Charles Taylor, in his essay 'The Politics of Recognition' (1994), is centrally concerned with the question of multiculturalism, which he relates to the idea of misrecognition. The work of the German philosopher Axel Honneth has also been deeply influenced by Hegel's account of recognition. In his book *The Struggle for Recognition* (1995), originally published in German in 1992, Honneth ponders whether an absence of recognition leads to psychic injury or hurt.[10]

Where, then, does Butler sit in this debate, and what is her distinctive contribution to the debate on recognition? I want to suggest that Butler's distinctive contribution to the debates on recognition is twofold: first, she establishes a connection between recognition and corporeality; and second, she connects recognition with a discussion of the idea of liveability (see also Chapter 2). Remarkably, even though recognition is central to Butler's political philosophy, she is not commonly referenced as a key contributor to the debates. This lack of acknowledgment is especially noteworthy if we consider that Butler's first systematic engagement with the topic, in *Subjects of Desire*, was published in 1987, several years before Honneth's and Taylor's contributions, both of which are often regarded as inaugurating texts of the contemporary recognition debate.[11] It is only more recently that Butler's work on recognition features more prominently in the wider scholarly debate on recognition, and that a critical commentary on her treatment of recognition is beginning to emerge.[12] I begin by sketching the elements of Butler's theory of recognition and its relation to the recognition discourse.

As I have argued, a key feature and widespread depiction of the struggle for recognition relates to its intersubjective aspect, building on the presence of two consciousnesses who, via conflict and struggle, reach an agreement that provides recognition for both. Although this relational aspect is crucial to Butler's work, she revisits Hegel in *The Psychic Life of Power* (1997b), in order to track the significance of the unhappy consciousness, also articulated in the *Phenomenology*, on the development of the subject. Producing a convergence of Hegel, Nietzsche, Foucault, Althusser, and Freud, Butler argues that the subject must desire its own subjection in order to persist in its being. This subjection manifests itself in two ways: via a passionate attachment to those on whom the subject depends, and via an attachment to norms. As she argues, '[t]o desire the conditions of one's own subordination is . . . required to persist as oneself' (*PLP*, 9). *The Psychic Life of Power* travels further with Hegel's own text, moving on to the next section in the *Phenomenology* on the unhappy consciousness, but, as I intimated in the previous section, she adds a distinctive reading, which stresses the paradoxical nature of subjectivation. In *The Psychic Life of Power*, she ponders the role of norms and the subject's submission to norms in the struggle for recognition, and the threat posed by the prospect of dissolution. This development in Butler's textual work allows her to develop a distinctive Hegel interpretation that comes to frame her account of the subject, and that draws on the insights of Nietzsche, Freud, and Foucault. Thus, Butler's neo-Nietzschean reading of Hegel, already commenced in *Subjects of Desire* ([1987] 1999), allows Butler to utilize Hegelian ideas in the development of her account of the paradoxical or ambivalent subject.

Butler returns to the question of recognition with *Antigone's Claim: Kinship between Life and Death* (2000a), where she gestures towards a reading of Antigone as a figure transgressive of heterosexual kinship arrangements, the ethical sphere, and the state. Pondering Antigone's significance for contemporary renditions of kinship, specifically those articulated in the context of non-heterosexual relationships, Butler challenges both Hegel and Lacan.[13] In fact, it is largely in relation to kinship matters, and to the critique of heteronormative kinship arrangements, that *Antigone's Claim* has been read. Such readings lead to important discussions on the question of recognition, specifically on the recognition of kinship structures.[14] Moreover, they pose the question of the human, which Butler develops more fully in

Undoing Gender (2004a) (I will discuss this in more detail in the next section). Such gesturing towards kinship and sexuality resurfaces in *Undoing Gender*, where Butler takes up the thread of recognition and develops it further, this time in the context of the so-called 'New Gender Politics' and the misrecognition of sexual minorities, specifically trans- and intersexuals (see also Chapter 2).

What interests me in Butler's discussion is the distinction she makes between recognition and recognizability (see *FW*): while recognition, in Hegelian fashion, is said to refer to reciprocal acts or practices that involve at least two subjects, recognizability denotes the general condition where recognition can take place. In other words, recognizability frames recognition: recognition presupposes awareness of the norms of intelligibility established by recognizability, so that recognition can only ever take place on the field of recognizability. However, even though the normative ontology of the frame, and with it the acts of recognition and field of recognizability, aim to circumscribe the subject, it should not be surprising that the Butlerian subject tends to exceed the limits imposed upon it by the frame. The iterability of the frames of recognition and schemas of intelligibility produce the conditions for extending or breaking the limits of the frame. Such subversive citationality also points to the structural weakness of the frame: as Butler points out, the intelligibility of the framed subject is contingent upon its outside, that is, on what lies outside the frame. That is, frames can never fully control, contain, or 'frame', recognition. As Butler contends, '[t]he frame never quite determine[s] precisely what it is we see, think, recognize, and apprehend. Something exceeds the frame that troubles our sense of reality; in other words, something occurs that does not conform to our established understanding of things' (*FW*, 9).

CHALLENGING RECOGNITION

I intimated that Butler's work on recognition does not feature prominently in the broader recognition debates; however, this aspect of her work has received attention from those engaging specifically with Butler's ideas. Three concerns surface in the critical commentary on Butler's account of recognition, relating to her treatment of the state (see Lloyd 2005, 2007; see also Chapter 5), to the relationship between recognition and redistribution, and to her alleged conflation of dependence with subjection. It is the latter two aspects that occupy me in this section. Not surprisingly, a large part of Butler's work on recognition explores the way it relates to questions of gender and sexuality. This focus is foregrounded in her exchange with Nancy Fraser, which centres on the relative merit of recognition over redistribution. Fraser (1995) ponders what she terms the 'redistribution—recognition dilemma'. In brief, she points up an alleged blind spot of recognition theories towards social inequality. As she argues, recognition and redistribution are two analytically separate forms of injustice, with recognition (which she conceives of as 'recognition for difference') articulating patterns of cultural or symbolic injustices, while redistribution attends to socioeconomic injustice. The crux for Fraser lies in her claim that struggles for recognition take place in the context of material inequality. Recognition struggles are thus derived from, or secondary to, struggles for redistribution.

The rendering of Butler's work as inattentive to questions of material equality, and to the economy more broadly, is a persistent feature of the critical commentary of her work, and I explicate and assess some of the criticisms further on. As I argue in the next chapter, Butler's recent attention to questions of precarity, which articulate unequal conditions of vulnerability, including material conditions, goes some way towards redressing the accusation of a neglect of the economy and social equality. For now, I want to focus on Butler's criticism of Fraser. In her response to Fraser, Butler rebuts the claim that struggles for recognition, specifically those expressed by sexual minorities, are 'merely cultural'. As she asks, 'is it possible to distinguish, even analytically, between a lack of cultural recognition and material oppression, when the very definition of "personhood" is rigorously circumscribed by cultural norms that are indissociable from their material effects?' (Butler 1997c, 273). Furthermore, Butler charges Fraser with instituting a binary between culture and economy, which, in Butler's view, exerts a violent subordination of one to the other, and which enforces a false unity that must be challenged by left democratic politics.

While Fraser's critique of Butler centres on the relationship between recognition and redistribution, Amy Allen (2006) focuses on a problem internal to Butler's account of recognition. Allen detects a broad ambivalence in Butler's work on recognition, which is said to arise from a perceived tension between some of Butler's earlier efforts to account for recognition, specifically as it is articulated in *The Psychic Life of Power* (1997b), and some of her more recent texts (here Allen draws on *Precarious Life* (2004b)).[15] Allen contends that in the earlier text, Butler equates subordination with dependency. Given the subject's passionate attachment to its own subordination, Allen (2006) worries that such an account is normatively problematic, and that it cannot provide answers to her key concern. This is the challenge to consider how subjection to normative femininity can be resisted (201). For Allen, the deeply entrenched structures of subjection constitute an impasse that prevents the generation of more positive forms of recognition. She is more open to the stress in Butler's recent work on relationality, corporeal vulnerability, and ethical obligations. Such emphasis, according to Allen, reformulates recognition as a non- or less subordinating normative ideal. However, this normative reorientation is undermined, Allen contends, with Butler's critique of intersubjectivity, formulated in her engagement with Jessica Benjamin's work. Towards the end of the essay 'Longing for Recognition', included in *Undoing Gender* (2004a), Butler identifies her insistence on the ek-static notion of the self as a fundamental difference to Benjamin's account of a dyadic structure of recognition. As Butler argues there, the self is defined by an 'ontological ek-stasis', 'beyond itself from the start' (*UG*, 150). Consequently, recognition is 'a question of so much more than the two of us': 'the "we" who are relational do not stand apart from those relations and cannot think of ourselves outside of the decentering effects that relationality entails. Moreover, . . . the relations by which we are defined are not dyadic, but always refer to a historical legacy and futural horizon that is not contained by the Other . . . who we "are" fundamentally is a subject in a temporal chain of desire that only occasionally and provisionally assumes the form of the dyad' (*UG*, 151).

One of the aims of *Undoing Gender* (2004a) is to displace the dyadic structure of recognition in order to imagine gender and sexuality outside or beyond such dualism (or beyond the triangular structure of Oedipalization). This approach carries additional significance for thinking the complex web of recognition under global conditions of plurality. Such global dimension of the recognition debate is key to some of Butler's most recent work. If Hegel's struggle for recognition centres on two consciousnesses, post-Hegelian thinking expands this concept by looking at the context of collective politics. Thus, an exclusive focus on the internal dynamics of contemporary societies glosses over recognition's global significance as well as the fact, pointed up recently by O'Neill and Walsh (2009), that struggles for recognition do not stop at national borders. Such insight into the global significance of recognition struggles, and of the global ramifications of the concept of recognition, motivates some of the 'foundation' texts of contemporary scholarship on recognition, such as Taylor's (1994) discussion of the politics of multiculturalism, its consideration of transnational migration processes and their centrality to contemporary disputes over multiculturalism, and migration internal to contemporary societies. In her most recent work on bi-nationalism, Butler connects the question of recognition in the context of multi-ethnic societies to the practices and forms of institutionalization of citizenship that, potentially, transcends or reconfigures state boundaries (see Chapter 5). Here I want to reflect on a further dimension that features prominently in her work: her critique of the unequal distribution of recognition on a global stage, and its association with racialized discourses on civilization (see Chapter 3).

Butler's discussion centres on two related aspects. These are first, the ramifications of the war on terror on the politics of recognition and on constituting global structures of recognizability, and second, the impact of unequal distribution of recognition on a global level. I assess the claims made on violence in Chapter 3, while Chapter 5 attends to conceptions of post-sovereign politics. Here I want to focus on *Frames of War*, her book from 2009, because it is there that Butler refines her discussion of recognition and clarifies various developments in her ideas since 9/11. As Butler declares, *Frames of War* is a collection of essays written between 2004 and 2008, all of which deal with contemporary war and with the regulation of our responses to war and violence, which Butler calls a frame. The notion of the frame surfaces repeatedly in some of her previous work, specifically in *Precarious Life* (2004b) and in *Giving an Account of Oneself* (2005), but it is in *Frames of War* where this concept finds its most explicit application. As I already have intimated, Butler seeks to elucidate why and how we respond to particular acts of violence,[16] and she connects this question with the notion of recognition.

Here I wish to pause for a moment: so far, I have mapped Butler's account of the subject in relation to the concept of desire and to the ek-static structure of subjectification, and I explicated some of the main features of the recognition debate. Butler's reading of recognizability and of recognition, coupled with her previous work on norms and with the new emphasis on the frame, offers a compelling way of approaching the problem of recognition. It allows her to articulate the paradoxical conditions under which recognition takes place, embedding the practices of recognition deeply within the structure of recognizability. This interpretation is also put to work in the global context. Although I have mapped some of the key parameters of Butler's political philosophy of the human, I will develop this discussion further by attending to the following aspects: the constitutive role of violence in the production of the subject (see Chapter 3), the material conditions of liveability (see Chapter 2), and the ontological anchors of Butler's work. It is this latter aspect that I address in the remainder of this chapter.

BUTLER'S (RE-)TURNS? ONTOLOGY AND ETHICS

Three aspects, previously underdeveloped in Butler's writings, have received significant attention in her recent work and have contributed to a notable change in approach: her explicit engagement with questions of ontology, her discussion of ethics, and, interwoven with these two, her turn towards an explicit endorsement of normative political theorizing. In this section I address these developments, beginning with an examination of Butler's alleged turn to ontology, before attending to the status and significance of ethics in her post-9/11 writings and to the focus on normative theory and its relationship to critique. I suspect that Butler's densely plotted argument regarding the relationship between ontology and ethics and its implications for politics may not always appeal to those who continue to subscribe to critical, or genealogical, perspectives. However, regardless of how we evaluate Butler's 'ethical ontology' (Murphy 2011), it has significant bearing on her conception of politics, including politics beyond the nation state.[17]

As a path into Butler's ontological reflections I draw on Stephen K. White's (1999, 2000) discussion of weak ontology. According to White, two mutually exclusive positions have dominated political theorizing and have led to discontent amongst critical thinkers: these are, on the one hand, strong ontology—essentially a form of ontology which grounds itself in metaphysical claims—and on the other hand, an alleged lack of ontological commitments, which he associates with liberalism. Navigating the extreme positions of metaphysical ontology on the one hand, and ontological nihilism on the other, contemporary political thought has begun to embark upon a turn to ontology that White refers to as 'weak ontology'. Although there is no agreed position amongst weak ontologists (White discusses several thinkers, including Butler, with his own favourite version of weak ontology represented in William Connolly's work), weak ontology shares a number of characteristics: it is said to be anti-metaphysical, critical of the alleged liberal neglect of ontological reflection, and located in an interpretive-existential terrain that rejects naturalization, reification, and unity, emphasizing instead contestability and reflection. This ontological turn is centrally engaged with the question of human being and its struggle with ontological givens, such as bodily needs and mortality on the one hand, and with the contingent constitutive forces of language, such as culture and history on the other hand.

It is easy to relate White's depiction of weak ontology to Butler's work. For example, the emphasis on contestability and practices of the cultivation of the self, as well as the engagement with the other and the world are key themes in Butler's oeuvre.[18] A more sustained reflection on questions of ontology is presented in her recent work, especially in *Frames of War* (2009a), where Butler attends to the ontological conditions of human life (in fact, to the question of the human), including those material givens that White regards as crucial, and where Butler, in critical fashion, distinguishes between universal human requirements and existential experiences of dependency, mortality, and susceptibility to violence (which she terms precariousness), and the differential, indeed unequal, distribution across different populations (which she terms precarity; see my discussion in Chapter 2). Ontology for Butler is thus inseparable from the social and political context in which it operates; it is a function of power, insofar it disguises its naturalizing effects, but it is also an effect of the relation to the other. Thus, ontology is 'always given over to others, to norms, to social and political organizations that have developed historically in order to maximize precariousness for some and minimize precariousness for others' (*FW*, 2–3). Ontology, in other words, is social; what's more, it is implicated in a structure of ethical relationality that comprises both obligation and dependency. Thus, Butler's increasing explicit emphasis on questions of being is mirrored in her concern for questions of being responsible, and it is captured in her turn towards ethics.

Butler's so-called turn to ethics has generated substantial interest in the recent scholarship on her work. In fact, there is some dispute over the nature of this turn and its relationship to ontology. For example Carver and Chambers (2008) conceive of Butler's turn to ethics as a turn, or (re-) turn, to ontology (93).[19] Although critical of the focus on moral philosophy as it is articulated in *Giving an Account of Oneself* (2005), they read Butler's ontology as political theory, and they contend, furthermore, that the realms of politics cannot be separated from those of ethics (117). While I

am sympathetic towards this interpretation, it leaves unexplained the genealogy of Butler's own account of the role of ethics and its relationship to
politics in her writings. In this respect, her 'turn' is all the more remarkable
because she has previously denounced ethics as non-political. For example,
in a well-known interview with William Connolly, Butler famously confesses
to worry about the turn to ethics. As she argues, 'ethics displaces from politics, and for me the use of power as a point of departure for a critical analysis
is substantially different from an ethical framework' (Butler 2000c). The
dualism she construes between politics and ethics, and the professed preference for a critical analysis (derived from the use of the concept of power)
over ethics is overcome with her later move towards ethics, specifically in
her ambition to challenge those who equate post-structuralism with moral
nihilism (*GAO*, 21). Her engagement with post-9/11 politics, as well as her
continued attention to questions of liveability in the context of the so-called
'New Gender Politics', which she addresses in *Undoing Gender* (2004a), has
generated a substantial output on material that deals with ethics (see Chapter 2). Ethical themes run through all of Butler's post-9/11 writings, but the
main source for this work is *Giving an Account of Oneself* (2005), the publication of Butler's Adorno lectures delivered at the University of Frankfurt
and her Spinoza lectures delivered at the University of Amsterdam. Three
broad parameters structure Butler's conception of ethics: first, building on
her reading of Levinas, she pursues the idea that we have ethical obligations
towards unknown others who make ethical demands upon us; further, we
are ethically required to respond to these demands. Second, Butler develops
her idea of ethics out of her wider thinking on the relational dimension of
the subject. That is, we emerge and persist because others have taken seriously their ethical obligations towards us. As she puts it, 'in the beginning
I am my relation to you, . . . given over to a you without whom I cannot be
and upon whom I depend to survive' (*GAO*, 81; italics in original). Such
relationality does not presume, however, the emergence of a self-contained
subject. Rather, we remain comported towards others, dispossessed and
ecstatic. Third, ethics is enmeshed with politics and thus with power.

While Butler's turn to ethics has acquired a significant role in her work,
it continues to cause considerable consternation amongst some of her readers, who struggle to reconcile this turn to ethics with her championing of
radical politics.[20] Some of her critics mirror the concerns originally articulated by Butler herself. For example, Jodie Dean (2008) worries about an
'ethics without politics' (110), which, she fears, is purchased at the expense
of recognizing the essentially antagonistic nature of politics. Others, such
as Diana Coole, are less concerned with Butler's turn to ethics as such,
but struggle with one particular source of Butler's ethics; this is, in Coole's
(2008) view, the abstractly normative philosophy of Levinas and Kant (27),
which, according to Coole, is at odds with Butler's otherwise genealogical
and existential phenomenological approach that dominated much of her
earlier work.[21] As I intimated in my introduction, Butler justifies her use

of Levinas, arguing that he provides her with a way of thinking of alterity that is of significance to her current intellectual undertaking. I share Coole's reservations regarding the deployment of Levinas, and I remain unconvinced that Levinas can provide Butler with a sufficiently rich account of alterity that is attentive to the historical and social context of alterity. However, as I argue in Chapter 4, Butler's deployment of Levinas should be seen in the context of her wider engagement with Jewish ethics and philosophy and with her effort to articulate a conception of ethical responsibility that is, at least partly, informed by the experience of the Holocaust.

Butler's subscription to a position of social ontology, coupled with her turn to ethics, has implications for the way she frames her political theorizing and philosophising within the context of normative theory. The question of normativity has occupied the reception of her work at least since the publication of *Gender Trouble,* and it turns on normativity's relationship to critical theory. In other words, against which standards or conceptions of normativity should critique develop? Although Butler's earlier work prioritizes critical practice, it would be wrong to conclude that critique, for her, is detached from normative theory. What interests me here is her later work, which takes an explicit normative turn, and which is underpinned by her interest in ethics and ontology. This normative turn is most pronounced in her recent writings on global issues, and there are two significant aspects pertaining to the methodological dimension of Butler's writings that I wish to highlight. These are (1) the relationship between a critical and a normative approach that I already have flagged up; and (2) the relationship of Butler's methodological approach to the analytical tradition.

References to a normative framework surface frequently in Butler's recent writings, which are peppered with a commitment to principles of justice (*PL*, xi;). Such references may appeal to those critics who have sought in vain for a normative dimension, and who have previously dismissed Butler's work for its lack of emancipatory compass or its inability to adjudicate on the desirability (or lack of it) of certain political practices. Moreover, whereas her earlier work failed to reconcile normative approaches with critical methodologies, this connection is more successfully achieved in her recent work. For example, *Frames of War* (2009a) acknowledges the importance of asking normative questions about social and political life (*FW*, 138). However, the normative framing of political analysis is not without its problems, especially when we consider that the norms at the centre of normative theory are themselves potentially problematic and in need of clarification and interpretation. Thus, normative commitments are mediated via the practice of critique, which seeks to uncover underlying ontological claims as well as the historical framework of the norm at play. As Butler argues, '[t]he point . . . is not to dispense with normativity, but to insist that normative inquiry take on a critical and comparative form' (*FW*, 162). Furthermore, '[i]t will be necessary to reconsider the relationship of ethics to social critique, since part of what I find so hard to narrate are the norms—social in character—that bring me into being' (*GAO*, 82). The relationship between norms and critique is a circular one: while norms facilitate my persistence, they are also subjected to critique that cannot be disentangled from yet another set of norms. Yet, while Butler's conscious move towards an acknowledgement of the significance (and limitations) of norms is to be welcomed, it sits, as I already suggested, uneasy with her ahistorical appropriation of Levinas's ethics and his conception of the subject.

ONTOLOGY, ETHICS, POLITICS

At the beginning of this chapter, I put forward a reading of Butler's account of subject formation as relational, ek-static, or dispossessed. As I intimated there, Butler's explorations of Spinoza, together with her broader references to the operation of social ontology, configure a relation between ethics and politics that I have, until now, not fully explored. This section attends to the broader vectors of Butler's critical thought, relating to her treatment of ontology, ethics, and politics. Butler's treatment of ethics, its relationship to politics, and her invocation of ontology have invited substantial criticism from her readers, and I want to use some of the critical commentary on her work as the foil against which I present my own reading of her. I begin by considering Ann V. Murphy's (2011) article 'Corporeal Vulnerability and the New Humanism', which foregrounds the intrinsic conception said to exist between the ethical dimension of Butler's writings and her portrayal of ontology. Proceeding to read this connection as an 'ethical ontology', Murphy highlights Butler's (and Adriana Cavarero's) stress on relationality (here I am only concerned with the reading of Butler), which she grounds in a bodily ontology that presupposes a vulnerability to violence and that predisposes ethical obligations towards the other (577). As Murphy argues, ethical ontology, that is, the 'co-implication of ethics and ontology . . . refuses the priority of either' (588).[22]

Murphy's reading of Butler's texts offers a faithful rendition of the spirit of Butler's arguments, stressing how ethical relationality and obligations are implicated in our fundamental vulnerability to her other. However, her focus on ethics and ontology brackets the question that occupies me: the question of politics. More critical receptions of Butler have focused on this relationship between ethics and politics and on the way that precariousness and vulnerability are anchored in this relationship. George Shulman (2011) detects a formalism in Butler's account of vulnerability, which is said to be selective in two ways: (1) by appealing 'to the powerful through their own vulnerability to injury', and (2) by giving attention to the existential fact of death while ignoring other threats, such as climate change or economic oppression. Moreover, it displaces politics by privileging ethical obligations to others at the expense of concrete political responses to the political foundations of precarity (see also Dean 2008). Janell Watson's (2012) critique of Butler turns on the relationship between (existential) precariousness and (the unequal distribution of) precarity. For Watson, '[p]recarity is the problem, but precariousness is not the solution'. She charges Butler with not addressing problems of production, distribution, and governance, and of inviting a 'laissez-faire liberalism', which weakens the state and further fragments the economy. Butler's alleged advocacy of 'vulnerability for all as an oppositional politics' remains unconvincing, according to Watson, because it displaces political intervention with a moral stance. While Murphy conceives of Butler's relational ontology as a critique of liberal individualism and of the subject as autonomous (and here I concur with Murphy's interpretation), Watson, and also Julian Reid (2011), construe Butler's social ontology and her insistence on vulnerability as deeply liberal.

Of course, such reading hinges on the way we understand liberalism, a problem I cannot fully address here. It suffices to refer to a recent comment Butler made, where she insists that 'this idea of a primary dispossession in and by the other works well as a critique of those forms of atomistic individuality that are bequeathed to us from the liberal political tradition' (Butler 2007c, 383). Before I present my arguments I want to turn to some of Reid's (2011) further assertions. As he suggests, to insist on vulnerability as a foundational condition of the subject leads to articulating demands for a state that protects us from vulnerability; it 'instantiates the very demand for protection on which liberal governance depends for its legitimation in relation to the subject' (773). I am not convinced that construing Butler's relational and ecstatic conceptions of vulnerability in Hobbesian terms is well judged. Isn't it precisely the refusal to insist on protection, to shield the subject from vulnerability, and to insist on the subject's openness, dispossession, and ekstasis that characterizes Butler's account of vulnerability? As Butler argues, it is the denial of vulnerability, which she depicts as a 'fantasy of mastery' (*PL*, 29), that furnishes military solutions and that entrenches unequal global distributions of vulnerability. The challenge, I believe, lies with drawing the distinction between existential forms of vulnerability, which constitute a point of departure for political life (*PL*, xii), and concrete and specific forms of vulnerability that are the product of power.

While Reid conceives of vulnerability as a problem of epistemology, not of ontology, for Butler the two are inseparable: persistence (as an ontological category) and recognition (an epistemological category) are intrinsically linked. I would like to put this objection into the context of Butler's own consideration of ontology and epistemology at the beginning of *Frames of War* (2009a). There, she asks how the question of comprehending a life is shaped by the issue of framing (an epistemological category), which influences what we can see and hear (an ontological category). Thus, epistemology operates alongside ontology: it seeks to determine what counts as a life. Reid's second objection pertains to vulnerability's quality as a basis for political resistance, especially when it is also conjured up by security states, which legitimize their actions through an appeal to the vulnerability of their populations. His invocation of the notion of masculinist protection in the face of vulnerability (see also Young 2003a; 2003b) misconstrues how Butler deploys vulnerability in the service of an ethics of relationality.

A more nuanced but critical appraisal is offered by Moya Lloyd (2008). Whereas Murphy considers the relationship between ethics and ontology, and Reid focuses on the linkage between ontology and epistemology, Lloyd attends to a tension internal to Butler's conception of ontology: this is the tension between a version of ontology as contested and contestable, which Butler refers to as social ontology, and her unacknowledged ontological premise (92). Much of Lloyd's criticism turns on Butler's deployment of Spinoza's conatus, specifically the unquestioned assumption of a desire to persist in one's being. Such deployment, Lloyd claims, fails to interrogate the terms of the social which construe the desire to persist in the first place. In other words, under what conditions, in which contexts, and in which language is persistence articulated? Butler, according to Lloyd, assumes rather than problematizes the ontological nature of the desire for existence (101): as she argues, '[w]hat is required, instead, is an exploration of the desire for existence as a discursive construction or cultural practice operating according to and constituted by certain historically specific norms and power relations' (101). This inquiry into the status of desire, and into Butler's unacknowledged ontological assumptions, also extends to Butler's conception of ethics. Lloyd queries in particular how Butler, prior to her turn to ethics, construes her opposition to ethics as a displacement of politics; moreover, whilst she is sympathetic to Butler's overall ethical project, she argues for the need to address its 'unexamined prediscursive assumptions' (104). As I already have suggested, such tension between unquestioned ontological premises and the formulation of a social ontology arises because of Butler's increasing interest in existential questions, and, I suspect, the tension between the two cannot be finally adjudicated.

Given the frequency with which the charge of a displacement of politics in favour of ethics is raised against Butler's work, it is apposite to address this matter here. As I already have suggested, the occasion for this criticism relates to her recent deployment of Levinasian ideas, and to an alleged privileging of ontological questions said to be pursued at the expense of historical and social analysis and their contingency. To further unravel the relationship between ethics and politics, I draw on Sara Rushing's (2010) recent article on Butler's ethical dispositions and their implications for Butler's political thought. Rushing argues that Butler does not prioritize ethics over politics; rather, she claims that Butler posits ethics as 'a form of self-cultivation that can be seen as preceding and informing the contingent, contestatory political interactions that she will never describe in advance for us' (285). To elaborate, Rushing reads Butler's politics as one of 'unsatisfaction', cultivating a virtue of restraint and not-doing in the face of political challenges.[23]

Although I sympathize with Rushing's reading of Butler, specifically with her stress on the ethics of the self as a way to inform politics, I wonder whether such reading gets Butler off the hook. In this respect, I am uncomfortable with Rushing's choice of terminology, specifically with her idea that an ethical disposition constitutes a way of '*preparing* for politics' (my emphasis). Such an assertion, like Murphy's (2011), cannot answer how, when, where, and in which discursive contexts these ethical dispositions emerge. Put differently, rather than asking for the ethical dispositions for politics, my question (and that of some of her other critics) is to ask after the political structures of ethics. Thus, even though Butler's relational account of the subject and her stress on the existential precariousness of human life has substantial merit, I remain unconvinced that the relationship between ethics and politics, as she currently presents it, is fully articulated. What is missing, furthermore, is a more fully developed acknowledgement of the genealogy of the ethical practices that Butler champions. To solve this conundrum requires more careful attention to the distinction between an existential ontology, which addresses fundamental bodily needs and the fact of bodily decay and mortality, and a construal of relationality as culturally and historically specific.

My aim in this chapter was to outline Butler's account of subject formation, which builds on conceptions of relationality, ek-stasis, and dispossession. Furthermore, I sought to demonstrate how this account of the subject informs her conception of ethics and ontology. In the next chapter, I develop this discussion by turning to Butler's attention to the concept of the human.

NOTES

1. The concept of performativity continues to exert influence on Butler's thinking. See for example the title of her most recent book, co-authored with Athena Athanasiou—*Dispossession: The Performative in the Political* (2013a).
2. In Chapter 2, I develop the discussion of Butler's account of subject formation by considering what I term Butler's political philosophy of the human.
3. As I discuss further later on, Butler's engagement with the concept of ek-stasis can be traced back to some of her early articles (see 1986; 1987).
4. On the relationship between critique and philosophy see Butler (2012b).
5. Butler deploys a variety of terms to account for such structures of intelligibility, including that of the norm and (increasingly in her recent writings) that of the frame.
6. Though see Lloyd (2007, 2008), where Lloyd renders Butler's deployment of Spinoza's idea of persistence as problematic, because it is said to lack an analysis of the social and historical conditions and the context of relationality and interdependency. As I will argue, such a flaw is substantially redressed by attending to the material conditions of life, captured by Butler with the term precarity (see below in this chapter) and, more specifically, through reference to the existential conditions of human life.
7. I return to this theme in Chapter 3, where I consider the claim of relationality in Butler's discussion of Laplanche.
8. As I argue in Chapter 4, Butler's more recent work foregrounds the specifically Jewish sources of the concept of ek-stasis. Her deployment of Levinas's concept of the face should also be read in the context of her formulation of the

subject as dispossessed. For the relevance of ek-stasis in the context of global politics, see my discussion in Chapter 5.

9. The reception of the Hegelian narrative of master and slave in modern and contemporary accounts of liberation is wide-ranging, including, amongst others, the works of Marx, Simone de Beauvoir, and Frantz Fanon.

10. Ferrarese (2011) suggests that contemporary theories of recognition operate with an ontology of the human as constitutively fragile and vulnerable. For a more fundamental criticism of the concept of recognition see McNay (2008).

11. See for example Thompson (2006), whose focus on contributions by Honneth, Taylor, and Nancy Fraser is symptomatic for the way that much of the recognition debate is framed. See also McBride (2013).

12. See Allen (2006), Ferrarese (2011), and Lloyd (2005; 2007).

13. See Hutchings (2003) for a reading of Butler in relation to Hegel.

14. See for example Steiner's (1984) reading of Sophocles' *Antigone* in the context of conflict and recognition. As he argues, the play articulates five constants of conflict, which comprise 'the confrontation of men and of women; of age and of youth; of society and of the individual; of the living and the dead; of men and of god(s)' (231). These constants, moreover, articulate what Steiner regards as '[s]elf-definition and the agonistic recognition of 'otherness' (of *l'autre*) across the threatened boundaries of self, are indissociable' (231–2; italics in original).

15. For a similar argument see also Ferrarese (2011), in which Ferrarese seeks to establish a convergence between Butler's theory of recognition (based on her more recent work) and that of Honneth.

16. I develop this discussion more fully in a forthcoming essay on 'Violence, Affect and Ethics' (2014).

17. As I discuss in Chapter 4, her recent consideration of Jewish philosophy requires, I believe, a further revision of the connection between ethics, ontology, and politics.

18. White asserts that Butler's early work, especially *Gender Trouble* (1990), has generated questions regarding the normative orientation and foundation of her project that have only been addressed in later texts; White considers in particular Butler's discussion of melancholia in *The Psychic Life of Power* (1997b), which is said to provide a more sustained and plausible account of the ontology of the subject. Although I am broadly in agreement with White's interpretation of the ontology of *The Psychic Life of Power*, I do not regard *Gender Trouble* as a text void of ontological considerations. Instead, I want to suggest that these considerations are present in her early work, albeit in implicit form.

19. In fact, Chambers and Carver refute the notion of a turn, as in their view ontological and ethical concerns have always figured in Butler's work. For a perspective which considers Butler's initial rejection of ethics see Lloyd (2008).

20. For a sympathetic reading of Butler's turn to ethics see Gutterman and Rushing (2008) and Rushing (2010).

21. See also Lloyd (2008) on the development of the relationship between ethics and politics in Butler's work.

22. Later in the text I return to Murphy's assertion that Butler's focus on ethical comportment towards the other acts as a barrier to violence: she develops a hesitation which is the hallmark of responsibility. See also Rushing (2010).

23. In Chapter 3, I return to the discussion of such a politics of not-doing, which lies at the heart of Butler's ethics and politics of non-violence, but for now I want to remain with the ethics-politics relationship.

2   The Political Philosophy of the Human

Have we ever yet known the human?
(*Undoing Gender*)

Building on my discussion in Chapter 1, where I examined Butler's account of subject formation based on the concepts of ek-stasis, relationality, and dispossession, this chapter focuses on Butler's recent work, which I propose to read as a political philosophy of the human. At first glance, interpreting Butler's work in relation to the human appears counter-intuitive, given her broad adherence to a Foucauldian framework, and its resistance to the idea of humanism. In fact, her fidelity to Foucauldian ideas dominates her choice of terminology, specifically her wide-ranging references to 'the subject', a notion which constitutes a prominent part of the rhetoric and conceptual repertoire of post-structural theorizing. Fundamental to her account of the subject is the concept of power. As she suggests, power pervades the conceptual apparatus that constitutes us as subjects (see Butler 1992). It governs 'what we are, what we can be' (Butler 2004a, 57), and in doing so, it saturates the regulatory categories of identity that produce us as intelligible subjects. Such narrative of subjectification renders the subject paradoxical. While becoming a subject is an enabling experience that allows us to engage in meaningful ways with others, it can also be deeply disabling and painful, because it entails subjection to the kind of conceptual apparatuses, identity categories, and norms that we have not—and possibly would not have—chosen for ourselves, and that we may never inhabit either fully or comfortably.

As I intimated in the previous chapter, Butler conceives of the subject as entangled with the processes of subjectification. In *The Psychic Life of Power* (1997a), she argues that the subject is the target of disciplinary power that, paradoxically, comes to enable its persistence while simultaneously subjecting it to hegemonic norms.[1] In this chapter, I further explore the significance of the shift in Butler's recent terminology that I alluded to in Chapter 1, from a concern with 'the subject' towards exploring the possibilities for 'the human'. My suggestion to read Butler's work as a political philosophy of the human draws on a terminological and semantic shift in her writings, which increasingly reference 'the human'. This shift, as we have already seen, is accompanied by a renewed attention to the notion of ek-stasis and to conceptions of relationality, dispossession, dependency, and liveability. Although Butler does not give up on the significance of power to the process of subjectification, her shift in terminology points towards a displacement of power, stressing instead the increased emphasis on and acknowledgement of the importance of alterity. Thus, this shift has important theoretical consequences: while it does not liberate the subject-human from constraint, it provides a closer focus on the idea of liveability. In doing so, it ameliorates the crushing experience of the constraining, indeed tragic, conditions of power and conscience.

To illustrate the significance of such discursive constitution of the human, I draw on recent examples from public political discourse on marriage equality. These examples, I suggest, elucidate uses of the term 'human' and its implications for a conception of human rights.[2] Here I develop my discussion in a different direction. Aiming to further clarify Butler's deployment of the human, I expound her concepts of life, liveability, and vulnerability. These themes, together with the concept of the human, have become increasingly significant to her political philosophy, and, as I already have suggested in Chapter 1, could profitably be read as the canvas for all of Butler's political-philosophical concerns. They obtain particular significance with her turn to ethics and her explicit move onto the terrain of normative philosophy (see Introduction). This terrain is densely populated, and one of my aims in this chapter is to establish which discursive space Butler occupies and how she furnishes it.

I also develop another matter already raised in the previous chapter. This is the significance of the material conditions of human life for conceptions of the human. To delineate this problematic, I read Butler's concept of liveability against the capabilities approach associated with the work of Martha C. Nussbaum (2011). This comparison allows me to gain purchase on a key criticism of Butler's work: her alleged neglect of the material conditions of human life. I also discuss her work on life and on the human in the context of her recent appropriation of aspects of Hannah Arendt's work ([1951] 1976; [1963a] 2006a; [1963b] 2006b). This lays the foundation for concerns addressed in later chapters. I conclude by unpacking her recent assertions on the human and her treatment of humanism, before discussing the implications for a politics of human rights. A main question that needs to be answered is whether Butler's endorsement of 'the human' leads her to subscribe to a form of philosophical humanism that rejects notions of the decentred subject. As I will argue, such a move would run against the gist of her early work. Rather, Butler's conception of the human remains attached to the idea of decentring, conceiving of the human as relational, open, ecstatic, dispossessed, and interdependent.

THE POLITICS OF LIFE AND DEATH: LIVEABILITY BEYOND RECOGNITION

Referring to the French Hegel reception in the wake of World War II, Butler declares that 'Hegel provided a way . . . to derive the transformative potential from every experience of defeat. The destruction of institutions and ways of life, the mass annihilation and sacrifice of human life, revealed the contingency of existence in brutal and indisputable terms' (*SD*, 62). The development of a philosophical framework that responds to the exposure of violence and that articulates the vulnerability of existence is a key theme in Butler's recent work.

As I indicated in the previous chapter, recognition struggles are manifestations of the subject's existential vulnerability and its dependence upon an other. In fact, the constitutive failure of recognition configures life as ontologically unstable and insecure, or, as Butler calls it, precarious (see below). It profoundly impacts the way we live our lives, resulting in what Butler, borrowing from Orlando Patterson (1982), refers to as social death.[3] Social death, or nonbeing, should not be equated with physical death, even though the socially dead are more vulnerable to physical violence than others. While the socially dead may continue in their biological persistence, such persistence takes place outside or beside the realm of human intelligibility, in a social space where biological life and physical survival are precarious. Thus, misrecognition and social death are linked to conceptions of life and to the notion of liveability, a theme that has obtained an increasingly important role in Butler's recent work. Even though her work is associated with the topics of desire and recognition, these concerns lead almost inevitably to her engagement with the notion of life.[4] This thread runs through all her discussion, from the journeying subject of *Subjects of Desire* ([1987] 1999) to her most recent consideration of life and liveability under conditions of war and in the context of heterogeneity and plurality (see my discussion in Chapters 3 to 5). This continued interest in the conditions of life interweaves several strands of Butler's concerns: these are philosophically and ethically inflected, borrowing from existentialist and post-structuralist ideas, and they guide her political analyses of some of the pressing issues of our time.

It is important to unpack this point further. Life, as Butler points out in *Frames of War*, is a loaded concept; it is not a natural or biological category. Claims to life are often associated with those movements and organizations that oppose or seek to restrict women's reproductive rights and autonomy, and that do so in opposition to an alleged 'culture of death'.[5] Not surprisingly, Butler rejects such uses of the term 'life'. As she insists, life cannot be considered in isolation from the terms and conditions that make life possible;[6] thus, it is 'liveability', understood as the conditions of life, that is more significant than life itself. Hence, challenging a position she ascribes to Agamben, Butler declares that life can never be considered 'bare' in any unmediated sense (see Agamben 1998), because 'bare' life is politically animated and differentially applied, operating through an ethnic and racial grid that distributes the conditions of life unequally (see also Chapter 5). The key question for Butler is 'what makes for a liveable life?' By posing the question of life in relation to liveability, or rather, by opening 'life' up to a critical investigation, she articulates a new conception of the human (see next section) that departs in significant ways from her previous emphasis on the subject and on structures of subjection.

What, then, are the key criteria for a liveable life? Life, according to Butler, is subject to the enabling constraints that make life liveable. These include a fundamental dependency on others, which makes us susceptible and vulnerable to their actions. Butler refers to this fundamental exposure, dependence, and vulnerability as 'precariousness', which she defines as 'a generalized condition whose very generality can be denied only by denying precariousness itself' (FW, 22; emphasis in original; see also *Precarious Life* (2004b)). She borrows the idea of precariousness from her reading of Levinas, whose conception of an ethical encounter with the face of the other constitutes the model for the conception of precariousness.[7] While precariousness is the shared condition of humanity, in fact of all life, it becomes mediated through the differential operation of what she terms 'precarity': this is the way the shared condition of precariousness is lived and experienced differentially, structured, for example, along lines of race, class, gender, or religious identification. The key conceptual tool through which the persistence of precarity can be unlocked is that of the frame, relating back to the question of recognition. What, then, is the link between recognition and the frame? Frames constitute a structure or scaffolding through which we view the world. As Butler indicates, they fulfil an epistemological function in that they filter and organize our view on the world. This epistemological structure moulds 'what we can see', and in this respect, frames do not facilitate a view from nowhere. Rather, frames are saturated with power, and they provide a differential, partial, or selective view on the world. Crucially linked to their epistemological role, frames produce ontological effects: they structure the question 'What is life?' as well as the answers to this question. This, according to Butler, has important implications: because the frame constitutes a structure or schema of intelligibility, it provides us with the norms that underpin the answer to the question of life and that generate the norms of recognizability (FW, 7). Put differently, frames contribute to the normative production of ontology that establishes some subjects as intelligible and others as abject. As Butler argues, 'our very capacity to discern and name the "being" of the subject is dependent on norms that facilitate that recognition' (FW, 4).

For Butler, the litmus test for a liveable life, and for the operation of an expansive frame that facilitates such a life, is the idea of grievability: that is, the acknowledgment of loss and the recognition of a life lived. It is through the grievability of death, understood as a future anterior, that a life is marked. Only those lives that will be grievable will be considered as having lived. And it is from the inevitability of death that Butler derives an ethical obligation towards life. Grievability contains two elements: it establishes first whether a life can be acknowledged as having been lived, and second whether grieving the loss of a life is publicly recognized. As readers familiar with Butler's earlier work will know, the consideration of mourning, as indeed an insistence on the melancholic structure of subject formation, is a key feature of Butler's work, stretching back to her critical reading of Freud in *Gender Trouble* (1990) and *The Psychic Life of Power* (1997b). There, Butler seeks to disclose the constitutive role played by a disavowed homosexuality in the constitution of (heterosexual) gender identity. Also, throughout her work Butler attends to the cultural prohibitions on mourning for those who succumb to HIV/AIDS, and more widely, those whose gender coherence is questioned by a hegemonic heterosexual culture based on a gender binary. More recently Butler has developed this discussion by attending to the question of mourning in the context of 9/11, the so-called war on terror, and the conflict in Israel-Palestine (I attend to this discussion in the following chapters). It is in this context of the grievability of death, understood as a future anterior, that, paradoxically, life is marked. Only those lives that will be grievable will be considered as having lived. And it is from the inevitability of death that Butler derives an ethical obligation towards life.

Perhaps counter-intuitively grief and mourning pose further challenges to violence (see Chapter 3), though of a different kind.

The importance accorded to grievability is equally significant to those who are left behind (allowing them to publicly express their loss), as it is to those who will have been lost (Butler insists on the use of the future perfect: those lives will be recognized as having been lived). Butler addresses this issue at length in *The Psychic Life of Power* (1997b), where the disavowal of a constitutive homosexual attachment results in the development of a melancholic psychic structure (in fact, of a culture of melancholy) that is build on the double barrel of what Butler terms the 'never-never': of never having lost a love object and never having loved the lost object. Following Butler, a similar psychic structure operates in the context of the war on terror. At the beginning of *Precarious Life* (2004b), Butler articulates her critique of the Bush administration's hasty willingness to embark upon violent conflict in Afghanistan, and she expresses bewilderment at President Bush's claim, expressed only days after 9/11, that the United States is done with mourning. Such swift abandonment of mourning, according to Butler, misses the opportunity to reflect upon our fundamental vulnerability towards the other's actions and to recognize our mutual dependence upon one another. Against this wilful invocation of the mastery of grief, Butler suggests that grief and mourning constitute important elements of a critical repertoire that enables a transformation of violence: they call to mind the ek-static nature of the subject, our susceptibility to being undone by the other, and our vulnerability towards the other's actions. Instead of mimicking the essentially superfluous attempt at establishing or regaining sovereignty, Butler invokes the necessity to recognize our mutual dependence upon one another. By reflecting upon my own vulnerability to violence, I may recognize how I am intermeshed with the other. In doing so, grieving also challenges conception of the subject as sovereign and autonomous (see Gilson 2011).

Yet how and where to grieve are matters of public dispute, especially in the context of conflict and its aftermath. In *Precarious Life* (2004b), Butler relates the story of an obituary for Palestinian victims of Israeli-state violence. This obituary, written for the *San Francisco Chronicle*, was rejected twice: first, on the grounds that the deaths could not be certified, and a second time because publication may cause offence. Thus, the grieving of some victims of violence could not be publicly accomplished and, according to Butler, a full recognition of a life lived was barred from consideration. Public grieving and commemoration is of course a highly contested issue, which is suggestive of the interweaving of the ethical and political domains. If grievability, as Fiona Jenkins (2011) suggests, expresses the need to mark a life, it also throws up questions over whose lives should be marked, where, and how. Which public sites, if any, should be dedicated spaces for public grieving? The differential responses to the losses from the wars in Iraq and Afghanistan are incisive. British army losses, for example, are publicly acknowledged upon their return to Britain. The repatriation of US service personnel is more low profile, haunted by images of body bags returning home that were associated with the Vietnam War. The grieving for enemy combatants and for Afghan and Iraqi civilians are not a constitutive part of the Western politics of grieving: no exact figures are obtainable, and only a few images or names enter the public discourse.

The importance that Butler accords to life and liveability, to precariousness and precarity, is underpinned by her profound commitment to ethics, and by an explicit shift to normative theorizing that marks a substantial departure from some of her earlier work, and that should put to rest those critics who have faulted Butler for not providing her readers with a normative compass against which to evaluate political claims (see for example Benhabib 1995; Nussbaum 1999). I will outline my own reservations towards this development below. For now, I further unpack the connection Butler makes between life and ethics. I already have suggested that Butler is not interested in life as such, but rather in the conditions of liveability that sustain life and that contribute to a reduction of conditions of violence (see Chapter 3). From her assertion of ontological dependency Butler deducts an obligation towards building and sustaining relations with others.

Closely related to such an appeal to ethics are Butler's explicit normative commitments. Her choice of vocabulary, of 'ought' and 'should', is indicative of such normative aspiration, expressed moreover by her appeal to 'inclusive and egalitarian way of recognizing precariousness' (*FW*, 13) and by her demanding concrete support in the form of food, shelter, and medical support that are generally regarded as the basic foundations for human flourishing (see my discussion in the next section). In *Frames of War* (2009a), Butler is occupied with the way that grievability intersects with the notion of precariousness and how this, in turn, comes to form our understanding of life. As she argues, recognition is not the only way, or the best way, to register precariousness. What is required additionally is to ensure human flourishing and persistence in the face of inevitable death.

What, then, does Butler mean by life? And how can the notion of life be rescued for left politics, away from conservative 'pro-life' positions that seek to restrict women's reproductive autonomy? Butler makes several claims that, at first glance, seem highly controversial, and that therefore deserve closer inspection. Her claims centre on the question of the right to life, and specifically on the conditions where such a right, if it exists, should be upheld. As Butler suggests, there are processes of life that 'require destruction and degeneration' (*FW*, 16). She further avers that '[n]ot everything included under the rubric of "precarious life" is . . . *a priori,* worthy of protection from destruction' (*FW*, 18; italics in original). To unpack these claims further, it is prudent to highlight those provisos that Butler introduces into her discussion. First, she approaches the question of life via a criticism of the anthropocentric assumptions that underpin much debate on the right to life. She stresses instead the significance of the biological dimension of life, which she refers to as *bios* and which connects the human with the animal. Second, life, according to Butler, cannot be thought without considering the conditions of life: in other words, the conditions where life becomes liveable. These conditions pertain to our fundamental dependency upon others and with them, our obligation towards creating liveable conditions for others. Thus, they include, as I already mentioned, the creation of material conditions that make such life liveable, such as food, shelter, access to medical care, or access to education (*FW*, 22). Hence for Butler, life normatively conceived requires egalitarian material conditions that acknowledge the ontological constraints that precariousness imposes on life and liveability, and that distribute fairly the effects of precarity. Such an egalitarian conception, moreover, must be conceived in a global context. However (and this is one of the key concerns in *Frames of War*), egalitarian conceptions are undermined by war. To reiterate a point I made previously, the geopolitics of war produce inequality along racial, religious, and gendered lines, and it occludes the view on its own production of inequality.

This insistence on egalitarian conditions and on obligations we have towards others also allows for a further modification of Butler's understanding of ethics. As she argues, '[o]ur obligations are precisely to the conditions that make life possible, not to "life itself", . . . there can be no sustained life without those sustaining conditions, and . . . those conditions are both our political responsibility and the matter of our most vexed ethical decisions' (*FW*, 23). I return to this discussion in the next section, but at this point I want to state that Butler's recent explicit attention to questions of material inequality should put to rest those views that accuse her of neglecting this topic. Admittedly, she does not provide concrete, detailed analyses of socio-economic questions and their global ramifications, but I suspect that is not her interest. Rather, she articulates from the perspective of normative political philosophy a critique of life and of liveability.

This brings me to a further criticism of the way she anchors the relationship between ethics and politics. As I indicated above, there are reservations regarding this development in Butler's work, and these revolve, in the main, around her use of Levinasian categories, specifically the idea of the structure of otherness/the face which is said to be void of any historical or social reference. While her genealogical-Foucauldian analyses as well as her existential-phenomenological work, which builds on de Beauvoir's ideas, are said to instigate concrete investigations into the constitution of the subject, her Levinasian analysis seems to lack such concrete specificity. I have already addressed the issue of Butler's unfaithful readings in the introduction, but I believe that it is too simple to rest here. What Levinas brings to Butler's analyses is a way to combine ethics and politics that is anchored in Jewish experience (I discuss this aspect in Chapter 4). In *Parting Ways* (2012a), Butler declares that her ethics (to be precise, she refers to practices of translation in ethical encounters) is derived from Jewish sources but modified for political philosophy. Ethics, she continues, is 'a relational practice that responds to an obligation that originates outside the subject'. Furthermore, by contesting notions of a sovereign self, ethics signifies 'the act by which place is established for those who are "not-me"'. Thus, it is a form of 'ec-static relationality . . . a way of being dispossessed from sovereignty and nation in response to claims made by those one does not fully know and did not fully choose' (*PW*, 9). Significantly, relationality and ethics arrive from the (historically concrete) experience of suffering, and they, in turn, inform one's ethical and political obligations. Such construal is not always explicitly spelt out in Butler's texts, but her most recent work will lead to a reformulation of some of the charges made against her.

MARRIAGE, THE HUMAN, AND HUMAN RIGHTS

The European Convention on Human Rights makes two provisions with respect to family and marriage life: Article 8 guarantees the right to respect for private and family life, whilst Article 12 guarantees the right of men and women of marriageable age to marry and found a family in accordance with national laws.[8] National laws, of course, differ, and while some convention states, including Belgium, Denmark, the Netherlands, Norway, Portugal, and Spain, have now legislated for marriage equality (and others are in the process of doing so), the topic of marriage has also become a contested issue in domestic politics and wider public discourse on morality, as has the role of faith in the formulation of public policy (see also Chapter 4). My aim in this section is not to rehash the arguments for or against marriage equality; rather, what interests me is how marriage equality is discussed in public political discourse. More specifically, I want to trace how public political discourse on the topic of marriage equality is informed by conceptions of the human. Using statements and interviews given by political and church representatives, mostly from Northern Ireland and Britain, I seek to demonstrate how assertions about the validity (or lack of validity) of such rights are informed by competing conceptions of the human. With reference to marriage equality, I suggest that while disputes over the implementation and institutionalization of human rights are significant, it is equally important to attend to the notion of the human. In fact, I want to suggest that it is primarily around the notion of the recognition of the human that human rights struggles need to be fought.

In August 2012, Ken Maginnis, a long-standing and senior member of the Northern Irish Ulster Unionist Party and a former member of Parliament for the Fermanagh-South Tyrone constituency in the United Kingdom, resigned from his party. One may conjecture that his resignation pre-empted a possible disciplinary investigation into an interview Maginnis has given to the BBC Northern Ireland's Nolan Show (BBC Northern Ireland 2012), which had not been cleared with his party's press office. I am not concerned here with the procedural matters of Maginnis's resignation; rather, what interests me are the substantive claims he made during the course of this interview. The subject matter of the interview was the possibility of an extension of the existing marriage law in Northern Ireland allowing same-sex couples the right to marry. During the interview, Maginnis expressed his opposition to same-sex marriage, but what is of particular significance is the justification provided by him. He described homosexuality as a set of 'unnatural and deviant sexual practices'. He repeated this claim in a subsequent BBC interview, where he also expressed a 'responsibility to speak', and where he bolsters this responsibility by relating it to his past public statements in relation to the conflict in the North of Ireland. As he continues, 'when people have been murdered in our streets, when people have been under attack in both sides of the community, I am not making any difference'. He grounds his outspokenness in his 'opposition to violence', which he equates to his opposition to the 'spectacle in Belfast, the gay pride parade, which really is offensive to me', and 'to other people, the majority of people think like me, they don't want to see an erosion of social and moral values that I have a right to protect'.

The analogies drawn up by Maginnis's comments are worth pondering for a moment. Homosexuality, the practice said to be underlying same-sex marriage, is described as 'unnatural' and 'deviant' (it would be worth considering the relationship between the unnatural and deviancy). Furthermore, speaking out (it is not clear whether against homosexuality or same-sex marriage) becomes a responsibility, equated to the imperative to speak out against violence and murder (again, it is not clear whether homosexuality, or same-sex marriage, or both, constitute a form of violence, or are a form of murder). That murder has happened 'in our streets' relates the conflict back to another use of the street in the forms of the gay pride parade. This is described as an offensive spectacle that may lead to the erosion of moral values, which need to be protected.

Such concern with an alleged erosion of values is also expressed by the Irish Presbyterian Church in a letter written to the Northern Ireland Assembly, the devolved legislative body of Northern Ireland. The letter claims that marriage equality will 'effectively demolish generations and centuries of societal norms', leading to a 'steady erosion of values' (Presbyterian Church in Ireland 2012). Such a position is not the exclusive remit of Irish politicians and church representatives. Cardinal O'Brien (2012), the former head of the Catholic Church in Scotland, has described marriage equality as 'a grotesque subversion of a universally accepted human right'. The Irish Catholics Bishops' Conference quotes Pope Benedict XVI's *Message for the Celebration of the World Day of Peace 2008*, which conveys his commitment to 'the natural family, as an intimate communion of life and love, based on marriage between a man and a woman'. It is said to constitute 'the primary place of "humanization" for the person and society', and a 'cradle of life and love' (Irish Catholics Bishops' Conference). In other words, the human person cannot emerge out of same-sex relationships, invoking the monstrous spectrality of the human. Likewise, the Church of England (2012) describes same-sex marriage as '[altering] the intrinsic nature of marriage as a union of man and woman, as enshrined in institutions throughout history'. It is said to be anchored, furthermore, in an 'underlying biological complementarity which, for many, relates to the possibility of procreation'.

One of the strongest recent statements on homosexuality comes from another Northern Irish politician, the former DUP MP for the Strangford constituency, Iris Robinson. In comments made during a House of Commons Northern Ireland Grand Committee debate on 'Risk Assessment and Management of Sex Offenders' in 2008, she draws up an analogy between the sexual abuse of children, homosexuality, and sodomy. As she argues, '[t]here can be no viler act, apart from homosexuality and sodomy, than sexually abusing innocent children. There must be sufficient confidence that the community has the best possible protection against such perverts' (House of Commons Northern Ireland Grand Committee 2008). As reported in the *Belfast Telegraph* on 22 July 2008, she subsequently declared that the recording of the debate, published on the Hansard website, did not accurately reflect her views,[9] but she is on record, again on BBC Northern Ireland's Nolan Show, of describing homosexuality as 'disgusting', 'loathsome', 'nauseous', 'wicked' and 'vile', and an 'abomination'.

The comments cited above anchor opposition to marriage equality in an understanding of homosexuality as a violation of the laws of nature and of the (moral) laws of society. According to these views, marriage cannot be a human right for LGBT people because such a marriage is regarded as a violation of the laws of nature and society. In contrast, the heterosexual family is portrayed as a natural unit where, paradoxically, the socialization into culture and the process of humanization is said to occur. Leaving aside the rather unreflective distinction between nature and culture (as, indeed, the question of why so-called natural, that is, straight families, can produce gay children), there is a clear need for a critical discourse on the human. Thus, as I have argued, human rights discourse requires a discussion about the human: how do human rights configure our current understanding of the human, and how can such configurations be changed, challenged, and expanded? Of course, human rights do not work exclusively in a juridical or sovereign way. Instead, they are taken up in unexpected ways, and in doing so, they themselves can become an instrument for transforming our notion of the human. I want to suggest that the theoretical vehicle for such a discussion is provided in Butler's work. Although her reflections on human rights are (still) limited in terms of scope, I aver that she furnishes us with an approach that allows us to imagine the human in new ways. To develop this argument further, I enquire into Butler's conception of liveability.

In the next section, I attend to Butler's conception of the human, and I ask whether her increasing use of the term 'human' allows us to speak of Butler's humanism.

THE HUMAN AND HUMANISM

As we have seen, dispossession, precariousness, vulnerability, and recognition are key vectors in Butler's analysis of the subject. As I intimated in the introduction, this account is accompanied by an explicit shift towards normative political theorizing and an expansion in vocabulary and ethical orientation. Whereas her earlier work is almost exclusively focussed on the question of the subject, on subjectification, and on practices of subjection,[10] her later work on liveability and on the human introduces the prospect of challenging those structures of subjection. In her exchange with Ernesto Laclau and Slavoj Zizek, published as *Contingency, Hegemony, Universality: Contemporary Dialogues on the Left* (2000b), Butler claims that the notion of the human has, historically, operated in an exclusionary fashion, excluding, amongst others, lesbians, gays, and women (*CHU*, 39). In *Antigone's Claim*, drawing on Agamben and Arendt, she asks about those abject beings that are outside the realm of the properly human. Recognition and intelligibility are the benchmarks for measuring the properly human, but it is important to stress that for Butler, the question of the human is essentially unanswerable; as she suggests, we no longer know the proper usage of the term 'human' (see *AC*, 81–2).

This openness, futurity, and unknowingness of the notion of the human informs her post-9/11 work, configuring two discussions in particular: her renewed consideration of questions of gender and sexuality, this time with reference to intersex, and her critique of US foreign policy in the wake of the interventions in Iraq and Afghanistan (I attend to both aspects in the following chapters). These discussions are, yet again, underpinned by her insistence on the importance of liveability and by the continued ethical and political aspiration towards securing liveable lives. In what follows, I address the question of whether Butler subscribes to a latent humanism (against the gist of much of her earlier work); I reconsider the role of vulnerability in the context of her discussion of the human; and I compare Butler's account of the human with the emphasis on the human in the capabilities approach, as represented by Martha C. Nussbaum (2011).

Butler's construal of the human as a topic for scholarly enquiry connects her work to recent discussions that go by labels such as critical humanism or post-humanism. Notwithstanding the distinctions between different versions of these enquiries, they all regard as deeply problematic conceptions of the human that are anchored in nature-culture dualisms or in rigid distinctions between human and other forms of sentient life.[11] Is Butler a critical humanist, though? Judging by the attention that the critical enquiry into the meaning of 'human' receives in her recent work, there are strong lines of convergence between her work and that of critical humanism. This connection is further reinforced by her attention to questions of ontology and ethics. At the heart of her conception of the human is her assertion of the ontological features of embodiment, precariousness and corporeal vulnerability, relationality and dispossession, and grievability. Yet, I aver that Butler's discussion of the human does not seek to develop humanism. In this respect, I would also disagree with claims that interpret Butler as redefining the human (see Arteel 2011). Rather, I want to suggest, she explores realms of liveability, applying an increasingly global lens. Butler's 'humanism', if we can call it that, is anchored in her account of corporeal vulnerability, not in any preconceived notion of the human.

There is a significant shift from her early work to her later work, relating to the way she attends to and frames the problem of the human. Her early work, steeped as it is in the language and thinking of post-structuralism, is at pains to criticize any notion of the human and of humanism that could be interpreted as prescriptive. In fact, her objective is to unsettle the notion of the human and to challenge any accompanying notions of humanism that underpin this concept (see Arteel 2011). However, as I discussed in the previous section, already her early work is guided by a notion of liveability that challenges those conditions that create and sustain the realm of abjection. This focus on liveability, as I have demonstrated, is a key feature of her recent political theorizing and her efforts to articulate the conditions of a globalized world, where life chances are unequally distributed.

As I already have discussed, Butler's philosophy of the subject is centrally concerned with questions of precariousness, precarity, and vulnerability. These constitute the ontological anchors of Butler's conception of the human. Of particular significance to her discussion is the concept of vulnerability. Increasingly in her recent work, Butler attends to the idea of the vulnerability and precariousness of bodies. That is, Butler is at pains to stress that it is primarily via our bodies that we become vulnerable to the actions of others. This vulnerability, which underscores the precariousness of life, introduces a structural egalitarianism into the conception of the human: no human is immune to vulnerability and to the—potentially—violent actions of others; in fact, to be human is to be vulnerable (see also Chapter 2). However, Butler recognizes that this vulnerability is unequally distributed along geographical and geopolitical axes, along gendered, sexed, and racialized lines. In *Frames of War* (2009a), she further articulates this differentiation by distinguishing between precariousness, understood as the shared ontological condition of vulnerability that characterizes all human life, and precarity, understood as the unequal distribution of vulnerability and precariousness.

Vulnerability and precariousness highlight a further dimension of the human: the dependence on known and unknown others who, in the best of cases, provide care for the vulnerable subject. This dependency is anchored in a fundamental relationality of the human, understood not as the connection of two or more autonomous subjects, but as the formation of the subject-human in and through its dependence on others. Such a version of subject formation is already formulated in *The Psychic Life of Power,* where Butler, building on Freud, accounts for the formation of the subject through the internalization of social taboos and gender images. While relationality plays a constitutive role in the formation of the human, it can also, however, profoundly unsettle the human, captured by Butler with her notion of ecstasy and dispossession.[12]

One of the key issues that this recent discussion has brought to the fore is the way that the human is underpinned by a set of ontological claims (see Introduction). As Butler outlines in *Precarious Life* (2004b) and in *Frames of War* (2009a), the ontology of the subject is to be understood as a social ontology, that is, as contingent. It is in this context that her reference to the human must be seen: the human, and humanity, are contingent categories of the 'not yet' rather than prescriptive accounts of what human life is or should be. To illustrate this point further, Butler draws on her recent discussion of the human form. The backdrop to this discussion is Kafka's story of Odradek, which Butler narrates in *Giving an Account of Oneself* (2005). Odradek is a figure lacking human form, although tied into the network of human relationships (see also Butler's statements on disability in a recent interview (2009c); see also her discussion of materiality in *Bodies that Matter* (1993)).

The idea of the human, understood as a futural conception, requires attention to the question of universality. Hence, apart from the few ontological characteristics previously outlined, what are the features of this human, and, more importantly, what kind of politics could be derived from this concept? Not surprisingly, given her critique of the state and of state-centred attempts at social transformation, Butler has been reluctant to embrace a politics of human rights. It would be misleading, though, to account for this reluctance exclusively with reference to Butler's post-structuralist leanings. In fact, the idea of human rights, as is well known, is contested within political thought, and the thinker most commonly associated with scepticism towards human rights is Hannah Arendt.[13]

In what ways does Butler's philosophy of the human compare to an approach that self-consciously puts the human at the centre of its analysis? (This is the human development or capabilities approach advocated in different ways by Martha C. Nussbaum [2011] and Amartya Sen). As I want to suggest, the capabilities approach throws up a series of challenges, questions, and concerns that overlap with those of Butler. Before I develop a comparison between the perspectives of Butler and Nussbaum, I want to briefly outline the main features of the capabilities approach. These include individual empowerment, making life fully human, positing the human independently of his or her particularistic attachments, universalism, and cross-cultural comparisons of development indicators. Central to the capabilities approach is its dual emphasis on policy relevance and moral philosophising. Nussbaum's work in particular is firmly anchored in Aristotelian philosophy. At the heart of her approach, as in Butler's recent work, lies the notion of the human. However, in the work of Nussbaum in particular, the human is not a question but an empirical reality that needs to be accommodated through adequate welfare and human rights provisions. Nussbaum's particular configuration of capabilities generates a range of interesting questions, especially if we compare her work with other approaches in the wider field of development studies. My concern here, however, is more narrow and has to do with Nussbaum's framing of the human and of life, and with the accompanying set of rights. Nussbaum's (1997) work is motivated by a concern to make 'life fully human' (286). Being human, furthermore, is said to be independent of one's belonging to particularistic groups, associations, and communities (292). Indeed, this assertion lies behind her driving motivation, which she shares with Sen, to instigate cross-cultural comparisons. More specifically, capabilities are meant to locate empowerment in the individual, 'in this life and in that life' (285; italics in original) and to articulate what people are able to do—in short, 'in enabling people to function in a fully human way' (285).

This summary, admittedly too brief to do full justice to Nussbaum's work, illuminates parallels but also differences in the way that both Butler and Nussbaum frame the notion of the human, what they consider to count as life, and what significance they accord to cross-cultural perspectives (on this latter point see also Sen 2004).[14] For the moment, I want to develop this comparison further before attending to its implications towards an understanding of human rights. What is evident is that for Nussbaum, the human is not a question for further investigation; rather, her emphasis lies with ensuring the capabilities of a fully lived human life. Similarly, Sen, although attuned to the dispute over the metaphysical grounding of human rights, is equally unconcerned with providing a foundation of the human. If anything, the human is said to participate in the kinds of 'unobstructed discussions' (Sen 2004, 349) that he regards as the benchmark for testing the ethical claims that underpin human rights. On the surface such line of reasoning seems attractive, yet it cannot answer, in my view, some of the fundamental questions posed in Butler's work.

Despite these fundamental differences, though, both Butler and Nussbaum orientate their work towards the notion of life and of making life liveable. For Nussbaum (1997), this occurs through the compliance with a list of key requirements, such as bodily health, bodily integrity, life, respect (287–8). For Butler, on the other hand, the question of life cannot be answered once and for all, for one, not only because it will be continuously posed anew but also because it will be challenged anew.

For example, while Nussbaum poses the right to bodily integrity as both aim and object of her take on capabilities, Butler interrogates the body in its relation to conceptions of human intelligibility. As Butler argues, there are some 'bodies that matter', complying with normative conceptions of human morphology, whereas other bodies fall outside the realm of hegemonic conceptions of intelligibility. She discusses the significance of bodily morphology and the implications of being differently embodied at length in *Undoing Gender* (2004a), where she narrates the life of David Reimer, better known as the child in the John/Joan case. Following a failed circumcision procedure that led to the burning of his penis, David underwent a series of psychological, surgical, and hormonal treatments that were meant to aide his/her socialization as a girl. This experiment in implementing a norm of gender failed, however, and David wished to return to a male body. Tragically, in 2004, David took his life. As Butler argues in the postscript to her essay on David Reimer, it is difficult to determine the reasons for his suicide. However, as she repeatedly points out, normative conceptions of human morphology have profound implications for the way we conceive of and recognize the human: they generate normative conception of the human. Thus, 'embodiment denotes a contested set of norms governing who will count as a viable subject within the sphere of politics' (*UG*, 28). This argument, though made in relation to her discussion of the New Gender Politics in *Undoing Gender* (2004a), is not restricted to the politics of gender broadly conceived. As she argues, with reference to the war on terror, racial embodiment plays an equally significant role in conception of human intelligibility, '[undergirding] the culturally viable notions of the human, ones that we see acted out in dramatic and terrifying ways in the global arena at the present time' (*PL*, 33).

Such racialized corporeal differentials are as significant in the domestic arena as they are in relation to global politics. To be precise, they surface or even constitute the nodal points where the domestic, or national, and the global intersect. For example, racial profiling and stop-and-search practices targeted, in the main, at young Black and Asian males remain a persistent feature of policing in the metropolitan areas of Western Europe and North

America. The recent controversial shootings in London of Mark Duggan by officers from the London Metropolitan Police triggered serious riots in London in the summer of 2011. It also continues to raise questions regarding the racialized politics of urban policing and of the discursive construction of male Black criminality in wider public debate on law and order. The operation of such discourses have also inflected public debates on the shooting of another young Black male, Trayvon Martin in Florida. As I have intimated, distinctive of the wider public debate on such killings is the way that the deaths are often legitimized by resorting to an alleged threat or suspicion of criminal activities on behalf of the victims. Such discourses of criminalization also feature in recent debates over the lifting of work restrictions for Bulgarians and Romanians in the European Union. These have triggered heated public debates over immigration in general and over access to public services, abuses of the welfare state, and crime in particular. Thus, narratives of Black criminality, of East European welfare scroungers, or of Muslim terrorists constitute the racialized subtexts of debates on the human, perceived as a challenge to a sanitized conception of national purity.

These examples illustrate that 'the human' cannot be the unquestioned foundation of political practice; rather, 'the human' is constituted performatively and in contest with hegemonic and exclusionary conceptions. How, then, do Butler's political-philosophical reflections speak to some of the key issues of concern to contemporary politics? In the final section of this chapter I attend to the way that Butler's discussion of the human can inform our understanding of human rights, and specifically how Butler's critical humanist perspectives could inform the politics of human rights.

THE HUMAN AND HUMAN RIGHTS

In *Excitable Speech* (1997a) and *Antigone's Claim* (2000a), Butler laments those, especially feminist and other progressive political movements, who seek recourse to the state in order to redress injustices (see also Chapter 5). Such a call for state support is often articulated via a demand for laws and legislation intended to restrict or criminalize the actions (and sometimes words) of those who engage in discriminatory or offensive behaviour. Demands for state action and intervention are also often connected with a wider call for the establishment of a robust and effective human rights regime. As is well known, Butler has repeatedly expressed reservations regarding such state-centred strategies, but her recent work has undergone a shift in perspective. I explore the relationship between law, state, and violence in Chapter 3, while I attend to a discussion of developments in Butler's wider views on the law in Chapter 5, where I assess in particular her acknowledgement of the importance of international legal protection in the context of war and the treatment of prisoners. As I will demonstrate there, in recent years, Butler has come to endorse at least partially a politics based on state support.[15] My focus in this section is not with the law, the state, or with rights, but with the effects of human rights discourses, specifically with the way that human rights discourse generates normative conceptions of the human that tie in with struggles for recognition.

Despite the enormous output of work published in the field of human rights, it is remarkable that until recently, comparatively little attention has been accorded to the concept of the human as the subject of these rights.[16] In fact, many human rights discourses presume the human as the unquestioned foundation of human rights. As one contributor to contemporary human rights scholarship, Jack Donnelly (2007), puts it, human rights are 'the *rights* that one has simply because one is *human*' (21; italics in original). Put differently, being human, as Donnelly suggests, gives rise to rights. Such framing of human rights does not provide any insight into the concept of the human that underlies the idea of human rights, though. As Donnelly concedes, human rights rest on a particular account of human nature, on what it means to be human, and this account remains contested within moral philosophy. The hyphenated construction of human rights, such as women's human rights, gays' and lesbians' human rights, or children's human rights, points towards the underlying problematic: it attests, albeit implicitly, that the human at the centre of human rights remains a contested concept. Put differently, it acknowledges the contested status or human quality of some populations within the wider framework of human rights.

My discussion in this section is located within these wider discourses; it is my aim to investigate and construe the relationship between the human, which I read as an urgent topic for political-philosophical enquiry, and human rights. Specifically, what interests me is whether human rights and human rights discourse play a constitutive role in the creation of the human—in other words, whether 'rights make humans' (Douzinas 2002). I begin by drawing on Hannah Arendt's famous critique of 'naked humanity'. As I want to suggest, Arendt offers a path into the conundrum that I am posing: whether humans constitute an ontological, that is, unquestioned, and sufficient foundation for human rights. However, whilst Arendt ([1951] 1976) poses the question of the relationship between the human and human rights, she identifies the problems as lying exclusively with human rights. I want to suggest that Butler's recent writings provide a more fruitful perspective on the topic: unlike Arendt, Butler reads the human as a political problem, and in doing so she helps to answer the question I am posing. Building on this discussion, I want to suggest that even though disputes over the implementation and institutionalization of human rights are significant, it is also around the notion of the recognition of the human that human rights struggles need to be fought.

As an entry into my topic, I review Hannah Arendt's famous passage from her book *The Origins of Totalitarianism* ([1951] 1976) entitled 'The Perplexities of the Rights of Man'. In this section, Arendt considers the failure of human rights protection in the face of political turmoil in the interwar years, based on her reading of the notion of human rights and their relationship to the notion of the human. As is well known, Arendt champions the political or public sphere as the terrain of human freedom. Freedom, for Arendt, emerges in tandem with the existence of a political community: she conceives of this community as a polity where humans strive for excellence and where public speech and action unfold. The emergence of the modern nation state, however, with its accompanying nationalisms, has upended the public sphere, and in this process has created national minorities on the margins of the nation state who are vulnerable to expulsions or a complete loss of their rights. According to Arendt, this vulnerability intensified during the interwar years, when national minorities, refugees, and the stateless found themselves outside the protective shield of a political community. It reached its apex during World War II and the Nazi policies of extermination. Those without the protection of a political community were thrown back to what Arendt refers to as the 'abstract nakedness of being human' (297). Faced with genocidal policies and practices, human rights, intended to protect humans from violent or arbitrary state actions, failed utterly. For Arendt, human rights can only function in the civic framework of a political community; in fact, they only become meaningful as rights within the context of the polity. Her emphasis on the polity opens up a distinction between the human on the one hand, here understood as a biological category, and the citizen on the other (*zoë* as the biological condition of being human, *bios* as the life told through a narrative). In fact, it is the polity that bestows human dignity upon the citizen and that turns biological life into a full life, lived and narrated in the context of the polity.

The importance that Arendt accords to the political community has recently been challenged by Lechte and Newman (2012), who argue that it constitutes an obstacle in the defence of human rights, especially in an era of global interdependence, migration, and ongoing statelessness (526). Furthermore, they question the efficacy of the polity. As they argue, it is the polity itself that generates, or at least fails to prevent, the problem of statelessness (527). Whilst they share Arendt's concerns regarding the anchoring of human rights in a natural law tradition that presupposes a notion of the human as a biological entity, Lechte and Newman emphasize the importance of 'bearing witness', which they borrow from Agamben, in conceptualising the human and human rights. In my view, such emphasis on 'bearing witness' is consistent with Arendtian conceptions of narrative (see for example Adriana Cavarero's (2000) reading of Arendt). It also circumvents the need for bounded communities, allowing for the possibility for human rights practice in our globalized world. Thus, while I agree with Lechte and Newman's key criticism, I also wish to add to it. It should be stressed, that despite inducing a breakage between 'the human', understood as a biological category, and the political actor, Arendt's political philosophy is not unambiguously anti-humanist. Rather, she displaces the political work of humanization, relegating it into a pre- or extra-political realm. The political quality of the political actor and the polity is contingent upon a realm of 'mere life', of *zoë* in the Arendtian sense, whose needs, requirements, and dignity are not protected by the polity.

I want to suggest that unlike Arendt, Butler furnishes us with an account of the constitution of the human that circumvents some of the blind spots that plague Arendt's ideas, that offers a theoretical toolkit which allows for rethinking the relationship between the human and human rights in a critical way, and that articulates possibilities for human rights struggles by those located on the margins.

While for Arendt the notion of the human does not require sustained analysis, Butler offers a sustained investigation into the genealogy of the human. The human, for Butler, is a futural project, never fully realized and always deferred. Some of her recent work has developed this theme further by asserting that violence operates in the constitution of the human. Such a claim throws up serious challenges for human rights discourse: after all, if the human is the effect or product of violence, then where does this leave an effective human rights intervention, especially one that opposes the use of violence?

Butler's interest in the human relates back to her discussion of recognition, struggle, and conflict, culminating in a narrative of subject constitution that posits the subject's fundamental dependency upon others, a vulnerability towards the—potentially violent—actions of others, and that claims the centrality of norms to our sense of selfhood.[17]

Butler argues that we can neither predict nor necessarily prevent the violent actions of others. Thus, vulnerability and the susceptibility to violence are inscribed into the human, but she distinguishes between such a foundational violence and its unequal social and geopolitical distribution, which circumscribes the gendered and racialized conditions of liveable lives. An important conclusion drawn by Butler is the question of the human, of who I am, which must grapple with the paradox that we are not just subjected to violence, but that we are also subjects of violence. Thus, for Butler, violence simultaneously threatens and facilitates our existence or intelligibility as human beings. Hence, there is no human without violence.

Violence's constitutive role in the production of the human does not just work through norms, though. It also operates in a direct fashion, and Butler discusses such uses of violence in her deliberations on the American occupation of Iraq and the practices deployed in Abu Ghraib. In *Frames of War* (2009a), Butler contends that the violent practices of torture are central to the development of a hegemonic narrative that constructs a progressive Western sexual subject, which becomes juxtaposed to a pre-modern Islamic subject, tied to religious-conservative values. A key part of the book is her discussion of the intersection of narratives of civilization and modernity with the operation of violence and torture of orientalized others. As Butler contends, torture is 'a technique of modernization' (*FW*, 130), which is embedded in the Western civilising mission, and which presupposes a narrative of sexual freedom that construes Islam as the other of this freedom. Western sexual freedom, however, is integral to the production of the Arab subject as pre-modern. It is a discourse of homophobia and misogyny, articulated so cruelly in the sexualized sadistic practices of Abu Ghraib.

What, then, are the implications for human rights, and how should we conceive of the relationship between the human and human rights? In an article that considers the relationship between the humanities, the human, and human rights, Butler (2006d, 5) asks whether human rights presuppose the human (as suggested by Donnelly), and she challenges us to engage in a critical archaeology of the human understood as the ground of human rights. As she continues, it is essential to be critical of 'the human' in order to assert human rights. Furthermore, the human is said to be inaugurated on the basis of norms of exclusion, which leave the violence of its own emergence illegible, demonstrating the naturalizing effects of ontology. Thus, the human comes into being at the expense of the non-human, as an effect of juridical law (as alluded to by Douzinas, 2002). However, while human rights may form part of such juridical law, they also conjecture a future possibility of the human. Human rights, according to Butler, do not take the human as their ground, but they query the human as a site of power differentials. She argues that '[a]t stake is not only the assertion of humanity as the differential between the human and the monstrous or inhuman but also the ability of human rights discourse to pursue a path that is at once rigorously critical and committed to effective intervention' (Butler 2006d, 1661). As I suggested in this chapter, it is precisely such a critical investigation into the human which is relevant in the current debate on marriage equality.

NOTES

1. A crucial supplement to Butler's concept of power is the idea of passionate attachment to one's subjection. See her discussion in *The Psychic Life of Power* (1997b).
2. Butler's treatment of human rights occupies me again in Chapter 5, where I attend to its significance in the context of the war on terror and international law.
3. In his discussion of slavery, Patterson (1982) distinguishes two conceptions of social death, which he terms 'intrusive' and 'extrusive'. In the intrusive mode, the slave was an outsider who did not belong to the community, while in the extrusive mode the slave became an outsider because he no longer belonged to the community.
4. This concern with life is reflected prominently in the titles and subtitles of several of her books, including *The Psychic Life of Power: Theories in Subjection* (1997b), *Antigone's Claim: Kinship between Life and Death* (2000a), *Precarious Life: The Powers of Mourning and Violence* (2004b) and *Frames of War: When is Life Grievable?* (2009a).
5. The idea of a culture of death is ascribed to the late Pope John Paul II. It captures the Catholic Church's position on abortion as a practice of death. Conservative Republicans and other New Right politicians in the United States

have borrowed this terminology. In more recent years, the term 'culture of death' has been applied to suicide bombings in the Middle East. See for example Victor (2004).

6. See her discussion of Walter Benjamin's essay 'Critique of Violence' in *Parting Ways* (2012a).

7. In a recent interview (2011a) Butler cites her upbringing as a Jews as a source for her attention to precariousness (see Chapter 4 for a fuller discussion of Butler's engagement with Jewishness).

8. See European Court of Human Rights, *European Convention on Human Rights*, Strasbourg. (www.echr.coe.int/Documents/Convention_ENG.pdf). Although my discussion pertains to the issue of marriage equality as it applies to couples in same-sex relationships, Article 12 also raises questions regarding its presumption of stable gender categories.

9. The Hansard record has not been amended.

10. In *Giving an Account of Oneself* (2005), Butler critiques the version of the subject presented in *The Psychic Life of Power* (1997b), suggesting that she 'perhaps too quickly accepted this punitive scene of inauguration for the subject' (*GAO*, 15).

11. See for example Bourke (2011), Plummer (2001), and Sloterdijk (2009). For a consideration of social relations between the human and the non-human world, including animals and cyborgs, see Donna J. Haraway (1989, 1991). On animal studies see also Wolfe (2003).

12. As I mentioned briefly above in the chapter, grievability constitutes a further element in Butler's conception of the human. For a more detailed discussion, see Chapter 3.

13. Given recent developments in Butler's thinking, I return to the ideas of Arendt frequently throughout my book.

14. See MacKenzie (2009) for a comparison of Butler's and Nussbaum's deployment of the concept of universalism.

15. She has served on the International Gay and Lesbian Human Rights Commission (see *UG*, 34).

16. For an exception see Douzinas (2002).

17. I have already explored this in Schippers (2009).

3   The Paradox of Violence

What would it mean, in the face of violence, to refuse to return it?

(Giving an Account of Oneself)

[W]ithout the capacity to mourn, we lose that keener sense of life we need in order to oppose violence.

(Precarious Life)

Matters of life and death, and of desire and persistence, are key motifs of Butler's political philosophy. Her pursuit of existential questions, which, as I suggested in the two previous chapters, configure her account of the subject, also underwrite her discussion of those broader policy issues that have ramifications for global politics. Nowhere is this connection between her philosophical suppositions and her claims on global politics more pronounced than in her criticism of US foreign policy in the wake of 9/11: her condemnation of the wars in Iraq and Afghanistan, and of the treatment of prisoners in the detention centres and camps associated with the names of Abu Ghraib and Guantánamo Bay, constitutes a powerful theme in her recent work. Butler gains purchase on these global events via her critique of violence. In *Precarious Life* (2004b) and in *Frames of War* (2009a), she present her response to the war on terror, to the racialized and gendered discourses on terrorism, and to the—equally racialized and gendered—framing of bodily vulnerability, loss and grieving. These texts should be read alongside her analysis of violence's role in the constitution of the subject and in the ethical encounter with the other, presented in *Undoing Gender* (2004a) and *Giving an Account of Oneself* (2005). Of course, this is not to suggest that violence does not figure in her earlier texts. In fact, violence is a central theme in her oeuvre, and its importance to her ideas predates her post-9/11 writings, emanating from her work on the violent operations of the norms of gender (see Butler 1990; for an assessment see Chambers 2007); but it obtains renewed weight in the engagement with post-9/11 politics, where she pursues the prospect of non-violence and ethical responsibility in the face of violence.

Butler's interest in the concept of violence connects her work with a wider discourse community in political philosophy, where the topic of violence has received considerable attention in recent years.[1] Three issues occupy work generated in this field: these are, first, the relationship between politics and violence, including violence's role in the generation of politicized subjectivities, as well as conceptual work on key texts (see Frazer and Hutchings 2007, 2008, 2011); second, the distinction between legitimate and illegitimate uses of violence, and the uses of the term 'terrorist' (see for example Asad 2007, 2010; Brassett 2008; English 2009; Finlay 2009); and third, the normative critique of violence (see Bufacchi 2007; Keane 2004; Schwarzmantel 2010).

I want to suggest that Butler adds to this discussion with her insistence on violence's paradoxical role, which she construes as simultaneously destructive and productive. The second distinctive aspect of Butler's work on violence is her consideration of the transformation of violence into non-violent, or less violent, political practices. I discuss Butler's account of violence as constitutive of subjects and communities, and I query whether she offers a conception of violence that articulates the prospect of the creation of the polity. I suggest that Butler poses fundamental questions about the role of violence in the formation of the subject and about the prospects of establishing non- or less-violent relationships with others. To unpack these claims briefly, for Butler, violence is indispensable to the constitution of the subject. While such a reading circumvents problems that arise from framing violence in moral or instrumental terms, it does not elucidate how a critique of violence or an ethics of non-violence arises out of such persistence of violence.

Thus, developing an implicit claim contained in Butler's work—that violence is constitutive of politics—I am interested in the way she addresses the political regulation of violence, and I examine this aspect by looking at her treatment of grieving and non-violence. As we have seen in the previous two chapters, Butler has already pursued some of these issues in relation to sexual politics on the one hand (such as the losses from AIDS and from sexual violence; see Butler 1990, 1997b, 2000a, 2004a), and in the context of the war on terror on the other hand (see Butler 2004b, 2009a). Drawing on examples from Butler's writings, my inquiry considers the politics of grieving against the backdrop of the West's intervention in Iraq and Afghanistan and in relation to the Israeli-Palestinian conflict.[2] Thus, I assess the prospect of an ethics of non-violence and of articulating non-violent political relationships that Butler intimates in her work. I focus on two questions: what is the role played by violence in social and political transformation or revolution? And, what is the role of violence in the creation of politicized subjectivities and new beginnings?

VIOLENCE, FREEDOM, AND THE FOUNDATION OF THE POLITY

What role does violence play in the constitution of a polity and in struggles for political transformation? Is violence a catalyst for new beginnings? And what is the political significance of revolutionary violence? As I intimated above, one could profitably construe the history of modern political thought as an effort to grapple with the phenomenon of violence in politics (see Frazer and Hutchings 2007). These responses include a focus on existential questions and matters of survival and on the sublimation of violence in the institutions of the state; pacifist responses that object to any use of violence on moral grounds; and revolutionary responses that seek to utilize violence in the service of radical transformation. My interest in this section lies with two responses that consider the relationship between violence and political transformation. To pursue this discussion further, I draw on the writings of Hannah Arendt and Frantz Fanon. Both Arendt and Fanon constitute the foil against which I want to assess Butler's political philosophy of violence. Furthermore, they have both posed, albeit each in different ways, the question of violence in the context of political transformation. Like Butler, they reject instrumentalist and moralistic conceptions of violence. Instead, they consider violence in it relation to politics, aimed at what Arendt calls 'new beginnings'.

Arendt and Fanon have served as interlocutors to Butler's political-philosophical discussions, with Arendt surfacing increasingly in Butler's most recent writings (see Butler 2007a, 2007d, 2011b, 2011c, 2011d, 2012a). Here I want to suggest that Arendt and Fanon, like Butler, consider violence in its relation to politics, not with respect to questions of morality. Considering its function in the constitution of the subject, violence plays a role in conceptions of new beginnings that have occupied strands of political thought and that relate, furthermore, to the idea of a philosophy of freedom which Butler alludes to in *Undoing Gender*. How each of these three thinkers conceives of freedom in the context of violence, and how violence may generate the possibility for freedom and for the creation of a new conception of the human is a further theme that occupies me here. Thus, the following questions guide my investigation: what work does violence do in the writings of Butler, Fanon, and Arendt, and what is its relationship to politics? How does violence come to form the human? And how do they conceive of the relationship between violence and ethico-politics?

I want to begin with a brief sketch of Arendt's ([1951] 1976; [1963a] 2006a; see also Schippers 2011) theory of violence. It is probably fair to state that all her writings deal at their core with the crisis that is modernity. Her attempts to illuminate our understanding of this crisis, which in her view culminates in the various manifestations of twentieth century totalitarianism, keep bringing her back to the polities of the ancient world, whose political culture, including the glorification of politics, civic virtue, and public duty (generally speaking, attributes to do with masculinized conceptions of political citizenship and the public realm) is juxtaposed to the perceived decline of politics in the modern era. Arendt's studies of the ancient world constitute the foil against which she criticizes the modern world. What, then, according to Arendt, is wrong with the modern world? In short, in the modern world the concerns of the *oikon*, the household, and the rise of society, triumph over the concerns for the *polis*, the public realm of politics.

For Arendt, this reversal has existential implications. Politics, for her, is concerned with the plurality of citizens and the well-being of the polity; its aim is freedom. Society, on the other hand, is concerned with the interests of groups and individuals. Moreover, the modern era is characterized by the dissolution of old ties and communal bonds, such as religion and social class. It generates a mass society without communal bonds and inhabited by isolated individuals. It is in this context that the conditions for the rise of totalitarianism are found and that politics and freedom disappear. As Arendt contends, totalitarianism plays on the dispersed crowd of the mass society which lacks sustaining connections and bonds. In doing so, it destroys the common world inhabited by the plurality of political actors, all of whom have shared responsibility for the world. Totalitarianism's main tools are violence and terror; it destroys what Arendt regards as the uniquely human characteristic: the ability for spontaneity and new beginnings. Yet despite her criticism of the modern era, Arendt ([1951] 1976) seeks to identify possibilities for new beginnings, which find their anchor in the birth of each man and in man's capacity to refound and recreate politics. As she argues, 'every end in history necessarily contains a new beginning . . . the supreme capacity of man; politically, it is identical with man's freedom. . . . This beginning is guaranteed by each new birth; it is indeed every man', 479).

How, then, does Hannah Arendt theorize the relationship between violence, politics, and the subject? Even though she is commonly read as a thinker who construes violence in opposition to politics, it is important to stress that Arendt does not offer any principled objections to the use of violence as such. Crucially, for her, violence and politics are diametrically opposed, but, as argued by Breen (2007), such relegation of violence to outside politics is only possible because Arendt reverses the relationship between the public and private realms: the private realm, for Arendt, lacks the characteristics of politics, namely freedom, plurality, equality, and disclosure. In other words, the public realm of freedom and politics is a realm of non-violence, while violence persists in the unequal and unfree conditions that characterize the realm of the private sphere. Yet to locate violence in the dualistic scheme of private and public realms, as Arendt does, ignores how the realm of the public, and with it freedom and politics, is contingent upon the existence of the private sphere. Thus, by relegating violence to the outside of politics, that is, the private realm, it becomes paradoxically constitutive of politics: without violence, there can be no politics.

Notwithstanding Arendt's lament for the loss of politics in the modern era, she insists that the refoundation and recreation of politics, and hence of freedom, always remain possible. Two events in the modern era capture her imagination: the American Revolution and its immediate successor, the French Revolution, which she contrasts with the American Revolution. Here I am not concerned with the intricacies and indeed idiosyncrasies of Arendt's comparison of these two events. Rather, what interests me is something that puzzles Arendt and on which, I suggest, her critique of violence flounders.

This is the generative or productive function of violence in the revolutionary events of the eighteenth century. As I outlined above, Arendt is commonly read as a thinker who regards violence as anti-political. Yet, she grapples with the role played by violence in the revolutionary events of the eighteenth century. As she argues in the opening pages of *On Revolution* ([1963a] 2006), violence is a 'marginal phenomenon in the political realm' (9), but whilst she accords violence a prominent role in wars and revolutions, these are said to lie outside the political realm. This is in itself a problematic claim, but I want to pursue further to what extent the new order can be justified if it is founded with the help of violence. As she suggests, 'where violence is used to constitute an altogether different form of government, to bring about the formation of a new body politic, where the liberation from oppression aims at least at the constitution of freedom can we speak of revolution' (25).

We are left with the paradox that revolutions use violence to create a new society; in other words, the human capacity for new beginnings cannot bypass the problem of violence. It is this aspect that is problematic in Arendt's account of violence. Violence becomes a boundary phenomenon of politics, its constitutive outside, which Arendt disavows and rejects. Furthermore, notwithstanding Arendt's disavowal of violence in the generation of freedom, for Arendt violence plays no role in the creation of the human, and it is in this respect that she differs fundamentally from Fanon and Butler. For Arendt, the idea of the human, conceived as *zoë*, that is, as biological life, is pre-political. *Bios,* on the other hand, the narrated life of the public sphere, is, by definition, exempt from violence. Thus, as humans we enter the public realm fully formed, so to speak. In fact, Arendt strongly rejects the notion that politics could or should create a new human; for her, this is the stuff of totalitarian nightmares. It is not about creating better men but institutions that guarantee freedom. This is but one claim that sets her apart from Fanon.

Fanon's writings, like those of Arendt, respond to the conditions of the world that he finds himself in. Unlike Arendt's world, his is not the world of the unfolding European disaster of World War II and the Shoah, but of the persistence of (European) violence against the colonized. His two best-known publications, *Black Skin, White Masks* ([1967] 1986) and *The Wretched of the Earth* ([1965] 2001), both document and theorize the political and psychological violence of the colonial condition. In this respect, his approach differs significantly from Arendt's: Fanon tracks the operation of violence and its marking of the subject, displayed in the physical and psychosomatic effects suffered by those involved in colonial struggle, colonizer and colonized alike. He shares with Butler a significant debt to Hegel, specifically to Hegel's narrative of the master-slave dialectic and the struggle for recognition. Although Fanon has been denounced as an apologist for terrorism and as providing a wilful endorsement of perpetrating violence against the colonizer, such an interpretation misreads how for Fanon violence is an instrument of transformation. Central to Fanon's critique of colonialism were the politics of race and its practices of dehumanization. His famous assertion that 'the black is not a man' ([1967] 1986, 10) captures how the status as human is denied to him through the actions of the white man, who constructs the image of 'black man' as racially inferior, below the radar of intelligible humanity, and as 'a white man's [artefact]' (16). Thus, Fanon's whole project could be read as philosophy of racial struggle towards achieving human status for Black men. Struggle and conflict lie at the heart of *Black Skin, White Mask* ([1967] 1986), where Fanon offers a detailed philosophical discussion, but the more significant text for my purpose is *The Wretched of the Earth* ([1965] 2001).

This book contains a lengthy and famous opening chapter entitled 'Concerning Violence', as well as a series of case studies of mental disorders experienced as a result of colonial war. Fanon presents three interrelated dimensions of violence: first, it has an epistemological function, because it illuminates the colonial condition to the colonized. As Fanon ([1965] 2001) declares, 'violence committed by the people, violence organized and educated by its leaders, makes it possible for the masses to understand social truths' (118). Second, violence also has a transformative function: violence alone can lead to liberation from the colonizers. This transformative function also operates through the individual, allowing violence to become a cathartic or 'a cleansing force' (74) that liberates the colonized from the psychological damage inflicted upon them by colonialism, such as their alleged inferiority complex and passivity. Finally, violence could be described as ethico-political; it binds the colonized together as a whole. As Fanon claims, 'each individual forms a violent link in the great chain, a part of the great organism of violence . . . The groups recognize each other and the future nation is already indivisible (73).

Fanon distinguishes between two types of violence: while revolutionary violence is the instrument of 'Man's' liberation, colonial violence subjects and oppresses. For example, he documents carefully the extent and brutality of the French colonial regime, and he highlights how this violence returns back to the colonizer and affects both colonizer and colonized via psychosomatic suffering. This dualism can be overcome by challenging both colonizer and colonized to create 'a new history of Man' (Fanon [1965] 2001, 254) and by leaving behind the ideas, practices, and institutions of the colonizers. As Fanon states, 'Leave this Europe where they are never done talking of Man, yet murder men everywhere they find them, at the corner of every one of their own streets, in all corners of the globe' (251). Imitating Europe, copying its institutions is not an option. Rather, 'for ourselves and for humanity, comrades, we must turn over a new leaf, we must work out new concepts, and try to set afoot a new man' (255). There is a utopian element in Fanon's thought: he advocates the use of violence as a tool to overcome violence and to create new concepts, including the new man, but he offers nothing about the path it takes to move from (violent) struggle to the new history of 'Man'. This idea of creating new concepts is also central to Butler's ideas, and it is to her writings that I return now.

SUBJECTS OF VIOLENCE: NORMS AND THE OTHER

In the previous two chapters, I mapped the key parameters of Butler's political philosophy of the human, which, I suggested, build on her insistence on relationality, ek-stasis, and vulnerability. I now want to add the remaining pieces to this philosophical jigsaw puzzle by considering the role of violence in Butler's account of the human. Given her recent focus on war, it is not surprising to see that the treatment of violence features prominently in her writings. Yet underlying these considerations, violence exercises a more fundamental role in Butler's texts: it plays on the constitutive dependency and vulnerability of the subject, and while it is oppressive, crushing, and disabling, it also simultaneously provides the subject with a primary intelligibility. It bestows an 'unwilled recognition' upon the subject, even though it may undermine the subject's desire for recognition. For Butler, violence is anchored in her claims about the human and the social operation of power, and in an ethical struggle which is said to lie at the heart of violence (hence her interest in Levinas). As I argue, Butler's deployment of violence as a category constitutive of the subject must be read alongside her deconstructive account, which demonstrates how the vulnerability that makes us susceptible to violence also undoes violence (see my discussion below). I explicate and examine Butler's deployment of the category of violence in her account of subject formation, the formation of communities, and political coalitions.

Butler's recent writings offer an intriguing account of the relationship between violence, regarded as constitutive of liveability, and the emergence of the human. I am broadly sympathetic towards Butler's emphasis on the constitutive dimension of violence, and I want to suggest that Butler offers a nuanced account of violence that is sensitive to its paradoxical role as being both productive and repressive. Such an account, I argue, helps to understand the role of violence in political transformation and in the generation of new political subjectivities.

Butler's framing of the subject in relation to dependency, ek-stasis, and vulnerability is further developed in her post-9/11 writings, where it undergoes two important developments: vulnerability, understood as a generalized condition of life, connects with her attention to ethics (I attend to this aspect further on). Furthermore, vulnerability obtains global significance. This focus is, primarily, her response to the political climate in the United States after 9/11, to war, military intervention, and possible non-violent responses to violence (see Butler 2004b, 2009a). Her acknowledgement of the importance of the global constellation and global feminism also bears upon her discussion of the framing of liveable lives in the context of the so-called 'New Gender Politics', which Butler addresses in relation to the development of international human rights for sexual minorities (see Butler 2004a; see also Chapters 1 and 4).

In *Excitable Speech* (1997a), Butler outlines the injurious, even crushing, effect of violence on the subject. There, she accounts for the interpellative force of language that may constitute the subject in a manner that is, potentially, at odds with the subject's sense of self. As I outlined previously, at the heart of this account of the subject-human sits the assertion of a fundamental precariousness and vulnerability that makes the subject susceptible to the potentially violent actions of others. Out of this constellation of fundamental dependency, Butler concludes that violence is constitutive of the subject. This claim adds force to her assertion of the paradoxical nature of subjectivity: the attachment to subjection is a precondition to the subject's emergence (see *PLP* and my discussion in Chapter 1). Linking this claim to her discussion of the operation of hate speech, Butler concludes that injurious language is simultaneously demeaning to and inaugurating of social existence. The capacity of language to exercise such power over the subject is rooted in what Butler terms an 'enabling vulnerability' (*ES*, 2), which turns on the subject's fundamental dependency on an other. *Excitable Speech* grounds this dependency in the speech or address of the other, where vulnerability to being named is a founding condition of the subject.[3]

The interpellative force of violence crystallizes around two related nodal points: these are the operation of norms and the pervasive existence of an—always potentially violent—other. While norms regulate the subject's compliance with hegemonic norms of identity, the other exploits a foundational precariousness and vulnerability that leaves the subject permanently exposed. Both dimensions of violence work in tandem, and they contribute to the constitution of a subject of violence. This fundamental dependency accounts for what Butler terms the social ontology of life, that is, the constitution of the subject in its exposure and vulnerability towards others, which is always shaped by the operation of power. I shall discuss both features in turn, beginning with a discussion of norms.

Samuel Chambers (2007) reads *Gender Trouble* (1990) as a political theory of violence, and he approaches this text through the concept of normative violence. Normative violence is said to articulate the regulating and disciplining function of identity categories. In *Gender Trouble*, Butler accounts for the formation of gendered subjects in relation to norms of gender in a heterosexual matrix, and for the performative displacement of that norm through subversive bodily practices. The question of bodily coherence and its relation to gender norms takes centre stage in *Undoing Gender* (2004a), where Butler defines norms as '[operating] within social practices as the implicit standard of *normalization*' (*UG*, 41; italics in original). Furthermore, they tend to remain implicit, concealing or displacing how we see the world.[4] As she intimates, norms are linked to violence and taken together; they are deployed in the regulation of gender. Such epistemic violence emanates from the nexus of power-knowledge, the politics of truth that is deployed by the medical establishment. Butler refers to the forceful and violent 'correction' of those bodies that do not comply with normative conceptions of masculinity and femininity. Drawing on the famous example of the Joan/John case (see Chapter 2), Butler argues that such surgical interventions constitute a 'violent attempt to implement the norm' (*UG*, 68). This is an important discussion, but I want to pursue further how Butler maps her account of the social ontology of life, including her assertion that violence is intrinsic to our emergence as intelligible human subjects. *Undoing Gender* identifies the problem of a normative operation in our conception of the human that classifies and categorizes those considered as intelligible and those who are abject. The failure to qualify or to be recognized as fully human, Butler argues, points towards the precariousness of human life, underwritten by a fundamental vulnerability to violence. However, while violence is inflicted upon individuals (and in this respect it remains external to them), violence is also constitutive, as it is said to form and be enmeshed in the shaping of bodily morphology of those considered as intelligible.

Although norms and ethical principles matter in *Giving an Account of Oneself* (2005), it is the question of the other that increasingly occupies Butler. She ponders the role of ethics in contemporary critical thought. She develops Adorno's claim (that ethics constitutes at least potentially a form of repression and violence) to suggest something she terms 'ethical violence', which she defines, again drawing on Adorno, as a 'collective ethos that has become anachronistic. The ethos refuses to become past, and violence is the way in which it imposes itself upon the present' (*GAO*, 5). Violence, according to Butler, is always potentially inherent in ethics and by extension in norms. Norms, however, as we have already seen, are instrumental to the establishment of the subject. Hence, the following questions, which Butler directs at Adorno, implicitly contain her answers: '. . . did Adorno consider that norms also decide in advance who will and will not become a subject? Did he consider the operation of norms in the very constitution of the subject, in the stylization of its ontology and in the establishing of a legitimate site within the realm of social ontology?' (*GAO*, 9).

In Chapter 1, I discussed Butler's turn to ethics and ontology, and I mapped how she increasingly ponders questions to do with the shared condition of humanity. This focus does not constitute a radical break with some of her earlier work. Rather, it is grounded in her insistence on the corporeal condition of human experience. Thus, the body and its susceptibility to violence remains a leitmotif of Butler's writings, albeit one that has undergone significant modifications in her recent work. Aimed at the horizon of post-9/11 politics, *Precarious Life* (2004b) illuminates Butler's broader conception of bodily vulnerability in relation to war and torture (see below). This assertion of bodily vulnerability builds upon two further related claims. These are, first, the claim of the primacy of the other, and of our fundamental exposure to others, which Butler derives from her reading of Jean Laplanche (see Caruth 2001) and Levinas (1996), and from Adriana Cavarero's (2000) concept of address, and second, Butler's deployment of the notion of ek-stasis. I have already attended to the significance of ek-stasis; here I want to unpack the notion of the address in more detail. *Giving an Account of Oneself* (2005) develops Laplanche's claim that '[t]he other is prior to the subject' (see Caruth 2001; see also *GAO*, 73). As Butler argues, 'we are, from the start, ethically implicated in the lives of others' (*GAO*, 64); thus, the other precedes the 'I'. As she puts it, 'I am authored by what precedes and exceeds me' (*GAO*, 82), where, 'in the beginning *I am my relation to you*' (*GAO*, 81). Furthermore, she ponders in particular the role played by the address of an other to the constitution of the self. Aiding her in this undertaking is the work of Adriana Cavarero (2000) and her dialogic notion of the self and ethical responsibility, developed as an alternative to identitarian conceptions of the self. At the heart of Cavarero's narrative sits a question borrowed from Arendt: 'Who are you?', which, following Butler's reading, establishes a relational politics, 'one in which the exposure and vulnerability of the other makes a primary ethical claim upon me' (*GAO*, 31). How such an ethics relates to politics will concern me further below; for now, I remain with the prospect of reading Butler's Cavareroean encounter. This linguistic address points up a further paradox in the fundamental structure of subject constitution: while the proto-subject requires an other in order to come into being and to persist in its being, this other and his/her address is always, at least potentially, violent (see *PL*, 39 and *ES*). Her account provides an important insight into the way she conceives of the temporality of subject constitution: as she argues repeatedly, the other and his/her speech precedes me. Laplanche's work allows Butler to circumvent a puzzle generated by the Hegelian struggle for recognition, specifically the presupposition that an 'I' precedes its establishment through the process of recognition.

While questions pertaining to gender and sexuality dominate Butler's writings in the 1990s, she broadens her focus in the 2000s with her reflections on US policy in the wake of the war on terror. This thematic emphasis brings to the fore her interest in questions of loss and grievability that follow the violent actions of state and non-state actors in the context of political conflict. Implicitly, it returns us to the question of recognition, that is, to the question of who is grievable and hence recognizable as being lost. What Butler poses in explicit form in these writings is the question of the ontology of the human, which she refers to as a social ontology and which, according to her, is grounded in our fundamental vulnerability and susceptibility to violence. As she claims, we are fundamentally dependent on some specific other, a primary carer or carers who, under ideal conditions, guide us through the vulnerable stages of our lives. This dependence persists into adulthood, as we continue to rely on the recognition of others. If, in the best of cases, others protect us from violence, then in the worst of cases violence is done to us by others. These violent others, whether known to us or not, raise the spectre of an unwanted violence visited upon us. Butler concludes that because we can neither predict nor necessarily prevent the violent actions of others, we can therefore no longer hold on to any notion of sovereignty. Violence undermines conceptions of a sovereign subject.

Notwithstanding Butler's insistence on the political or strategic value of autonomy, exposure and dispossession undercut those philosophical claims that assert the autonomy of the individual, and they point to the subject's implication and investment in an other. It is out of this account of the subject's dependence that vulnerability, understood as a susceptibility to violence, emerges.[5] Thus, violence, for Butler, does not merely operate on the subject, exploiting the subject's vulnerability. Rather, for her, violence obtains a constitutive or generative function, as it comes to form the subject, and in fact generates the subject in the first place. These concerns lead her to produce a narrative of subject constitution that posits the subject's fundamental dependency upon others and a vulnerability towards the—potentially violent—actions of others, and that claims the centrality of norms to our sense of selfhood.

Violence, according to Butler, is effective because human beings are fundamentally dependent upon others and hence susceptible to a primary vulnerability. Furthermore, we can neither predict nor necessarily prevent the violence impressed upon us by others. Such violence occurs in physical form, as I intimated above, but it also operates at a symbolic level, for example via the use of language. Yet, while vulnerability and the susceptibility to violence is inscribed into the ontology of the human, Butler also distinguishes between such an 'ontological' vulnerability and susceptibility to violence on the one hand, and its unequal social and geopolitical distribution on the other. This distinction is captured with her categorical distinction between precariousness, defined as our fundamental vulnerability, and precarity, which describes the social allocation of vulnerability and violence to marginal groups (see Chapter 1). Such unequal distribution circumscribes the gendered and racialized conditions of liveable lives, singling out populations who are more vulnerable. I already alluded to the discussion of intersex, which features in Butler's more recent work, while her writings on US foreign policy and the conflict in Israel-Palestine illustrate the unequal geopolitical and racialized impact of violence on populations and recognition globally, and in regions torn apart by conflict.

Furthermore, it allows Butler to engage in a critique of US foreign policy, which she maintains holds on to the myth of a non-vulnerable, sovereign subject that undermines the sovereignty of others in the name of its own. Erinn Gilson (2011) refers to the denial of vulnerability as an 'epistemology of ignorance'. Such ignorance, or denial, in her view, is ethically and politically dangerous, because it misses the opportunity to undo violence and oppressive social relations. In fact, 'openness to being affected and affecting', according to Gilson (31), is essential. It is easy to see how Butler's reflections on the vulnerability and misrecognition of sexual minorities, and the violence inflicted upon them, transfers to her geopolitical considerations. These explain why certain populations, for example in the Middle East, Iraq, and Afghanistan, as well as those looking 'like Arabs' in the US, suffer disproportionately from violence. There is, at this stage, an important conclusion to be drawn: as Butler suggests, the question of the human, of who I am, must grapple with the subjection of the human to the violence of others; more significantly, perhaps, is her insight that, as humans we are subjects of violence. In this respect, violence is paradoxical: it simultaneously threatens and facilitates our existence or intelligibility, our recognizability as intelligible subjects. Hence, there is no subject without violence.

It is only in the context of her discussion of violence that Butler's emphasis on conceptions of vulnerability and relationality, ecstasy, and dispossession obtains its full significance. As I indicated previously, what I find attractive about Butler's discussion is her account of the subject as relational and dispossessed (see Chapter 1), and its susceptibility and exposure to the potentially violent actions of others. Configuring the subject in its exposure and vulnerability to others allows Butler to develop an ethics that emerges out of vulnerability (see below); it also facilitates an analysis of structures of dependence, vulnerability, and violence on a global scale, whether in the context of war or in relation to the unequal distribution of the material conditions of liveability. Thus, vulnerability and interdependency are woven into the structure of global politics, where one's vulnerability may be the target of geographically distant or unknown others (see also Zehfuss 2007). Crucially, ethics and politics, and vulnerability and relationality are corporeally underpinned; as 'fleshy' categories, they convey the needs of the body for survival, and the way bodily needs depend upon the actions of others. Hence, the ontological parameters of human being and human life, defined as precarious, are modified or heightened by the unequal distribution to vulnerability. To further develop my argument, I attend to the discussion of state violence in the context of the war on terror.

STATE VIOLENCE, WAR, AND TORTURE

One of the most persistent disputes to emerge out of discussions on conflict and war is that of the distinction between legitimate and illegitimate violence. Furthermore, efforts to differentiate between legitimate and illegitimate violence are frequently mapped on discussions over the use of the term terrorism, where 'terrorism' stands for the use of illegitimate violence exercised by non-state actors.[6] Not surprisingly, Butler is critical of this distinction. In her essay 'Indefinite Detention', included in *Precarious Life* (2004b), she regards usages of the term 'terrorism' or references to 'terrorist' as problematic because they dehumanize those who engage in acts of violence defined as terroristic (see also her discussion in *Frames of War* (2009a)). I attend to this aspect of her discussion later on. For the moment, I want to focus on a related point. Of particular pertinence to Butler's unease with the term 'terrorism' is the way that the distinction between legitimate and illegitimate (or terrorist) violence is mapped upon a further distinction: that between violence exercised by the state and violence exercised by non-state actors. Following the logic of this distinction, violence exercised by states becomes, by definition, legitimate, while violence engaged in by non-state actors is categorically defined as illegitimate (and terroristic).[7]

In this section, I unpack these claims further, attending to Butler's discussion of state violence in the context of war and torture. Her focus on state violence and the ethical imperative to critique it is a recurrent theme in her recent work, which connects with her wider reservations regarding all matters to do with the state. In fact, it is plausible to claim that for Butler the state is the violent institution par excellence, and that all other forms of violence are secondary, derived in one way or another, from the violence that emanates from the state. It follows that, for Butler, the critique of state violence becomes a critique of the state, conceived as an institution that engages in violence and operates according to exclusionary principles (see also Chapter 4). I am broadly sympathetic towards Butler's critique of state violence, but I have several reservations. Her association of the state with violence is problematic, in my view, because it restricts the view on non-violent instances of state action;[8] furthermore, it construes the deployment of violence by non-state actors as merely derivative; and third, it clouds the way that the boundaries between states and non-state actors are blurred.[9]

Although the critique of the state constitutes part of the radical tradition in modern and contemporary political thought, it is important to remember that the equation of the state with violence is in and of itself not the exclusive hallmark of radical theory. Rather, to associate the state with violence, or, to be precise, to locate the legitimate use of violence in the institution of the state is the inaugurating move of modern political philosophy, beginning with Hobbes and stretching at least to Weber's famous definition of the state as the institution that embodies the legitimate use of violence.[10] Building on an implicit acknowledgement that equates the state with violence, Butler is at pains to articulate a critique of violence as state violence. As I suggest towards the end of this chapter, she calls on Walter Benjamin to aid her in this undertaking. In this section, I am concerned with the manifestation of state violence in war and the use of torture as a tool in the war on terror.

If violence is understood to reorder the international arena, it also has domestic implications. To be precise, it blurs or even dissolves the boundaries between the domestic and the global. As Butler suggests, war frames domestic policy and discourses on domestic policy. Thus, one of the key themes emerging from the wider debates on the war on terror pertains to the way that the actions of the US government abroad have reconfigured the nature of the state at home. As Kaufman-Osborn (2008b) argues, '[t]he aggrandizement of executive power at home and abroad has over time corroded the very distinction between domestic and foreign, and that in turn has vitiated a key premise undergirding liberalism's affirmation of power's accountability'.[11] Brad Evans (2011), in an introductory essay to a special collection on liberal war, lists among the key principles of twenty-first century bio-political warfare the claims that liberal wars (1) operate according to bio-political imperatives, (2) collapse the distinction between local and global, and in doing so universalize war, and (3) produce political subjectivities. Related to this point, Reid asks 'how to resist the forms of subjectivity [that liberal wars] produce' (770). The relationship between governmentality and sovereignty in the context of the liberal security state and the wider framework of the state of exception will occupy me in Chapter 5. For now I want to map briefly what possible responses or resistances arising out of Butler's ideas could look like.

To begin with, against bio-politics (understood to be integral to the conduct of liberal war and centrally concerned with the management and regulation of populations) Butler posits the notion of life and liveability. Recall that liveability articulates the idea that conditions of precarity must be exposed; in other words, if liveability is one aim of radical politics, then it must concern itself with the egalitarian distribution of the material conditions necessary for a liveable life, and a recognition of the fundamental precariousness of all life (see Chapter 1). Insisting on liveability thus reformulates the collapse between local and global that liberal war is said to institute: its acknowledgment of global vulnerability and interdependence dismantles the civilizing mission and the military expansionism that lies at the heart of liberal war. To further delineate how war produces forms of subjectivity, I turn again to Butler's discussion of torture.

Butler dedicates much space to the discussion of American foreign policy in the wake of 9/11. In her writings she delineates a critique of US foreign policy that draws on her political reflections and puts to work her ethical principles. This work has two dimensions: first, it challenges just war theory (she refers explicitly to the writings of Michael Walzer) and presents in its place a critique of war, foreign policy based on war, and its domestic significance in the context of the US. Second, it develops, more broadly, a critique of the state and of state violence (which also includes her critique of Israel). War, according to Butler, prevents reflection on our fundamental vulnerability, our relationality, and our dependence on the actions of distant others. In this respect, war precludes reflection on and recognition of a global constellation of interdependence, leading to the formation of international coalitions. In their place, war puts an essentially futile conception of mastery and sovereignty that seeks to prize one's own precarity at the expense of others. To consider war in such a way leads Butler to reflect on the conditions of global responsibility (I return to some of this in the next section). Such responsibility, as Butler avers, should not be confused with conceptions of global mission to bring democracy to distant parts of the world. Rather, global responsibility needs to challenge 'imperialist appropriation' (*FW*, 37) and to reflect on the constitution of a 'we' in global terms.

In fact, much of Butler's discussion concentrates on state violence and the ethical imperative to critique state violence. Here I want to map briefly her key claims before outlining my critical reading of these assertions. Given that Butler posits relationality, dispossession, and dependence as the central features of human existences, violence, and war, could be seen as undercutting human existence. Yet, because violence is simultaneously destructive and constitutive, it plays an important function in constituting those regarded as abject or indeed themselves violent. It is in this context that Butler turns to the discussion of torture and its deployment in the various holding centres of the US military, such as Abu Ghraib prison and Guantánamo Bay. In *Frames of War* (2009a), Butler argues that torture plays a constitutive role in the discursive construction of those who are perceived as dangerous, as terrorists. With reference to the prisoners held at Guantánamo Bay, Butler deconstructs the discourse of the US military and officialdom, referring to the way that the prisoners are conceived of as 'pure vessels of violence' (*PL*, 88–91), related to the insane or to animals, and thus denied their status as human (see Chapter 2).

An important element of the discussion pertains to the use of gendered practices in the disciplining of prisoners, playing on cultural traditions of shame. Forced nudity, the forced staging of (homo-)sexual acts, the wearing of female underwear, as well as the use of fake menstrual blood during interrogations became elements of a technique of discipline that operated, as Timothy Kaufman-Osborn (2008a) asserts, under what he terms a 'logic of emasculation', aimed at '[stripping] prisoners of their masculine gender identity and turn them into caricatures of terrified and often infantilised femininity' (210). Thus, the staging of US masculinity grew in inverse proportion to the attack on Iraqi masculinity: violence constitutes a feminized Arab subject as well as a masculinized US military subject (see also Young 2003a, 2003b). I return to this discussion of torture in the next chapter, where I focus on its role in discourses of civilization.

Before I move to the final sections of this chapter, I wish to pause for a moment and recap the themes that I have discussed so far: I have mapped Butler's account of the constitutive nature of violence, and I related this account of violence with her emphasis on precariousness, vulnerability, and interdependence. I also tracked her critique of state violence, specifically its articulation in the context of US foreign policy and the war on terror. In the remainder of this chapter, I enquire into the prospects for transformative engagements with violence. To do so, I draw on Butler's treatment of the topic of grieving and grievability, her exchange with Catherine Mills and Fiona Jenkins on the idea of non-violence, and her reading of Walter Benjamin's conception of divine violence.

IS NON-VIOLENCE POSSIBLE?

Despite her insistence on violence's productive capacity in the generation of subjects, Butler holds on to the aim of non-violence. In the remainder of this chapter I want to consider how violence can be transformed into non-violence. I will ask whether, given the seemingly all-pervasive role accorded to violence, there is any space for non-violence in Butler's account. I also enquire into its relation to violence. These questions, which aim at the horizon of ethics, run up against two challenges: if non-violence is intrinsically and structurally linked to violence, how can the two be disentangled? If a struggle to '[wrestle] ethically with one's own murderous impulses' (*PL*, 150) lies at the heart of the subject, then non-violence is not an easy task, and in her writings Butler herself wrestles with the ethical demand of non-violence. Thus, how can we escape violence or lessen its impact if our very existence is bound up with the operation of violence? This question lies at the heart of her recent venture into the field of moral philosophy, articulated in *Giving an Account of Oneself* (2005), but it is also dispersed in some of her other recent writings.

Recall Butler's claim that life is precarious: we are connected with others on whom we depend for our survival, and for whom we are responsible. These, as I aim to demonstrate here, develop from her insistence on critique as a strategy of non-violence, her proposal to induce a breakage between violence and non-violence, and practices of public grieving. Thus, countering violence with non-violence fundamentally transforms our relationship with the other. It should be stressed, though, that practices of non-violence must not be confused with pacifism, which Butler condemns as a form of ethical violence: ethical principles may exert their own form of violence. Instead, she links ethics to the wider question of our responsibility towards the other, and she locates non-violence in the relation to the other.

What, though, is the other of violence? Can non-violence emerge out of the seemingly all-pervasive account of violence? Here I want to examine the categorical status of non-violence as the other of violence. At various points in her recent work, Butler alludes to the prospect of a less or non-violent world. If violence demarcates the limits of a liveable life, does non-violence erase those limits, making lives more liveable? These questions have been the subject of a recent debate between Butler and Catherine Mills.

If violence obtains a paradoxical role in Butler's political thought, constituting the subject while also subjecting it, then the imperative of non-violence is equally paradoxical: how can it be possible to escape violence or to lessen its impact if violence enables the existence of the subject? Would non-violence undo the subject? For Butler, ethics is bound up with the wider question of the possibility of responsibility in the context of a decentred notion of the self. Drawing on her discussion of Laplanche and Levinas, Butler locates non-violence in the same paradoxical frame that generates the subject. It is in the relation to the other that the prospect for non-violence originates. As she asks, '[w]hat might it mean to undergo violation, to insist upon *not* resolving grief and staunching vulnerability too quickly through a turn to violence, and to practice, as an experiment in living otherwise, non-violence in an emphatically nonreciprocal response?' (*GAO*, 100; italics in original).

This possibility of non-violence in the face of a violent assault is embodied in the notion of responsibility, which includes one's responsibility for the violence one is subjected to. Laplanche's work enables Butler to circumvent a puzzle generated by the Hegelian struggle for recognition, specifically the presupposition that an 'I' precedes its establishment through the process of recognition. This is an important claim to make, and it challenges those critics who allege that the decentred subject is incapable of exercising ethical responsibility (*GAO*, 19).

These considerations of violence and non-violence formed part of a recent exchange between Butler and the philosophers Catherine Mills and Fiona Jenkins (see Butler 2007b; Jenkins 2007; Mills 2007). I want to begin by taking a closer look at Mills's criticism of Butler. Mills, I believe, shares many of Butler's assertions, including the claim that violence plays a role in the formation of the subject. However, she is critical of Butler's effort to develop a 'non-violent ethics' (Mills's term). According to Mills (2007), Butler's account of normative violence does not square up with her effort towards a non-violent ethics (135). As Mills asks, how can we comply with a non-violent ethics if we are constituted by violence, that is, if we depend on violence in order to persist? On the surface, this seems a legitimate concern, and Butler's response to Mills that we are 'at least partially formed through violence' (*FW*, 167), is rather ambiguous, opening up further questions. For example, which parts of us are formed by violence and which aren't? Are some of us more the product of violence than others? Butler's distinction between precariousness and precarity, between a foundational vulnerability and its unequal distribution across differentiated populations may go some way towards answering the question, but it cannot respond adequately, in my view, to the claim of partially violent formation in precariousness.

Developing her rejoinder to Mills, Butler declares that while we are formed 'partially' through violence, we must induce a 'breakage' between the violence that forms and subjects us and turns us into subjects, and the violence that we inflict upon others. It is in this breakage that an ethics of non-violence and responsibility for the other is located. Butler's answer to this question introduces the idea of a 'breakage' between the violence that subjects us and forms us and the violence that we engage in and inflict upon others. It is in this breakage that she locates her ethics of non-violence. What would such a breakage look like, though? I want to suggest that this refusal to return violence creates a kind of temporal and civic breakage that allows for a different way of broaching the problem. Taken together, the time for reflection on how to respond to violence and for gathering up courage to speak out form the basis of social critique. Speaking out against violence requires 'collective courage' (*PL*, 127). As she asks, 'will we be silent (and be a collaborator with illegitimately violent power), or will we make our voices heard (and be counted among those who did what they could to stop illegitimate violence), even if speaking poses a risk to ourselves?' (*PL*, 103).[12] Thus, Butler establishes a connection between critique and violence, specifically the critique of (state) violence, but also critique as a response to violence. It is this latter point, that is, the insistence on a critique that is not just of violence but also is a response to violence, together with Butler's insistence on the constitutive role of violence and civil courage, that in my view is Butler's most significant contribution to the topic to date.

Furthermore, for Butler, such an ethics of non-violence differs from Mills's allusion to a 'non-violent ethics', which imposes a set of principles that are themselves violent, constituting paradoxically a form of ethical violence (*GAO*, 5). Thus, the 'practice of non-violence' (*GAO*, 64) should not be confused with pacifism, which Butler condemns as a morality that exerts its own form of ethical violence. Much could be said about Butler's reading of pacifism, specifically her association of pacifism with a form of violent morality based upon abstract principles.[13] Countering this ethical or normative violence with non-violence fundamentally transforms our relationship with the other. If violence seeks to install the mastery of one subject over another, then the refusal to engage in violence opens up the prospect of establishing ethical relationships. As she argues, '[i]f violence is the act by which a subject seeks to install its mastery and unity, then non-violence may well follow from living the persistent challenge to egoic mastery that our obligations to others induce and require' (*GAO*, 64). It is in this respect that non-violence undoes the subject. However, such undoing does not erase the subject or its intelligibility; rather, it brings to the fore the subject's ek-static relationality to the other.

As I sought to suggest, Butler posits the susceptibility to corporeal vulnerability as a formative feature of human life. This corporeal vulnerability provides the opportunity for a resignificatory body politics that contests and expands those norms regulating and governing bodies. As argued by Butler, it constitutes the basis for the development of ethical relationships with others based upon the recognition of a shared corporeal vulnerability as a shared feature of human life. Butler envisages the development of communities and coalitions arising out of this shared corporeal vulnerability, especially on the international stage. This focus on the development of community and coalitional politics grounded in shared bodily experience constitutes an important development in Butler's work, which goes beyond her previous emphasis on the exploration of gendered bodily practices and which grounds transformative body politics in an ethics of vulnerability.

I want to return to Mills's criticism. Towards the end of her essay, Mills (2007) asks whether the distinction between non-violent ethics and foundational violence requires us to distinguish between different modes of violence (151), drawing in particular on Benjamin's notion of a divine violence that destroys violence. A similar thought is introduced by Fiona Jenkins, who, instead of holding on to the necessity of violence, suggests an adherence to injurability and vulnerability as foundational categories. Moreover, as Jenkins stresses, rightly in my view, we are not condemned to remain in the thrall of violence, especially normative violence, since norms can be played, changed, or, as Butler calls it, resignified. Thus, practices of non-violence can be ethical, in their relationship to the other, as much as political, in terms of their status vis-à-vis the norm.

For Butler, there can be more than one form of violence, and there are also multiple forms of non-violence (understood as violence that refuses violence), and I want to map them briefly. These include the resignification of norms, especially in those cases where norms impose themselves violently onto the subject. Moreover, the care of the self and the self-forming of the subject as an ethical project is a way of resignifying normative violence. The refusal to return to violence constitutes another form of non-violence, articulating one's responsibility for the other. The practice of critique constitutes another important form of non-violence. As I outline below, Butler draws on Walter Benjamin's conception of critique as a critique of state violence. Unsurprisingly, one of Butler's sources for her account of ethical life draws upon her reading of the later Foucauldian understanding of an ethics of the self, embedded in practices of critique. For her, critique itself becomes a challenge to violence. As she discusses in her essay 'The Charge of Anti-Semitism: Jews, Israel, and the Risks of Public Critique', speaking out against violence, in this case against violence perpetrated by the state, poses a challenge to violence that requires 'collective courage' (*PL*, 127).

I have much sympathy for Butler's account of responsibility, and her articulation of a concept of global responsibility that is grounded in the relationality to unknown others puts forward an attractive conception of global ethics. I wonder, though, whether the link she makes between relationality and non-violence requires a leap of faith. After all, why should non-violence follow from dependency? Why should I spare those on whom I depend in some vaguely conceived way, especially if such dependency is obscured by geographical distance? What kind of breakage does relationality place on my aggression? While these questions can be answered within the context of Butler's ethics, I remain unconvinced that, taken on their own, they aid a further understanding of politics. In Chapter 5, I discuss how Butler's reappraisal of international law and human rights provides a more promising path into the problematic of responsibility. To remain with the question of grievability— although insisting on grievability as a practice of non-violence also throws up the kind of challenges that I just sketched—allows, I believe, for a more carefully constructed political consideration of the question of non-violence.

DIVINE VIOLENCE AND MESSIANIC EXPIATION

Violence's paradoxical nature, articulated in its most enigmatic form, converges in Butler's reading of Walter Benjamin's (1999) dense and difficult essay 'Critique of Violence'. Butler's motivation for engaging this text is twofold: first, it provides her with an account of violence that reaches out to non-violence and holds out the prospect of resolving the problem raised by Catherine Mills (see previous section), namely, how we can articulate non-violence out of its intrinsic link with violence. In other words, it throws up what Butler terms 'the paradoxical possibility of a non-violent violence' (*PW*, 71) (I attend to this aspect in this section). Second, Benjamin's essay contributes to Butler's recent interest in Jewish ethics and philosophy, and it allows her to examine Jewish sources that will aid her articulation of a critique of Zionism and Israeli state violence (which I discuss in Chapter 4). Although Butler's reading of the Benjamin essay could arguably be interpreted as introducing a new set of abstract ethical principles, especially in her consideration of the question of responsibility, I want to suggest that its focus on the critique of state violence enables her to circumvent the dilemma that a critique of violence based on Levinasian ideas generates, namely a hollow ethics void of politics. It is problematic, however, insofar as it further entrenches her association of violence with the state. Before outlining my reading of Butler's text, it is prudent to provide a brief exposition of Benjamin's essay on violence.

In 'Critique of Violence', Benjamin (1999) develops a critique of violence out of his critique of the state and law through the use of conceptions of the messianic.[14] Throughout his essay, Benjamin operates with two sets of distinctions. These are the distinction between lawmaking and law-preserving violence, and the distinction between mythical and divine violence. To unpack these distinctions briefly, lawmaking violence deals with the problem of foundations: it relates to those acts of law that bring a polity into being without providing further legitimating foundations. Law-preserving violence is the kind of violence that underpins every lawful act and that is exercised, in the main, by the police and the military. In addition to the differentiation between lawmaking and law-preserving violence, Benjamin also sets apart what he calls 'mythical violence' from 'divine violence'. Mythical violence, according to Benjamin, is lawmaking. Divine violence, on the other hand, is law destroying. As I will outline now, these distinctions are significant for Butler's discussion of violence, because they allow her to articulate her own critique of violence with her critique of the state and the prospect of non-violent political practices.[15]

As is well known, Benjamin's critique of violence and the law develops out of his discontent with the politics of parliamentary democracy.[16] Thus, pondering his equation of law with violence, he argues that law must be undone. Helping him to develop this connection is the work of Sorel, whose ideas have significantly influenced Benjamin and whose distinction between political and proletarian strike underpins Benjamin's critique of the state. Sorel famously suggests that the political strike, which he associates with the Jacobin revolutionary transformation, merely strengthens state power, replacing one form of power with another. The proletarian strike, on the other hand, is said to aim at the destruction of power. Taking up Sorel's distinction, Benjamin argues that the proletarian strike is non-violent and anarchistic because it aims at the destruction of state power and violence; it constitutes a form of non-violent destruction.

To further develop this notion of non-violent destruction, Benjamin introduces the distinction between mythical and divine violence. As he outlines: 'if [mythical violence] sets the boundaries, [divine violence] boundlessly destroys them; if mythical violence brings at once guilt and retribution, divine power only expiates; if the former threatens, the latter strikes; if the former is bloody, the latter is lethal without spilling blood.' (Benjamin 1999, 297).

To elaborate his conception of mythical violence, Benjamin draws on the myth of Niobe; tempting fate by insulting the gods, she was turned into stone and had to watch the killing of her children. Guilt is the knot around which Niobe's punishment turns; only the expiation and atonement brought by divine violence can untie this knot of guilt. Two aspects of Benjamin's discussion are of particular significance to Butler's work, and I will address both in turn. These are first, Benjamin's claim of the constitutive nature of violence in the production of the guilty subject, and second, the prospect of a non-violent violence (Benjamin's divine violence). The production of the guilty subject, which emerges in submission to the law, is a theme that has already occupied Butler in *The Psychic Life of Power* (1997b). There she drew on in particular the work of Nietzsche and Althusser to make sense of the subject's emergence in and through subjection.

Elements of these themes return in her engagement with Benjamin. Drawing on his work, Butler delineates yet again the emergence of a guilty subject, whose guilt is produced through the law, specifically via the prospect of punishment. Thus, the violence of the law operates in the formation of the subject; it also works on the subject. As Benjamin (1999) asserts, '[m]ythical violence is bloody power over mere life for its own sake' (297). And yet, whereas the subject of *Psychic Life* is forever caught in a melancholic circle of guilty conscience, the Benjaminian subject can hope for expiation, a release from guilt through the operation of divine violence. Such hope, following Benjamin, is articulated with the notion of the messianic (see also Chapter 4). According to Butler's reading of Benjamin, the messianic introduces forgiveness and expiation into the consideration of violence. In this respect, it becomes an important category for thinking through the use of state violence, specifically state violence that justifies itself through the claim of self-defence. Butler's critique here aims directly at Israeli policy, specifically in relation to the 2006 war in Lebanon. Critique (of Israeli state violence) becomes a 'political ethics' (*PL*, 103) that requires a public space in which to debate and exercise one's critique (*PL*, 126). The messianic contains a further aspect. Again drawing on Benjamin, it facilitates a rethinking of temporality, of progress and development. These become important tools in Butler's consideration of the narratives of civilization (see Chapter 4).

Much of Butler's discussion of Benjamin draws on a solitary battle with the divine commandment 'Thou shalt not kill'. At first glance, conceiving of the ethical struggle with violence (see also Levinas) in such a way lends itself to a reading of an individualistic battle with one's own violent, even murderous impulses. Such an account runs counter to Butler's persistent emphasis on the relational aspect of the subject. It is only towards the end of her essay on Benjamin that she returns explicitly to such a reading (Butler 2006a). Drawing again on the example of Israel's policies, Butler problematizes the notion of self-defence and the border as phenomena that must be cultivated through military institutions and practices. As she argues, defence is a mode of disavowed subjugation without which the self cannot survive.

Consequently, resistance to subjugation leads to the self's undoing. However, as she continues, boundaries are sites of multiple relations, and the denial of the insight of the subject's enmeshment with such relations can only leave two paths: destroying or destruction.

As I hinted at the beginning of this chapter, one of the compelling features of Butler's conception of violence is its depiction as paradoxical. Thus, the simultaneously productive and destructive nature of violence allows Butler to theorize this concept beyond the consideration of moral categories that so often feature in political-philosophical reflections. Furthermore, by shedding light on violence's structural implication in the state, Butler is able to articulate a more detailed and sophisticated account of the operation of war in contemporary (global) politics than some of her analytical critics can. Violence becomes a bio-political tool that is just as significant in the operation of the microphysics of power as it is in the global arena. In fact, as I sought to demonstrate, Butler's discussion deconstructs the boundaries that are said to lie between the subject, the realm of the domestic sphere, and international relations, broadly conceived.

Furthermore, her account of violence is both politically and ethically compelling. By positing critique as an important element in the repertoire of non-violence, Butler articulates an enlarged conception of critical citizenship that includes reflection (what Dana Villa calls Socratic citizenship) and civic courage, and that goes beyond the usual reflections on rights and participation. Her consideration of grievability is equally attractive, and it successfully integrates, in my view, what could otherwise be perceived as the disparate realms of ethics and politics. Thus, to consider critique and grievability in the context of violence goes some way towards addressing what I consider to be shortcomings in her argument. These include some of her considerations of non-violence that in my view lack logical force, as well as the Levinasian appeal to ethical struggle. My discussion in the next chapter aims to complete the consideration of the relationship between ethics and politics. As I will argue there, Butler's recent reflections on Jewish philosophy close the gap between these two, at times disparate, areas of her thinking. Furthermore, she adds to her already existing work by considering the role for religion in the discursive formation of the subject. I return to the question of violence in Chapter 5, where I consider Butler's treatment of international law.

NOTES

1. The scholarship on violence is extensive. For two recent, useful anthologies see Bufacchi (2009) and Lawrence and Karin (2007). See also Bufacchi (2007); Frazer and Hutchings (2007, 2008, 2011); Keane (2004); Schwarzmantel (2010); and Žižek (2008). The interest in violence and war has also spawned a re-engagement with just war theories (see Elshtain 2003; Walzer 2004). For new scholarship on the concept of liberal war see Evans (2011) and Reid (2006, 2011).

2. Butler's account of violence as paradoxical mirrors her account of the paradoxical structure of subjectification. Her writings on violence are influenced by Walter Benjamin, Theodor W. Adorno, and Emmanuel Levinas. Other thinkers who surface include Arendt, Fanon, and Sartre (see Butler 2006b), as well as, more implicitly, Sorel. Significantly, their respective contributions to Butler's articulation of violence are intrinsically linked with her ideas on ethics, which I discuss throughout this chapter. Related to the question of violence's paradoxical operation is that of the origin of violence, which Butler delineates in dialogue with Melanie Klein's account of aggression (see Butler 2004b, 2009a).

3. Butler is at pains to argue that language does not operate in a sovereign or unidirectional way (see also Chapter 5); rather, while language exploits the subject's vulnerability to linguistic interpellation, it is tied into a chain of signification that obscures the speaker's absence of sovereignty, and that keeps language open to challenge through practices of resignification.

4. See my discussion of the role of the frame in Chapter 1.

5. Operating at a deeper level is an existential vulnerability of the body, susceptible to illness, decay and, ultimately, death.

6. For recent critical engagements with the notion of terrorism, see for example Asad (2007, 2010) and English (2009). See also Benjamin (1999) on the distinction between legitimate and illegitimate violence in the context of his critique of violence.

7. See Finlay (2010) for a discussion of this problem from an analytical perspective.

8. Admittedly, one could plausibly argue that every state action is backed, in the final instance, by the threat of violence, and it is in this context that the state could justifiably be described as a violent institution. However, this is not the same as to argue that every state action is violent.

9. Recent work on new wars and on asymmetrical warfare, although not without problems, seeks to reflect on the blurring of boundaries between different agents of violence. See for example Kaldor (2012).

10. In the original, Weber uses the term 'Gewalt', which implies both force and violence.

11. I consider Butler's reflections on the blurring of the boundaries between governmentality and sovereignty, articulated in *Precarious Life* (2004b), in Chapter 5. See also Loizidou (2007).

12. On the wider issue of civic courage see also Butler's recent conversation with Cornel West on *Honoring Edward Said*, held at Columbia University on 30 October 2013 (www.youtube.com/watch?v=jF5mYvjDp3U).

13. Given Butler's insistence on practices of resignification, it should be asked whether pacifism could also be subjected to resignificatory, transformative practices.

14. As Derrida (1992) points up in his reading of the same essay, the English translation of the original German 'Gewalt' as violence bypasses the complexity that the German allusion of 'Gewalt' as both violence and force carries. Butler's reading of Benjamin is exclusively occupied with the association of 'Gewalt' with violence.

15. Although, as I discuss in Chapter 5, it also generates a new set of challenges, given Butler's recent endorsement of the import of international law.

16. For a critique of Benjamin's essay on violence see Derrida (1992).

4 Towards a Post-secular World?

[A]s a Jew, I was taught that it was ethically imperative to speak up and to speak out against arbitrary state violence. That was part of what I learned when I learned about the Second World War and the concentration camps.

(2011a)

In the previous chapter, I discussed how Butler derives her critique of state violence, which she conceives as a structural feature of the state, from her ethical concern for the precariousness of the other. I connected her fundamental critique of the state as an institution of violence with her particular criticism of US foreign policy, which she has articulated over the last decade. This specific criticism of the violence exerted by successive US governments also chimes with her criticism of the violence perpetrated by the state of Israel, specifically with the occupation of Palestinian territory, and it relates to her concerns regarding the exclusionary ethno-religious basis of Israeli citizenship. In this chapter, I attend to Butler's reflections on Jewishness, her critique of Israel, and her engagement with allegations of anti-Semitism. As she has outlined on several occasions (see for example Butler 2000d; 2006e; 2011a), there are pressing biographical factors that account for her commitment to these topics; they include the loss of family members in the Holocaust, as well as an educational formation in her synagogue that launched her philosophical instruction and responded to her interest in questions of responsibility, arising out of the lessons learnt from the Holocaust. This biographical impetus, which underpins Butler's reflections on Israel and Jewishness, is embedded in her broader political-philosophical engagements, such as her work on loss and grieving (see Chapter 2), her effort to articulate an ethics of non-violence (see Chapter 3), and her work on sovereignty (see Chapter 5).

To unravel this recent development in Butler's thinking, I begin with an exposition of her discussion of anti-Semitism and I assess her effort to develop a specifically Jewish critique of Israel, derived from her engagement with Jewish sources. This discussion leads me to assess her consideration of Jewishness, which she construes in a framework of relationality and which,

I suggest, sheds further light on her articulation of the relationship between ethics and politics. The focus on Israel and Jewishness also opens to a broader reflection on political theology, on the role of religion in public life, and on the relationship between religion and secularism. As I demonstrate, what is particularly pertinent about this intervention is Butler's refusal to frame the discussion in terms of a dualism between religion on the one hand and secularism on the other hand. Rather, she insists on the historical specificity that is necessary for any evaluation of this issue. The ideas which inform her position are those of scattering, dispossession, diaspora, and exile. Much of Butler's writing in this area builds upon recent work on secularism and religion in public life; in this respect, she does not significantly add to this particular debate. I want to suggest that the added value of Butler's contribution to this debate lies with her critique of a 'blunt' secularism that clouds over its own investment in theological ideas. What is of interest, in my view, is the way she relates these debates back to the question of war and violence and how she ties them in with a consideration of civilizational narratives.

A significant aspect of Butler's recent reflections on religion and secularism relates to their respective relation to progressive sexual politics and the implications for public policy and the public realm. Here I utilize the work of Okin (1999) to develop the aspect of coalitional politics. I am particularly interested in Butler's claim that a critique of the secular constitutes the necessary frame for any progressive politics that also draws on the demands of race and gender. This assertion, I suggest, offers a persuasive contribution to recent work on multiculturalism and a key challenge to those positions, especially within feminism, that posits the demands of progressive sexual politics and minority ethnic and religious cultures as mutually exclusive. It is pursued at the level of national politics, where Butler's intervention into recent debates on multiculturalism pertain to its relationship to feminism and the politics of progressive sexual politics. This discussion leads me to consider the philosophical orientation of her debates on the politics of cultural translation and the dispute over universality.

Closely related to this discussion is my assessment of her critique of narratives of violence, which are said to be framed in relation to dominant accounts of civilization. To illustrate my discussion, I introduce a series of examples on the role of religion in public life. An important element of Butler's recent engagement with religion (and to my assessment of her work) is her critique of the orientalist framing and religious coding of minorities associated with Islam. Its global significance consists of Butler's challenge to the idea, most prominently associated with the work of Huntington (1997), of a clash of civilizations. Developing this discussion further, I demonstrate how depictions of progress and civilization come to regulate the prevailing understanding of the relationship between progressive sexual politics on the one hand (embodied, for example, in policies of gender equality and the rights of sexual minorities), and recent positions on multiculturalism on the other, embodied in a conceptualization which construes Muslim communities as antithetical to progressive politics. Building on my discussion of coalitional politics, I consider the work on cultural translation. This aspect has already featured in some of Butler's earlier work, such as her contributions to *Contingency, Hegemony, Universality* (2000b), and it has been considered in the critical literature (see Lloyd 2007). I revisit this theme in light of her work on religion.

ANTI-SEMITISM AND THE JEWISH CRITIQUE OF ISRAEL

Whereas *Gender Trouble* (1990) provided the occasion for Butler's trouble within sections of the feminist scholarly community (see my discussion in the introduction), Butler's recent interventions into public political debates on Israel-Palestine, and her involvement in the Boycott, Divestment and Sanctions (BDS) activities and Jewish Voice for Peace have embroiled her in controversies beyond the academy. Several of her recent public speaking engagements, such as her acceptance speech at the Adorno Prize ceremony in Frankfurt, Germany, in 2012,[1] her participation at a BDS event organized by Students for Justice in Palestine at Brooklyn College, New York, in February 2013, and her receipt of an honorary doctorate by Canada's McGill University in May 2013 have led to hostile reactions from Zionist and pro-Israel groups, who have denounced Butler as a 'self-hating Jew' who articulates 'pro-terror' and 'anti-Israel' positions (see Barney 2013). Frequently invoked in these denunciations is a comment Butler made at a teach-in organized at Berkeley in 2006, where she referred to Hamas and Hezbollah as part of a global left political project. Although she qualified her comments with an implicit criticism of Hamas and Hezbollah that called for non-violent forms of politics, this qualification did not make an impact on her critics.[2]

Underlying the public quarrel over Butler's position is, as I already intimated, her critique of Israel and her support for movements that seek to reach a peaceful settlement between Palestinians and Israelis on the basis of a critique of Israeli policies towards Palestinians. My interest in this section does not lie with Butler's specific criticism of Israeli policies, though. Rather, I want to unpack how she construes her critique of Israeli state violence as specifically Jewish.[3] At first glance, the specifically Jewish character of Butler's critique of Israel may derive from the identity of her interlocutors, who happen to be Jews (she draws on writings by Arendt, Benjamin, and Levinas, as well as Martin Buber, Franz Rosenzweig, and others). Butler insists, with reference to the work of Walter Benjamin, that her critique not only qualifies as Jewish because of the critical resources that her interlocutors draw from (*PW*, 74–75), but also because it builds on the practice of criticism, which she conceives of as a Jewish value derived from Talmudic tradition. More significant, in my view, is a further explanation that Butler offers: as she suggests, each of the thinkers she engages with articulates conditions of heterogeneity, dispossession, and diaspora. These ideas, as we have already seen, underpin Butler's political philosophy of the human, and they inform her conceptions of ethics and politics; it is within the parameters of this immanent interpretation that Butler's political philosophy could also be depicted as a Jewish political philosophy. What is crucial to Butler's thought is the framing of the diasporic and ek-static principles, formulated in Butler's sources as specifically Jewish, which puts them fundamentally at odds with the policies of the Israeli state; for the purpose of my discussion in this section it is significant to stress that they refute, by the nature of their 'Jewishness', the claim that criticism of Israel should be regarded as anti-Semitic. Furthermore, by claiming the ecstatic structure of the subject and the conditions of diaspora and dispossession from Jewish sources, derived from and applied to her analysis of Jewishness, Butler re-articulates the relationship between ethics and politics that allows her to think through the politics of bi-nationalism (see Chapter 5). My critique of Butler's deployment of Jewish philosophy is immanent: I seek to draw out the ethico-political implications for her political philosophy. Thus, while a critical enquiry into Butler's appropriation of Judaic ideas is now due, I cannot provide such work here. Furthermore, given the relatively recent publication of some of this work, there is as yet no critical commentary to draw on. What I offer here are exploratory investigations that I believe shed light on recent developments in Butler's political philosophy, and the way she construes the relationship between ethics and politics and between theological and political ideas.

As I intimated above, Jewishness, according to Butler, construes ethics based on ideas of relationality and diaspora, but it also formulates a political critique that she deploys in her discussion of Israel. As a point of entry into my discussion of her reflection on the relationship between Jewishness and the critique of Israel, I begin by attending to her critical response to comments made by the former president of Harvard University, Larry Summers. In a speech given on the occasion of Morning Prayers, Summers averred that 'profoundly anti-Israeli' views are gaining increasing support 'in progressive intellectual communities' (Summers 2002). He went on to describe certain actions as 'anti-Semitic in their effect if not their intent'; these include student fundraising for 'organizations of questionable political provenance that in some cases were later found to support terrorism', as well as a petition calling for divestiture of endowment funds from businesses operating in Israel. Thus, in Summers's view, to critique Israel constitutes anti-Semitism 'in effect if not intent'.

In her essay 'The Charge of Anti-Semitism: Jews, Israel, and the Risks of Public Critique', included in *Precarious Life* (2004b), Butler presents a forceful rebuttal of Summers's assertions. Drawing on some of the themes developed in *Excitable Speech* (1997a), Butler questions Summers's invocation of the efficacy of the speech act, and its alleged 'effective' and 'intentional' anti-Semitism. As she argues, for Summers effective becomes intentional, but this conflation depends upon what she terms 'the field of reception' of the

86 The Political Philosophy of Judith Butler

particular criticism of Israel. Furthermore, 'what we can hear' (this is also the title of one of her other essays included in *Precarious Life* (2004b)) is filtered through the frame of an anti-intellectual climate that is not receptive towards certain forms of criticism, or in fact to the idea of criticism as such (see Conclusion). At the heart of her discussion lies another concern to do with the complex web of relations between Jews and Israel, the criticism of the state of Israel articulated by Jews, and the relationship of such a critique to anti-Semitism. Butler locates her critique of Israel within a Jewish ethical tradition, which is, she avers is 'wrought from experience of suffering' (*PL*, 103–104). It derives from the experience of the Shoah and the political obligations for civic courage. As she argues, 'it was imperative that we [were] able to speak out. Not just for Jews, but for any number of people. There was an entire idea of social justice that emerged for me from the consideration of the Nazi genocide' (Butler 2011a, 214). To conceive of Jewishness in the historical context of suffering, struggles for social justice, and civic courage has fundamental implications for the reading of Butler's ethics: her emphasis on relationality and the responsibility that arises from my implication in the other is formulated against the backdrop of a history of suffering. Furthermore, the Jewish tradition that Butler invokes is anchored in the heterogeneity of Jewish thinking; as she contends, the range of Jewish attitudes and feelings towards Israel is broad-ranging. Hence, there can be no equivalence between Jews and Israel. Contra Summers, who equates the critique of Israel with anti-Semitism, she claims the criticism of Israel as part of a Jewish tradition and ethical obligation.

While Butler acknowledges that criticism of Israel can and sometimes does derive from anti-Semitic positions, she argues that not all criticism of Israel is by definition anti-Semitic. What kind of work, though, does the accusation of anti-Semitism perform? And where does Butler's critique of Israel leave the charge of anti-Semitism? As Butler argues, the accusation of anti-Semitism has a terrorizing effect, especially if it is made against Jews. It evokes, she avers, the spectre of the Jewish collaborator with the Nazis, and in doing so, it controls and curtails public speech: it produces 'a climate of fear through the tactical use of a heinous judgment with which no progressive person would want to identify' (*PL*, 120–121). In fact, it does more than limit the type of public speech that is permissible. It actually demarcates the boundaries of those public spaces where speech is possible, and in this respect it produces and indeed curtails the public realm. As Butler intimates towards the end of her essay on Summers, a similar criticism applies to those who seek to limit the critique of US foreign policy in the current climate of anti-intellectualism.

In contradistinction to Summers's equation of anti-Semitism with a critique of Israel, Butler develops her critique of Israel on the basis of her Jewishness. Out of a self-confessed emotional investment in the state of Israel (*PL*, 113), she argues for a radical restructuring of the current ethnic basis of the Israeli state and Israeli citizenship (see also Chapter 5) and for a decoupling of Jewishness and Israel, which will also lead to a re-valuation of the Jewish diaspora. As I already suggested, Butler's critical engagement with Israel and radical Jewish traditions also inform her thinking on the kinds of ethical obligations we have towards others, and it influences her ideas on state formation, nationalism, and citizenship (see Chapter 4). In the next section, I further develop her discussion of Jewishness and Israel. By locating her critique of Israel in the context of her own Jewishness and Jewish formation, Butler's dis-identification with Israeli policy becomes a way to articulate the prospects for a radical future that is ethically underpinned and that formulates the workings of a polity under conditions of difference and plurality (see Chapter 5).

WHAT IS JEWISHNESS?

In one of her earliest explicit engagements with questions of ethics, Butler (2000d) narrates the beginning of her philosophical career within the context of her Jewish education, 'one that took the ethical dilemmas posed by the mass extermination of the Jews during World War II, including members of my own family, to the scene for thinking ethicality as such' (16). This account has significance beyond the personal narrative it provides of Butler's formation as a Jewish philosopher (rather than a philosopher who happens to be a Jew). I have already attended to the wider significance of ethics in Butler's more recent writings (see Chapter 1). As I have demonstrated, this explicit attention to ethics has caused considerable consternation amongst some of her critics, not least because it has been perceived by some to be fundamentally at odds with her genealogical and existential-phenomenological commitments. This criticism, I want to suggest, should be revised in light of Butler's considerations of Jewishness and its mooring in the relation to the other and history. I intimated that Butler articulates a demand for ethics out of political conditions of violence and destruction. In doing so, she circumvents the false dualism of (abstract) ethics and (concrete) politics, instead anchoring ethical obligations in a life that is under existential threat from genocidal politics but that seeks to counter this threat by insisting on the sustaining quality of relationality. Since the publication of her critique of Summers (see Butler 2004b), Butler has developed her engagement with the complex relationships between anti-Semitism, Jewishness, and Israel, presented most recently in her book *Parting Ways: Jewishness and the Critique of Zionism* (2012a). Her initial objective articulated in *Precarious Life* (2004b), which was to disassociate Israel from Jewishness and challenge the claim that a critique of Israel constitutes anti-Semitism, also opens her discussion in *Parting Ways*. While this book is centrally concerned with the fundamental question of what constitutes a specifically Jewish critique of Israel that draws on Jewish resources, it is the question of anti-Semitism that continues to haunt her discussion.

What, though, is the status of Jewish critique, and, to return to an aspect I raised above, what is specifically Jewish about it? For heuristic purposes, it is helpful to invoke Hannah Arendt's famous exchange with Gershom Scholem, which took place in the wake of the publication of *Eichmann in Jerusalem*, Arendt's ([1963b] 2006b) book on the trial of Adolf Eichmann.[4] Scholem's criticism of the book concerns, amongst other things, Arendt's depiction of Eichmann and her criticism of the Jewish councils, as well as of aspects of the trial in Jerusalem itself. Of significance to my discussion here is Arendt's famous response to Scholem's accusation: that she lacks love for the Jewish people, and that he tries to claim her as a daughter of the Jewish people. As Arendt (2007) argues, '[t]o be a Jew belongs to me to the indisputable facts of my life, and I have never had the wish to change or disclaim facts of this kind' (466). She continues to express gratitude for what she regards as given, *physei,* as opposed to what is made, *nomō,* and she describes such an attitude as pre-political, albeit with political consequences.

I have already alluded to Butler's ambivalent relationship with Arendt (see Chapters 2 and 5): while she draws on Arendtian ideas of plurality and bi-nationalism to generate a Jewish critique of Zionism, she is also clearly at odds with Arendt's naturalizing portrayal of identity. For Butler, Jewishness is not fact, but rather an ethico-political encounter construed within the context of relation to the non-Jew. She refers to what she calls 'Jewish formation', which relates to upbringing, the initiation into cultural and possibly religious practices and rites, the attachment to language (whether Hebrew or Yiddish), or the formative influences of history, including the Shoah. This wider socialization into Jewishness is mediated and affirmed by the concept of relationality, which avows and simultaneously unsettles the concept of Jewishness. In *Precarious Life* (2004b), she insinuates that the ethical relation to the non-Jew is definitive of what is Jewish. This does not imply, however, that the conception of Jewishness arises out of a dyadic or antagonistic relation (she rejects Sartre's claim that it is the anti-Semite who 'creates' the Jew). In fact, the relational aspect alone cannot consolidate what is Jewish in this relation. Rather, Jewishness *is* relationality, and this relationality displaces any attempt to shore up substantive conceptions of the self. Thus, instead of asserting the substance of Jewish identity, Butler emphasizes the relation to alterity as constitutive of identity; with this emphasis, she seeks to interrupt the unitary character of the subject. Moreover, as she develops further, if Jewish ethics is Jewish/non-Jewish, then the meaning is said to lie in the conjunctive disjunction.

It is in the context of this discussion that Butler revisits her notion of the ecstatic character of the self: her insistence on the centrality of 'being given over', or dispossessed, provides her with a new perspective on the way that cohabitation beyond sovereignty and nationalism could lead to a polity that would accommodate Palestinian and Israeli lives. I discuss this aspect further in the next chapter, where I attend to wider questions to do with (global) governance, the state, nationalism, and sovereignty. For now,

I want to remain with the notion of ek-stasis, which, as we have already seen in Chapter 1, is central to Butler's narrative of subject formation. Key to her wider discussion on the subject, ethics, and politics is her critique of identitarian formations and their communitarian moorings. In their place, Butler stresses the constitutive aspect of relationality, the transformative dimension of interdependence, and the value of dispossession and scattering. These values, which, as I have intimated, inform her thinking about state formation and citizenship, also underpin her thinking about the subject and ethics (see Chapter 1).

Aiding Butler in further developing her account of dispossession and diaspora is Edward W. Said's discussion of the impure foundations of Judaism and Jewishness, which, according to Said, are centred in the figure of Moses. In *Freud and the Non-European,* Said (2003) posits the Arab origins of the figure of Moses. He asserts the relational aspects of identity formation and the way that seemingly disparate histories are implicated in one another, a move which, he claims, has been eliminated by 'official Israel' (44). Moreover, he advocates a politics of diaspora that can accommodate both Jewish and Palestinian life and that is not anchored in identitarian, and thus exclusionary, state formations. Said's rendering of the diasporic condition converges with Butler's, and it underwrites her effort to dispel an Israeli, or exclusively Jewish, narrative hegemony on the conflict. What she borrows in particular from Said is her insistence on the diasporic and dispossession, which, according to Butler, provides a condition for bi-nationalism. However, Butler is not satisfied with efforts that anchor the critique of Israel in Jewish sources. In fact, she argues for the need to question the sufficiency of a Jewish framework as the defining horizon of the ethical. Such an exclusively Jewish critique of Israel would extend a Jewish epistemological and political hegemony over the region, constituting a kind of benign counter-colonial project that excludes other voices, especially those coming from Palestinians, and that would frame the discussion about Israel in exclusively Jewish terms (see Said 2003). Butler's overall aim is to articulate complex and antagonistic forms of living together. How, though, do these ideas chime with those of other Jewish writers? Here Butler returns to the writings of Levinas and Arendt.

As I already have indicated, Butler's deployment of Levinasian ideas has puzzled some of her critics, not least because of its alleged abstract normativity that is seen to run counter to the phenomenological and genealogical investigations associated with her earlier work (see Coole 2008; see also her discussions in *Precarious Life* (2004b) and in *Giving an Account of Oneself* (2005)). What motivates this move is her effort to seek an answer to the problem of violence. More specifically, as she explains in *Parting Ways* (2012a), it is the contact with alterity, which incites an ethical scene that obligates me and which underlies her reading of Levinas. Thus, it is Levinas' decentring of the autonomous subject, together with his assertion of a radical alterity that lies at the origin of the subject, which animates Butler's appropriation of his ideas. It follows, according to her reading of Levinas, that the subject is only possible because an other exists prior to the subject's emergence. While these ideas, as I have stressed, exert a profound influence on Butler's thinking, she is deeply at odds with Levinas' framing of ethical obligations within the context of the Judaeo-Christian tradition, based on Levinas's alleged Zionism and an orientalized perception of Arab populations. Butler is equally dismissive of Hannah Arendt's ([1963b] 2006b) orientalising of non-European populations (including Arab Jews) articulated in her *Eichmann in Jerusalem,* but she is more sympathetic towards Arendt's critique of Zionism and her ideas on cohabitation.[5] From Arendt, Butler borrows ideas that come to inform her thinking on the formation of the state under conditions of plurality. Arendt's assertion of 'merely belonging' to the Jewish people refutes strong identitarian claims that seek to construct community and polity on the basis of shared history, cultural practices, and so on. Conceiving of Jewishness as relationality inflects Butler's philosophy of the subject, and it sits at the interstices of ethics and politics. As I will argue in Chapter 5, it is out of her reading of Jewish sources that Butler develops a conception of community as diasporic and dispossessed. Now I will turn to Butler's considerations of the role of religion in public life, broadly conceived.

POLITICAL THEOLOGY

As we have seen, the consideration of Jewishness and its relationship to Israel is central to Butler's recent work, but her discussion also enquires into the fundamental connection between religion and politics, the role of religion in the public realm, and the religious sources of secularism. These themes are addressed in three recent pieces: her book from 2009, *Frames of War,* her response to Talal Asad and Saba Mahmood on the question of critique and secularism (Butler 2009d), and her recent essay 'Is Judaism Zionism'? (Butler 2011d).[6] Butler's contribution to the debates on religion centres on three aspects: she considers the formation of religious subjectivities in the context of the war on terror; she explores how these subjectivities are mapped onto a narrative of modernity; and she critiques the theological framing of secular conceptions of the public sphere. My aim in this section is to sketch Butler's arguments in relation to this latter point, while I attend to the first two (and in my view the more significant and developed) aspects of Butler's work in the remainder of this chapter.

Recent years have seen much ink spilt on discussions pertaining to the role of religion in public life. As is well known, many of these debates—specifically their treatment in public political discourse—converge on the question of multiculturalism and the implication of immigration from ethno-religious minorities, and they attend to perceived challenges emanating from the existence of Muslim communities in Western societies. These

challenges revolve around issues such as cultural integration, broadly construed, a perceived danger to Western liberal (and secular) values, and the
spectre of Islamic terrorism. The attention on Islamic fundamentalism and
on violent spectacles that are associated with Islam has brought the public
interest in and perception of a rise of religion into sharp relief. Controversies
surrounding the wearing of religious garments, symbolized by the headscarves affair and various efforts to regulate its wearing in public, epitomize
the anxieties and perceived perils in the face of the existence of Muslim communities in Western societies (see Joppke 2009; Scott 2007). However, such
focus on Islam and its alleged threat to secular Western values clouds the
fact that Christian theology is deeply inscribed into the make-up of Western
polities and societies, and that from such inscription, notwithstanding differences between national political cultures, emanates a peculiar conception
of secularism that is inflected with Christian theology. How, then, should the
relationship between politics and religion be framed? What is the role of religion in public life? And how, and to what extent, are religion and theology
entangled in the make-up of what we refer to as secularism? Before dealing
with Butler's contribution to these debates, I begin to unravel this relationship by attending to the secularization thesis, which has gained renewed
impetus in recent political sociology. This will be followed by a brief map of
some of the key issues pertaining to political theology.

There are several points—let's call them sociological—that are worth
highlighting in the context of my discussion because they reveal enormous
differences in the way that secularization and the privatization of religion
are worked out differently around the globe. The secularization thesis,
broadly construed, articulates the idea that religious faith and adherence
undergoes a gradual decline in late capitalist societies.[7] Intimately linked to
the idea of modernity, adherents of the secularization thesis see religion as
a remnant of pre-modern, pre-Enlightenment, and pre-industrialized societies, and inherently at odds with the enlightened or disenchanted outlook of
modern, complex, and industrial societies. However, the upsurge in various
fundamentalisms, whether Christian, Islamic, Jewish or other, as well as a
growing interest in New Age ideas, have challenged the key assertions of
the secularization thesis. Religious or religiously informed ideas have also
entered the public political discourse of Western polities through the public
expressions of religious faith that have often been cited as a key motivating
force of the presidency of George W. Bush, and of the prime ministership
of Britain's Tony Blair. As is well known, both Bush and Blair deployed
religious rhetoric to justify the 'war on terrorism', infamously described by
Bush as a crusade just days after 9/11.

Of course, such public invocation of religion, even if articulated by political leaders, does not suffice to ring the death knell of the secularization thesis
claims. Drawing on empirical evidence, Pippa Norris and Ronald Inglehart
(2011) in their study of the global parameters of religion argue that a decline
in religiosity and an increase in secular orientations are typical of advanced

industrial societies; on a global scale, however, religiosity is on the increase. As Norris and Inglehart contend, 'the world as a whole now has more people with traditional religious views than ever before—and they constitute a growing proportion of the world's population' (5). They link this trend to existential security and vulnerability (see also Bruce 2013). Although the sociological context of the debate on religion and secularism is significant, this is not the place to pursue this argument further. Besides, what interests me is a question that the secularization debate glosses over: this is the question of the theological foundation of modern (secular) politics. It is here, I would suggest, that political theology upends political sociology.

Possibly the best-known representation of political theology is associated with the work of Carl Schmitt ([1922] 2009), who famously remarked that all significant concepts of modern state theory are secularized theological concepts (43). The work of Schmitt and others has significantly influenced the recent upsurge of interest in political theology (see for example Kahn 2011; see also Forrester 1988; Kirwan 2008; Lilla 2008; de Vries and Sullivan 2006). Political theology, as I use the term here, refers to the intertwining of religion and politics and to the theological foundation and legitimization of political authority. The historical origin of political theology lies in the pre-modern era, when theological or metaphysical justifications of political rule were common. In contradistinction to current debates over the role of religion in public life, these pre-modern forms of political rule did not repudiate their implication in theological categories. Rather, divine will constituted a central reference point for earthly political power. Notwithstanding attempts to revive or create traditions of civil religion in the modern age, religion and politics are said to have become separate spheres, and the anchor for political rule was no longer found in God but increasingly in the people.

In his critique of attempts to provide a secularized, and in his view sanitized, narrative of modern politics and modern political thought as a break from pre-modern, religiously anchored political orders, Paul W. Kahn (2011) wryly observes that the idea '[t]hat political concepts have their origin in theological concepts is, to most contemporary theorists, about as interesting and important as learning that English words have their origin in old Norse' (3). Given the recent upsurge of interest in the relationship between religion and politics, not least as a result of the events surrounding 9/11, Kahn's reminder of the significance of political theology seems highly pertinent in that it underscores the widely received perception that this revival of religion returns us to pre-modern forms of conceiving the world and organising collective life.

Kahn locates his take on political theology in relation to Carl Schmitt's work, and in contradistinction to Mark Lilla's thesis (2008) of a 'great separation' between a pre-modern religious political order and modern secularism. Kahn emphasizes Schmitt's famous assertion that all political concepts have their origins in theological sources. Challenging the view that modern politics and modern political thought perform a turn away from religion, Kahn claims that political practices remain attached to what he calls the sacred. Whereas Lilla, according to Kahn, reads political theology as a religious mapping of the political order, Kahn claims that the alleged break between a pre-modern religious political order and a modern, secular order never occurred. It should be stressed that Kahn does not necessarily advocate a religious configuration of politics. Rather, building on his critique of the idea of the social contract, he asserts that the claim of (modern) politics to replace the violence of the state of nature with the security of the law is misleading. Instead, modern politics replaces murder with sacrifice, articulated in the sacrificial practices and symbolic politics of the modern state. Kahn's insistence on the persistence of the theological within the discourse of modernity is an area of political inquiry that has also received attention in Butler's recent work.

It should be stated that Butler does not set out to offer a political theology; hence, her contribution to the debate is not as significant or as developed as the one proffered by Kahn and others. However, she makes three significant interventions into the wider discussion around religion. These are, first, her challenge to those notions of secularism that disavow its constitutive relationship to religion; second, her use of political-theological resources to rethink the conflict in Israel-Palestine; and finally, her insistence on the role of religion in the formation of subjects.

To revisit her narrative of her religious formation, she argues that 'prior to any questions of gender or sexuality, there were for me questions regarding the Jewish community, its history of persecution, its methods of expelling its own, its relation to violence, and the question of what of theology could remain after the Nazi death camp' (Butler 2006e, 277–8). Out of an engagement with religious texts and themes, such as the occupation with grief, community, and ethical responsibility, emerges the possibility of being Jewish in the absence of God. The practice of textual interpretation lies at the heart of this encounter. Thus, Butler argues, '[t]o know how to live, one had to know how to read, and one had to be able to develop an interpretation of what one would read' (278). Thus, liveability becomes linked to interpretation and indeed to contestation. Crucially, such questions of living are not merely ethical matters; they point Butler in the direction of a Jewish political theology that utilizes Jewish sources for a conception of politics derived from a focus on relationality, scattering, and diaspora, and they articulate a distinctive effort to develop a conception of politics out of political theology, specifically her articulation of forms of political community beyond the traditional confines of the nation state (see Chapter 5) as well as her critique of narratives of modernity that frame differential conceptions of religious subjectivities, which she deploys with the aid of Benjamin's conception of the messianic expiation and which challenges the juridical conception of the guilty subject. Thus, Butler's political theology converges on three related issues: her deployment of Jewish and Judaic sources in aid of a critique of (state) violence (I return to this point in the next chapter), her critique of orientalist discourses which juxtapose (Western) secularism with (traditional and pre-modern) Islam, and her reformulation of plurality in the aid of coalitional politics.

While religion, as Butler suggests, is a structure of subject formation, it is also the dissipated condition of the public space. Suggesting that the public sphere is a Protestant accomplishment, Butler (2011d) concludes that 'public life presupposes and reaffirms one dominant religious tradition *as* the secular' (71; italics in original). Such assertion challenges the way that the public-private distinction becomes mapped upon the secularism-religion divide. As Butler argues, if Protestantism privatizes religion, then both public and private are set up in relation to religion. As I discuss in the next section, such analysis has consequences when we enquire into the types of religions that may legitimately enter the public sphere.

SECULARISM, MULTICULTURALISM, AND SEXUAL POLITICS

At the moment of writing, there are heated debates on the prospect of changes to the abortion law and the possibility of extending access to abortion in both jurisdictions of the island of Ireland.[8] Most Christian churches oppose the widening of the current restrictive regime in Northern Ireland. The Catholic Church opposes any provision of pregnancy termination services, whether north or south of the border, and it has threatened elected representatives with excommunication. Prior to a recent by-election in Northern Ireland, the Catholic Church urged its congregations to support those politicians who oppose the opening of a private clinic offering sexual health advice and performing terminations.

In 2012, a regional court in Germany ruled that the circumcision of young boys on the grounds of religion constitutes grievous bodily harm and is therefore illegal. The ruling followed medical complications arising from the circumcision of a young boy. The ensuing debate saw Muslim and Jewish groups seeking to defend their religious and cultural practices and traditions, whilst opponents of circumcision argued from the perspective of the health of the child and the principle of informed consent. The German parliament has since passed a law that allows for circumcision if performed by a trained practitioner or a doctor.

In 2011, France introduced a ban on the wearing of a full-face veil in public. Non-compliance with the ban carries a fine of €150.00 or lessons in French citizenship. The ban comes after many years of debate over the wearing of religious garments in public. More recently, a new controversy emerged following the unlawful dismissal of a nursery employee for wearing a headscarf. According to media reports, the French government is concerned that the court ruling may dilute the principle of secularism, and is considering the introduction of further restrictions on the wearing of religious garments.

Although these three examples emanate from different political cultures articulating different conceptions of the relationship between religion and public life, they all highlight the ongoing significance of this relationship, and they challenge implicitly or explicitly some of the key assertions articulated in the secularization thesis. As we have seen in the previous section, political theology sheds light on the theological foundations and structures of the modern state and modern politics, but it cannot in and of itself deduce normative claims regarding the extent or desirability of religion's impact on public life (see Kahn 2011). The challenges that the relationship between religion and public policy throws up are all too familiar. For example, should religious belief systems inform public policy decisions? If so, how, and in what ways? Should religious organizations be tasked with carrying out public duties such as education and health? Also, how should we adjudicate between competing value systems of different religious groups, or between those of non-religious populations and religious groups? These disputes are not limited to societies widely regarded as religious, be they predominantly Christian or Muslim; they are equally pertinent to societies considered as secular. To gain purchase on this topic, this section and the next focus on the relationship between secularism, multiculturalism, and sexual politics in the context of the war on terror. Notwithstanding Butler's recent focus on war, violence, and Jewish philosophy, she continues to return to the topic of sexual politics and to issues pertinent to feminist theory and practice. Her most recent contribution to these topics is underpinned by some of her earlier assertions on the feminist disputes over the notion of the subject and representation. Building upon these debates, this section reconsiders the question of coalitional politics and its significance for feminism. My interest lies with the attention given to questions of political alliances, coalitional politics, and a conceptualization of politics grounded in the idea of plurality. I begin by offering a brief sketch of some of the key issues and controversies around the topic of coalitional politics. I challenge those positions that consider feminist goals to be incompatible with the principles of coalitional politics, and I argue instead for the openness and fluidity of feminist politics. I then propose a shift from pluralism, understood as group-based politics, towards plurality, embodied in shifting alliances and coalitions, and the creation of a non-sovereign understanding of feminism and feminist politics.

Although the feminist 'theory wars' of the late 1980s and 1990s have lost their vehemence in recent years, the dispute over difference and plurality has not been put to rest. If anything, these issues have emerged in a different form in feminist controversies over multiculturalism, where they obtained a particular poignancy in the wake of the war on terror. The emphasis on difference and diversity as paradigms of academic investigation has instigated a broader concern with the question of political alliances and coalitional politics. Much consideration has been given to the development of coalitions for progressive sexual politics, leading, on one hand, to the acknowledgement of an internal differentiation of feminism, and, on the other hand, to the need to develop political coalitions with similarly minded political groupings and movements. One of the most contested questions has been that of accommodating minority cultural rights and multiculturalism more broadly. This debate is epitomized by the so-called 'headscarves affair' (see Joppke 2009; Scott 2007). Over the last two decades, public political discourse and scholarly discourse alike have been grappling with the question of how to respond to the existence of Muslim communities within Western societies and the politics of Islam, said to be pursued by many Muslim communities and states outside the western hemisphere. Despite a wealth of scholarly writings on this topic, it continues to occupy feminist scholars. Further aggravated by the global events that have unfolded in the wake of 9/11, the question of multiculturalism has caused enormous anxiety within some strands of feminism, leading to diverse or even opposing responses.

I want to use this multicultural challenge to feminism as a point of entry into Butler's discussion. Drawing mainly on *Frames of War* (2009a) (and to a lesser extent on *Parting Ways* (2012a)), my aim is to assess three aspects that surface in these contributions and to address these (albeit in different degrees of detail) in the remainder of this chapter. These are her comments on the relationship between multiculturalism and feminism (and the prospects for coalitional politics that potentially emerge from this relationship), her articulation of the relationship between religion and secularism in the context of a narrative of progress, and her growing utilization of Arendtian ideas, specifically those of plurality and cohabitation (see Chapter 5). I begin with a brief sketch of the position articulated by Susan Moller Okin (1999), who rejects the desirability of creating coalitional projects between feminism and multiculturalism, before turning to a discussion of Butler's ideas. My reading of Butler is broadly sympathetic. I claim that she furnishes feminism with a conception of (coalitional) politics that circumvents the pitfalls of identity politics grounded in a pre-conceived notion of the subject. Coalitional politics is anchored in her rejection of pluralism, understood as group-based politics, and her endorsement of plurality, embodied in shifting alliances and coalitions and the creation of a non-sovereign understanding of feminism and feminist politics. Such emphasis, I want to suggest, aids feminism when confronting the challenges it faces in the age of the war on terror. Moreover, she more broadly articulates a critique of the civilizational narrative that grounds such a politics of the subject. Finally, notwithstanding my sympathy towards Butler's overall project, I also wish to articulate some reservations.

As I briefly have intimated, feminism has allied itself with a variety of other political movements; the existence of various hyphenated feminist projects and identities is testament to such alliances. Not surprisingly, much consideration has been given to the development of coalitions for progressive sexual politics. Without understating some of the problems that such alliances may bring, it is fair to state that it is the question of accommodating minority cultural rights, and of multiculturalism more broadly, that remains hotly contested. One outspoken critic of the potential alliance between feminism and multiculturalism is Susan Moller Okin (1999), whose well-known essay 'Is Multiculturalism Bad for Women?' articulates some of the key concerns of feminist critics of multiculturalism. Of significance to my discussion is the way Okin frames her arguments in an explicit feminist context. She detects a tension between feminism and multiculturalism, said to be grounded in multiculturalism's concern to protect cultural diversity. As she argues, 'I think we—especially those of us who consider ourselves politically progressive and opposed to all forms of oppression—have been too quick to assume that feminism and multiculturalism are both good things which are easily reconciled. . . . there is considerable likelihood of tension between them—more precisely, between feminism and a multiculturalist commitment to group rights for minority cultures' (10).

The focus of Okin's concern lies with the multicultural aim of granting group rights to minority cultures, including indigenous groups and minority ethnic and religious groups. Such group rights, according to Okin, are potentially inconsistent with liberal values of individual freedom; furthermore, they disguise the internal differences within minority cultural groups and also fail to tackle the privatized nature of women's oppression. She concludes that the connection between gender and culture is a troubling one, and that conflicts between feminism and multiculturalism are inevitable. Much could be said about Okin's arguments.[9] For example, she simultaneously builds on and rejects the notion of group identity (with gender becoming the signifier for 'women' and individual freedom, and 'culture' signifying group oppression). Her critique of cultural groups as internally diverse obfuscates her own levelling of group differences. Her implicit reliance on the concept of groups cannot account for overlapping group membership; finally culture becomes the baggage of minority groups and is juxtaposed to the autonomous individual free from cultural constraints. Rather than developing this discussion further, I want to examine how Butler conceives of the relationship between feminism and multiculturalism, and how she articulates a position that is, in my view, more compelling than Okin's. Although Butler does not contribute to the exchange with Okin, I want to read her work, specifically her arguments presented in *Frames of War* (2009a), *as if* she is directly responding to Okin.

Before I do so, it is important to acknowledge that both Butler and Okin explicitly articulate their discomfort at the idea of group homogeneity. It is on the basis of this discomfort that Butler cautions of the use of the term 'multiculturalism' when outlining her vision of coalitional politics. In fact, the idea of 'multiculturalism', conceived as an identity project that seeks to obtain rights and recognition for pre-established groups, is incompatible with Butler's wider philosophical and political commitments, including those articulated in her early work, such as the performative constitution of identity (see Butler 1990). With reference to her recent writings on war and violence, she proposes to think sexual politics together with questions of secularism and war. This, she suggests, requires a departure from identity-based political formations, to be replaced by alliances and coalitions that articulate alternatives to the developmental narratives of progress and struggle for conceptions of freedom that arise out of a critique of state violence. As she argues, '[t]he possibility of a political framework that opens up our ideas of cultural norms to contestation and dynamism within a global frame would surely be one way to think a politics that re-engages sexual freedom in the context of allied struggles against racism, nationalism, and the persecution of religions minorities' (*FW*, 133). Butler's critical reworking of multiculturalism also modifies her emphasis on recognition, which, as I suggested in Chapter 1, remains key to her overall political philosophy. As she contends, recognition, through the normative power it exercises, is part of the process of ordering and regulation. Without diminishing the significance of recognition as a political-theoretical category and recognition struggles as important tools in the repertoire for political transformation, recognition becomes problematic if it serves as the foundation for a politics that articulates its political demands on the basis of identity only. In this respect, Butler is particularly dismissive of the framework of cultural conflict, which is said to presume distinct identity categories or communities whose interests either clash or converge. Butler bypasses multiculturalism and cultural conflict as the parameters of an analytical framework, focussing instead on the way power, especially state power, operates to constitute and regulate the identity categories that are said to make up those distinct cultural entities.

Although her concern relates, in the main, to the prospects for articulating progressive politics under global conditions of war, she underpins these reflections with a renewed call for coalitional politics that is as significant for the formation for global coalitions, as it pertains to the conditions of heterogeneity within the realm of domestic politics. As I will argue in the next chapter, with reference to the *nuestro himno* movement,[10] Butler's impetus towards coalitional politics articulates conditions of diversity, plurality, and heterogeneity without seeking recourse to identity politics. As she argues, coalitions bypass the requirements of identity; they operate under conditions of antagonism and they coalesce around the critique of power and state violence. Thus, '[m]obilizing alliances do not necessarily form between established and recognizable subjects, and neither do they depend on the brokering of identitarian claims' (*FW*, 162). Understood this way, the subject of coalitional politics becomes, as Butler puts it, 'an active and transitive set of interrelations' (*FW*, 147). Such politics, Butler suggests, operates both nationally as well as globally, and it has the potential to underpin global subject formations as well as the production of political alliances amongst the legally disenfranchised. In this respect, Butler's insistence on coalitional politics constitutes a challenge to multiculturalism as the frame for understanding heterogeneity. As she argues in *Frames of War*, multiculturalism presumes distinct subjects capable of articulating distinct, possibly opposing views. Even though antagonism is a constitutive element of coalitional politics, it allows, in contradistinction to multiculturalism, for the possibility of coalescing around shared goals, without presuming a shared identity.

While undoubtedly an attractive option, it is less certain how effective such a conception is. I have already raised the issue of passionate attachments in Chapter 1, where I asked whether passionate attachment does not in fact stand in the way of coalitional politics. There is a further aspect to this conception, to do with the practice of cultural translation. As Butler avers, coalitional politics requires cultural translation. Mediating between the various demands and the always provisional and unstable elements of coalitional politics are practices of cultural translation. The question of how we frame the relationship between universality and particularity, which is central to the current disputes over multiculturalism, continues to occupy Butler's writings. Her engagement with this problem is not new; in fact it can be traced to her work of the 1990s. There, she frames this problem through reference to the idea of cultural translation, and it is this concept that re-emerges in her recent work on religion and the engagement with religious texts and concepts, specifically in relation to Jewishness. As I already have indicated in a previous section of this chapter, Butler challenges the idea that religion and secularism are diametrically opposed. Moreover, as we have seen, she insists on the centrality of (religious) formation, where religion constitutes a 'matrix for subject formation' (*PW*, 116) without determining the subject's future engagement with its religious history.

In this respect, practices of cultural translation are construed as ethical practices that connect to the encounter with alterity. Importantly, for Butler, cultural translation does not entail assimilation of religious meanings into a secular frame. Neither does cultural translation generate a new, common language that transcends the particularisms of its constitutive elements. Rather, cultural translation constitutes a re-articulation (and possibly misappropriation) of existing language into new contexts, and in this respect it always entails impurity and scattering. Alterity is at the heart of such practices, which also build on the idea of ecstatic relationality, leading to transformative encounters. As she argues elsewhere, universalization is negotiated as/at the conjuncture of discourses. How easy, though, is this? In his response to Butler, Chetan Bhatt (2008), although sympathetic towards her arguments, asks, '[w]hat expansive politics of time might speak to a Gujarati woman from Birmingham and a Turkish woman from Hamburg such that they apprehend each other as *European?*'(32; italics in original). While it is not necessary, I believe, to work towards the creation of a new, shared identity as the goal of coalitional politics and cultural translations, I wonder whether Butler eludes the structural obstacles in the path of coalitional politics.

IMPURE SECULARITY

Building on my discussion in the previous sections, I want to use the remainder of this chapter to focus on the way the relationship between religion and secularism is deployed in the delineation of distinct civilizational entities and the demarcation of their boundaries. It is in the context of this discussion that the global dimension of the current controversies over religion emerges most forcefully. As we have already seen, Butler challenges the way that the relationship between feminism and multiculturalism is framed. Specifically, she rejects how both feminism, with its pursuit of sexual politics, and multiculturalism become embedded, though each differently, in a civilizational narrative of progress that construes the historical development of the West as the unfolding of the project of individual freedom. Such narrative is contingent upon the abjection of an orientalized pre- or anti-modern Islamic other. As Butler declares, 'hegemonic conceptions of progress define themselves over and against a pre-modern temporality that they produce for the purposes of their own self-legitimation' (*FW*, 102). Two of the essays published in *Frames of War* (2009a), 'Sexual Politics, Torture, and Secular Time' and 'Non-Thinking in the Name of the Normative', offer a tightly argued analysis of the relationship between demands for progressive sexual politics, religiously coded views on immigrant communities (specifically those associated with Islam), the politics of secularism, and the practices of the US army in the war on terror.[11] Butler's wider theoretical aim in these essays is to critique those conceptions of modernity and progress that conceive of 'the West' as a modern and thus culturally and politically advanced political formation, which becomes juxtaposed to Islamic formations, construed as backward and anti-modern. More specifically, she challenges a conception of secularism understood as inherently progressive, demonstrating instead its potentially oppressive nature as well as its intrinsic link to conceptions of religion. Given the density of Butler's analysis, it is worth unpacking her points in detail.

The struggle for progressive sexual politics, as is well known, is a key concern of Butler's intellectual enterprise, but its relationship to the politics of immigration, and in particular to the war on terror, is at first glance unclear. Yet as she suggests, war blurs the boundaries between the domestic and the global (see also Chapter 3); it is around demands for progressive sexual freedom that the West's self-understanding as modern and progressive crystallizes and that the war on terror has been fought.[12] To illustrate her point Butler offers several examples, such as the Dutch civic integration examination, which equates prospective citizens' cultural ease with homosexuality with an acceptance of modernity and with their capacity to integrate into a modern, liberal society. Also cited is the example of France, where a self-consciously secular state equates a version of sexual politics with welfare policies targeted at immigrants and with the legal ban on the wearing of some forms of face cover in the public realm (see above). As Butler argues, these articulations of modernity marginalize those who either cannot, will not, or are perceived to be unable to embrace the values of modernity, embodied in the support for progressive sexual politics. Paradoxically, the apparent embrace of modernity is often coupled with homophobic politics, as seen in the reluctance to introduce adoption rights for gay couples into French law. As Butler suggests, such reluctance, justified with reference to the necessity of upholding a patrilineal and masculine symbolic order, resembles certain theological refusals to grant equal rights to sexual minorities. In this respect, the secular is contaminated by the religious, (and more specifically by a Catholic tradition) that, in turn, anchors itself in conceptions of a natural order.

She argues further that while conceptions of the natural serve as the legitimating ground for the religious opposition to sexual equality and reproductive freedom, civilization acts as a benchmark against which Islam, conceived as uncivilized and pre-modern, is judged. Such narratives are said to underpin recent utterances by the Catholic Church, but they are also said to be at work in US foreign policy and military practice. As discussed in the previous chapter, for Butler the paradigmatic expression of Western progress as it operates in the war on terror is the use of torture in the various detention centres and camps opened by the US military. Butler is clearly sensitive to torture's attempt at exploiting cultural vulnerabilities of the prisoners. However, rather than merely exposing how torture aims to break the prisoners, Butler suggests somewhat counter-intuitively that torture is also used to produce a subject—the Arab subject—as culturally inferior, anti-modern, and potentially a threat to life. As Butler intimates further, the sexualization of abuse that made Abu Ghraib so notorious must be understood as part of the civilizing mission of the US military. This mission, embedded in ideas of masculinism and homophobia, construes the populations under its control (and specifically the prisoners in its camps) as antithetical to Western ideas of progress and sexual freedom. In fact, they are construed as constituting a threat to Western culture. As she argues, these acts of torture should be understood as 'the actions of a homophobic institution against a population that is both construed and targeted for its own shame about homosexuality'; they are also 'the actions of a misogynistic institution against a population in which women are cast in roles bound by codes of honor and shame' (*FW*, 129). Butler concludes that in this context, torture becomes a 'technique of modernization' (*FW*, 130), which exposes the lawlessness and coercion of the civilizing mission it seeks to spread.[13]

Butler's analysis poses a key challenge to feminist scholarship: how should it respond to the war on terror if one of feminism's central tenets, that of the pursuit of progressive sexual politics, is utilized for a narrative of civilization with potentially racist and anti-immigrant implications? It is in this narrative that the progressive Western sexual subject is juxtaposed to a pre-modern subject, tied to religious, and by extension, conservative values that are instrumental in the oppression of (minority) women. What, though, are the implications for coalitional politics? Tying feminism into a political narrative that is contingent upon the abjection of religious and minority communities undermines the prospects for coalitional politics and, as Butler declares, it disarticulates the struggles for sexual freedom from struggles against racism and religious discrimination. Accordingly for Butler, coalitional politics cannot and must not be anchored in mutually exclusive rights claims (which is Okin's position). Instead, Butler proposes an account of coalitional politics that draws on a network of shifting alliances, which (a) do not presume cultural homogeneity, and which (b) develop around the critique of state violence. Thus, instead of a politics of pluralism, understood as an encounter between pre-constituted collective subjects, Butler envisages the prospect for a pluralization of shifting political struggles, networks, and alliances. Instead of focussing on the subject of politics, the emphasis lies with the prospect of politics understood as expanding the possibilities of liveability, seeking to undercut how state violence infringes on the prospects for liveable lives. As Butler states, 'the point is to establish a politics that opposes state coercion, and to build a framework within which we can see how the violence done in the name of preserving a certain modernity, and the conceit of cultural homogeneity or integration, form the most serious threat to freedom' (FW, 132).

I have much sympathy for the way that Butler conceives of the project of coalitional politics and for her critique of the cultural conflict framework, and there are empirical as well as theoretical and normative arguments to further support her claims. For example, the political protest against the invasion of Iraq illustrates the workings of coalitional politics, as it brought together individuals, communities and organizations from across a range of ideological, political, and faith perspectives. Likewise, a focus on coalitions provides a fresh look at the prospect of collective politics, and in doing so it circumvents many of the shortcomings of identity politics. This latter point is as much a theoretical as a normative claim in that it articulates both the conceptual possibility and the desirability of coalitional politics. However, as I already have argued, I wonder whether her persuasively and elegantly argued case for coalitional politics and against identity politics can fully account for the kinds of 'passionate attachments' that are said to be the hallmark of identity politics. In this respect, I am not fully convinced that the subject of identity and the coalitional subject are fully mediated.

As I intimated earlier, I am broadly sympathetic towards Butler's account, specifically towards her critique of the operation of discursive frameworks, her notion of a coalitional subject, and her sensitively argued case of the significance religious subject formation. However, I have some reservations which I will sketch here. For example, despite her criticism of positions artic-ulated by the Catholic Church (see Butler 2004a, 2009a), Butler evades some of the substantive issues raised in the wider debate on the role of religion in public life, specifically issues to do with the potentially oppressive mani-festation of religion and religious practices in minority communities. While I am in agreement with her effort to circumvent the traps of identitarian politics with a focus on state violence, such focus alone cannot, in my view, articulate how state violence works with and through religious communi-ties and organizations. Neither does she fully address genuine feminist con-cerns regarding concrete and specific gender-based violence emanating from within religiously motivated groups. I would also question her depiction of the self-understanding of the Western subject as sexually progressive. Such a depiction overlooks, in my view, the fiercely fought political battles over the role of religion in public life, including the pressure and intimidation that is exerted in some of these campaigns, especially in campaigns surrounding reproductive autonomy and access to abortion rights. It also generates, implicitly and perhaps unintentionally, a narrative of a homogenized Western subject that runs against widely differing levels of religiosity in the Western world, and in doing so, it is strangely at odds with Butler's own invocation of heterogeneity and difference. Likewise, her reference to 'the effort of secular elites to exclude religion from the public sphere', which she locates in class privilege and blindness to the cohesive function of religion for vulnerable populations (*FW*, 145), is not one that I easily recognize in public political discourse. To turn this argument around, one could just as well argue that religiosity works with and through class privilege, allowing various elites to evoke religion to legitimize their political agenda. Still, despite these reservations, I regard Butler's discussion as an important contribution to ongoing debates on multiculturalism and immigration, and it is a telling criticism of those feminist attempts to ally themselves to conservative positions that seek to push back progressive sexual and feminist politics in the West.

Given the density and complexity of Butler's argument, it is impossible to reach an overarching conclusion. Clearly, there is much in her discussion that should be commended, specifically the connection she makes between conceptions of time and progress, the instrumentalism of progressive sexual politics, religion, secularism and civilization, and war is a bold and original move. However, I am less comfortable with the 'broad sweep' approach that she deploys in parts of her analysis. For one, her depiction of 'the West' as the location of progressive sexual politics brushes over the contentious nature of sexual politics within the West. Given the often heated disputes over reproductive freedom, rights for gays and lesbians, and pornography, it is unclear to me where or who the champions of Western progressive sexual politics are. Second, while Butler is clearly right in highlighting the way that secularism is underwritten by religion, she also underplays the tension, often over sexual politics, that exists in the West between those who identify broadly as secular, and between certain branches of Christianity. Third, whilst pornography, misogyny, and homophobia, propagated under the disguise of sexual freedom, were central elements in the abuses at Abu Ghraib and elsewhere, it is problematic to deduct these practices from a wider alleged discourse of sexual freedom in the US. Finally, even though I am sympathetic towards Butler's effort to understand discourses on immigration in the context of civilizational narratives that abject immigrant communities, I would have expected some indication about her thinking on some of the issues pertaining to sexual politics within immigrant communities. Is it really enough to blame state policies, patrilineal versions of kinship structures, or Catholic theology?

Notwithstanding my reservations, I wish to return to some of Butler's substantive criticisms that, in my view, make important contributions to contemporary debates. As we have seen previously, the notion of the frame, understood as a discursive structure that articulates the normative categories which in turn regulate identity and politics, plays a central role in her discussion. She is equally critical of the frames of liberalism and multiculturalism, both of which are said to reify the politics of the subject, whether in an individualistic fashion (as in the case of liberalism) or in a communitarian way (as in the case of multiculturalism). Thus, neither the narrative of liberalism nor the narrative of multiculturalism provide Butler with the adequate resources for thinking through progressive politics, and neither of the two constitute adequate frames to criticise state violence. By shifting the focus on the critique of state violence away from the politics of identity and cultural conflict, Butler is able to address several issues that occupy her work: first, it circumvents the deadlock of identitarian and communitarian politics, especially if this is conceived to articulate incompatible positions. In doing so, it enables Butler to articulate possibilities for radical forms of politics that draw on the experience of subjugated groups and individuals, whether sexual or religious minorities. Second, it allows her to engage in a critique of the epistemological framework that underwrites the cultural conflict framework by highlighting the violence at work in the constitution of distinct identity categories. Third, it focuses directly on the role of the state (a key target of Butler's criticism) in the regulation of cultural conflict and the frameworks that underwrite them.

In sum, what, then, is Butler's key contribution to debates on religion, secularism, and sexual politics in the context of the war on terror? As I sought to demonstrate in this chapter, attention to religious matters, broadly construed, has obtained increasing significance in Butler's recent writings. This attention emanates from Butler's biography, including her philosophical formation in the synagogue and her current interest in the politics of the Middle East. Her deployment of Jewish resources in the dispute over Zionism, as I have argued, challenges positions that equate the critique of Israel with anti-Semitism. Of particular relevance for my discussion is the way that her utilization of Jewish philosophy and ethics facilitates a reworking of the abstract nature of Levinasian thinking that has surfaced in aspects of Butler's recent work. My discussion in the next chapter develops elements of Butler's 'Jewish' philosophy and ethics by looking at the implications for citizenship in a global context.

NOTES

1. The Adorno Prize is awarded by the city of Frankfurt, Germany, for outstanding services to philosophy, music, theatre, and film. The prize is awarded every three years.
2. According to a transcript published on the *Radical Archives* blog, Butler's comments respond to two questions on Hamas and Hezbollah, relating to their use of violence and their threat to Israel. Butler argues that Hamas and

Hezbollah as social movements are progressive and part of a global Left, though this should not prevent criticism of both movements, especially coming from those who are pursuing non-violent politics (see 'Judith Butler on Hamas, Hezbollah & the Israel Lobby (2006)', *Radical Archives* (blog), http://radicalarchives.org/2010/03/28/jbutler-on-hamas-hezbollah-israel-lobby).

3. I attend to the wider significance of the concept of critique in Butler's writings in my conclusion.

4. The initially private exchange of letters between Arendt and Scholem was published in *Neue Zürcher Zeitung* (October 1963) and *Encounter* (January 1964).

5. Butler's relationship with Arendt is a complex one and, in light of her recent, more sustained engagement with Arendt, is deserving of a separate investigation. For the purpose of my discussion it suffices to say that Butler's recent work, especially on the nation and on Israel-Palestine, has brought her to a more considered engagement with Arendt's work (see Butler 2007a, 2012a).

6. A revised version of this essay is included in *Parting Ways* (2012a).

7. For a recent consideration see Norris and Inglehart (2011).

8. Ireland, understood as a geographical entity, is divided into two jurisdictions, the Republic of Ireland and Northern Ireland, which is part of the United Kingdom.

9. For a critical engagement with Okin's position see the various responses included in Okin (1999).

10. *Nuestro himno* works towards the legalization of the status of migrants in the United States. See my discussion in Chapter 5.

11. The first of the two essays was originally delivered as the 2007 annual lecture for the *British Journal of Sociology* and was published in this journal in 2008, together with responses by Ali, Beckford, Bhatt, Modood, and Woodhead. I am using the version of Butler's essay included in *Frames of War* (2009a).

12. Recall that the name 'Operation Enduring Freedom' was used by the US government to refer to its military operations in Afghanistan.

13. I attend to Butler's treatment of (international) law in Chapter 5.

5 Undoing the State? Radical Politics beyond Sovereignty

Whereas some critics mistake the critique of sovereignty for the demolition of agency, I propose that agency begins where sovereignty wanes.

(*Excitable Speech*)

[T]he point is to be neither pro-sovereign nor to be anti-sovereign but to watch the ways in which sovereignty is invoked, extended, deterritorialized, aggregated, abrogated in the name of sovereignty as well as against the name of sovereignty.

(*Who Sings the Nation-State?*)

One of Butler's most significant contributions to contemporary political philosophy is her incisive critique of the operation of power and its workings on the subject and politics. In contrast to the depth, detail, and sophistication that characterizes this aspect of her oeuvre, it is fair, I believe, to describe much of her writings on the state and the law as disappointing. Even though she articulates important conceptions of radical politics, her treatment of state and law has evaded both detail and clarity and has been the subject of much criticism. On the surface, such evasion seems puzzling, given that the state constitutes the central foil for the development of her key claims regarding the efficacy and desirability of progressive and radical politics. Still, it is accurate to describe much of her work on the state as antagonistic:[1] she does not offer an explicit and detailed theory of the state, neither does she provide a fully developed account of that key feature of the modern state, sovereignty. Not surprisingly, her views on the state have received substantial criticism, charging her with an alleged lack of sophistication and grasp of the state's structure and workings, and with a refusal to see the state as a key site for political struggle (see in particular Passavant and Dean 2001).[2]

This chapter reconsiders Butler's treatment of the state and law in the context of her emphasis on relationality and dispossession and her critique of war and violence. One of my aims is to work through an ambivalence at the heart of her writings, which has also occupied the critical commentary on Butler's work: her presentation of the operation of sovereign state power, which is at odds with her critique of sovereign state power. It is my contention that even though this ambivalence is not fully resolved in her recent work, it is substantially redressed and reformulated in the increasing acknowledgment of law. Butler continues to advocate post-sovereign radical accounts of politics. Such a position, I suggest, does not sufficiently work the weakness in the state; it also overlooks the extent to which non-state forms of agency are mediated through the state. Building upon my discussion of coalitional politics from previous chapters, I return to the question of political alliances, which I now consider under conditions of global conflict. Of key importance to my discussion is an assessment of Butler's call for 'non-nationalist modes of belonging', which she ponders in the context of diaspora and cohabitation and, more specifically, in relation to the conflict in Israel-Palestine. Drawing on Butler's reflections on the situation in the Middle East and her appropriation of Jewish conceptions of diaspora and non-violence, I want to think through diasporic and cohabitative forms of statehood and nationhood and consider, furthermore, the prospects for critical forms of cosmopolitanism (she refers to this as 'new internationalism').

Despite Butler's lack of clarity regarding the nature of the state, however, she continues to grapple with the state, and it is this aspect that occupies me in this chapter. Thus, rather than turning her back on this topic, the state receives renewed attention in her recent work, and, as I suggest, she substantially redresses some of the gaps in her writings. Of key significance to Butler's rethinking of the state are her ontological categories of relationality, dispossession, and ek-stasis. These, I will suggest, configure the interaction between her existential concerns about the precariousness of life and the contingent structures of politics, as well as our ethical obligations across national boundaries. Several areas are particularly significant for my discussion. These are her critique of violence (which, as we have seen in Chapter 3, is intrinsically linked with the state), specifically her criticism of the violence that underpins US foreign policy, her recent writings on Israel (see Chapter 4), and also, more broadly, the violence inherent in the state's regulation of identity. Of key significance to Butler's work on Israel-Palestine is not just her critique of the formation and continued actions of a particular state, though. Rather, her discussion poses fundamental questions about the idea of belonging and forms of political agency and organization appropriate to conditions of heterogeneity and plurality. Heterogeneity and plurality cut across and beyond state boundaries, though, and Butler attends as much to conditions of diversity internal to the state as she considers forms of political organization that cut across state boundaries.

I consider the first aspect at the beginning of this chapter, where I attend to Butler's treatment of the state and the condition of statelessness. Like much in her recent work, this discussion is informed by her reading of Hannah Arendt, specifically by Arendt's critique of the nation state and its generation of statelessness, and it culminates in Butler's vision of a politics that transgresses the boundaries of the nation. I develop this structural critique of the state in two directions: first, by considering the 'dissonant voices' that operate within the state, and second, by exploring forms of bi-nationalism. The last two sections in this chapter explore the prospects of a politics 'beyond the state'. I begin by re-examining Butler's claims regarding sovereignty developed in some of her earlier work before attending to her treatment of this topic in some of her more recent writings. An important dimension of this topic is also the conduct of US policy regarding the detainees at Guantánamo Bay, and I discuss this aspect by attending to the role of law in Butler's recent work. I conclude with a discussion on what I call the ek-static cosmopolitanism in Butler's work.

REVISITING THE STATE

The criticism of Butler's treatment of the state, which I alluded to above, predates her post-9/11 writings. It focuses, in the main, on arguments presented in *Excitable Speech* (1997a) and in *Antigone's Claim* (2000a). In this section, I will briefly recap the relevant themes of both titles before I summarize, again briefly, the key criticisms of these two works. In this respect, this section serves a heuristic purpose: it provides the backdrop to the following sections, where I track and assess the development of Butler's account of the state in her post-9/11 writings.

In *Excitable Speech*, Butler ponders the primary dependency of the speaking being and its vulnerability to the injurious actions of others. Focusing on the workings of language, specifically in the context of the hate speech debates in the United States, Butler avers that language is at the same time injurious and constitutive; it both produces and exploits a 'scene of enabling vulnerability' (*ES*, 2), in which the subject emerges as an intelligible being who remains subjected to linguistic norms. At the heart of *Excitable Speech* lies the question of the sovereignty of language, what Butler terms 'sovereign performatives'. Seeking to displace the conception of sovereign language, Butler maps a model for radical and post-sovereign forms of politics out of her critique of the state and state censorship, and of those political movements which seek recourse to the state as a recompense for historical injuries. Her objective is twofold: by championing 'nonstate-centered forms of agency and resistance' (*ES*, 19), Butler also articulates the waning of sovereignty.[3] This challenge to efforts to invoke the state in the pursuit of progressive politics is a recurrent theme in her work, and the target of much of this critique is the work of Catharine A. MacKinnon. In *Only Words*, MacKinnon (1996) presents a forceful analysis of pornography, building on her claim that words are not merely representational but constitutive. That is, words do not merely refer to an independently existing reality; rather, they constitute or produce the reality they speak of. Thus, MacKinnon conceives of pornography as an efficacious performative that, through the expression of its ideas, produces women as subordinated and unequal. Butler's quarrel with MacKinnon is over the efficacious nature of the speech act; against MacKinnon, she contends that language can lead to unexpected and unintended effects, and she develops this claim further by pointing up the resignificatory possibilities of injurious language. It is this latter aspect that is significant for my discussion here: by challenging the claim that language is efficacious (that is, that language always does what it says), Butler also challenges conceptions of the speaker as efficacious and sovereign. Although the speaker remains responsible for the language uttered, the meaning of an injurious utterance always exceeds the intentions of this 'post-sovereign speaker'.

In essence, Butler makes two related claims: first, she provides an overall critique of the state, while, second, she is critical of those social movements that seek redress for their injuries by referring to the state. To begin with, Butler challenges those positions, including feminist anti-pornography positions such as those articulated by Catharine MacKinnon, that proceed from the assumption of the efficacy of a speech act. Butler elaborates on her deployment of the theory of performativity, which has been central to her discussion in *Gender Trouble* (1990), by distinguishing between speech acts that are efficacious and those that are not. Key to her argument is her insistence on the resignificatory capacity of 'words that wound', this is, the capacity of injurious words to take on new and unexpected meanings which change the intention of the speaker.[4]

This consideration of hate speech is significant, because it constitutes the backdrop against which Butler delineates her view of the state. Thus, she concludes that efforts to enlist the state in the fight against injurious language are pointless and even potentially dangerous. For one, censorship itself reiterates and proliferates injurious language and contributes to its circulation. What's more, the state, according to Butler, is not a neutral arbiter over conflicting interests. Rather, as she avers, censorship is applied unequally in political practice, for example by censoring the representation of gay sexuality while protecting the representation of heterosexuality as free speech. Thus, the extension of state power via censorship constitutes a threat to lesbian-gay politics (*ES*, 22). The differential application of censorship is also racially inflected, censoring for example sexual expressions in rap music.[5]

Without going into the details of Butler's arguments in *Excitable Speech* (1997a) on the topic of hate speech and censorship, I want to briefly summarize some of the key assertions presented in this book.[6] These are, first, the idea that language is generative, and that this generativity has (potentially unintended) injurious implications. Second, Butler challenges claims that posit the efficacy of language (in a sense the sovereign operation of language)—in other words, the claim that language always does what it says. Third, from this challenge to language's sovereignty, Butler derives the prospects for resignification. As she states, there is a gap between the intentions of the speaker (insofar as these can be defined) and the effects that his/her speech produces. Fourth, in addition to her effort at displacing the intentionality and sovereignty of the speaker and his/her speech, Butler also questions the equivocity of language. This questioning allows her to delineate her work on cultural translation and the contested nature of universality Finally, Butler challenges notions of the univocity of sovereign power allied with conceptions of agency. Instead, agency, for Butler, becomes displaced, emerging at the site (specifically sites outside or beyond the realm of the state) where power-sovereignty is said to disappear.

To what extent can Butler's discussion of the sovereign performative in the context of hate speech be transposed to the level of global politics? Is the sovereignty of the speaker comparable to the sovereignty of states? And do similar structures of criticism apply?

One of the most perceptive readings of *Excitable Speech* is offered by Paul A. Passavant and Jodie Dean (2001). Although sympathetic towards Butler's efforts to proliferate the sites for politics beyond the state and into the rich network of associations that goes by the name of civil society, Passavant and Dean wonder whether Butler is giving up on the state as a site for political action. Specifically, they ask whether the state and law provide opportunities for the kind of non-sovereign forms of political agency championed by Butler. This includes the possibility to subject law to 'the perpetual openness of linguistic action to reinflection'. As they argue, 'the image of the state and law that emerges from her discussion is, well, rather sovereign and univocal' (380). Insisting instead on the law's openness to interpretation, they suggest that law can, in fact, be deployed in the battle against racism (see also Lloyd 2007).

Excitable Speech's portrayal of the state as monolithic, its lack of attention to the divergent and competing branches of the state, and its privileging of forms of political agency that are located outside the state is not significantly redressed in *Antigone's Claim* (2000a). If anything, the personification of the state in the figure of Creon further props up a monolithic account of the state. Yet in other ways, *Antigone's Claim* develops *Excitable Speech*. It reconfigures some of the concerns of *Excitable Speech* in relation to the public-private dualism; it could also be read as a bridge between the earlier critique of the state articulated in *Excitable Speech* and the path into some of her more recent considerations on cohabitation and bi-nationalism. As Butler points out at the beginning of the book, the figure of Antigone has been repeatedly invoked as a feminist heroine who challenges the masculine-paternal authority of the state. Indeed, Antigone's insurrectionary speech acts and her disobedience challenge the sovereignty of Creon, and they upend the primacy of politics over kinship. In fact, one could argue that Creon's insistence on sovereignty contributes to the tragic unfolding of events. If read as a treatise on illicit love that fails to obtain the state's recognition, *Antigone's Claim* highlights the creation of what Butler calls 'partial zones of citizenship', populated by those abject beings who are not properly human and who lack the recognition of the state. Yet, by invoking Arendt's notion of a 'shadowy realm' which haunts the public sphere (*AC*, 81), Butler stresses how the existence and persistence of the public realm is contingent upon those who remain excluded or unintelligible against dominant norms of recognition. Yet Antigone is also, dialectically, linked to Creon, as her speech is contingent upon the edicts of the state. Of significance to my discussion in this chapter is the development of Butler's argument towards the end of *Antigone's Claim*.

Notwithstanding the important issues raised by Butler, neither *Excitable Speech* nor *Antigone's Claim* provide satisfactory answers on the role of state and law in political transformation. However, both books throw into relief themes that occupy Butler's post-9/11 writings and that deal with her attention to minoritarian forms of citizenship. Specifically, they prefigure her consideration of the state in its international context, challenging the claims to sovereignty and invulnerability that she detects in the post-9/11 discourses. I will return to these books in the next section (they add the notion of bio-politics). As I stated, although this discussion evolves against the background of what Butler perceives to be the heteronormative foundations of the public realm, it obtains added significance in her work on migration and ethnic heterogeneity.

Thus, the curtailed view on the state articulated in some of her earlier writings receives significant elaboration in some of her recent work. These elaborations can be grouped into three related approaches: first, Butler continues to grapple with the state as the locus of sovereignty, and she reformulates sovereignty in relation to governmentality (specifically in *Precarious Life* (2004b)).[7] Second, she ponders the role of the state as a 'container' for diversity and heterogeneity, and she thinks through modes of belonging that transcend the ethnic and physical confines of the nation state.[8] Third, she articulates approaches to the formation of international community and responsibility that build on a conception of international law, and that I want to call (building on Brassett (2010)) 'cosmopolitan sentiments'. Of significance to the development of my discussion is the context in which these changes unfold. These relate to her adherence to the ideas of relationality and dispossession, and they are located in the context of global politics. Butler offers an account of the state in the global arena, and specifically under conditions of contemporary war. Rather than engaging with the question of the efficacy of state power and potential resistance to it, Butler's key issues entail her discussion of sovereignty, this time in a global context and in relation to the modern war prison, the state's international obligations, human rights protection, and the emergence of a global politics of difference. I will begin with an exposition and critical assessment of Butler's writings on state sovereignty, after which I will turn to a consideration of the politics of difference in the context of state sovereignty and the global constellation.

SOVEREIGNTY AND GOVERNMENTALITY

As we have seen, the question of sovereignty, which informs much of her discussion in *Excitable Speech* (1997a), lies at the heart of Butler's discontent with the state. In fact, one could profitably read Butler's early work, specifically *Gender Trouble* (1990), as an attempt to displace the agentic, sovereign subject. What, though, happens to her critique of sovereignty if it is applied to the state and, more specifically, to the operation of the state in the global 'war on terror'? How should or could sovereignty be reformulated? Is it possible to imagine or articulate a politics beyond sovereignty? And if so, what would it look like? These are some of the questions that I put to Butler's recent writings.

In *Frames of War* (2009a), Butler suggests that insistence on sovereignty effectively forecloses the possibility of developing an ethical relation to the other. Such foreclosure operates through the use of state violence, which in turn conjectures a sovereign subject, conceived as one not impinged upon by others (*FW*, 178). The sovereign subject, Butler continues, denies its own constitutive vulnerability and precariousness while at the same time transferring this vulnerability onto others. According to Butler, to understand the attacks on the Twin Towers in New York on September 11 within the language of sovereignty, that is, as attacks on the sovereignty and borders of the United States, misses the opportunity to reflect on US vulnerability and precariousness and to articulate responsibility for violence in a global context. Yet instead of taking the opportunity to embark on such reflection, the United States entered a process of heightened nationalism (see below) and, as outlined in *Precarious Life* (2004b), a resurgence of sovereignty that manifests itself as lawless power (*PL*, 56). My aim in this section is to unpack her treatment of sovereignty further, attending to its relationship to governmentality. I will argue that out of her discussion emerges an important shift in her argument towards a more explicit acknowledgment of the role of the law and human rights.

The central reference point for Butler's discussion of sovereignty is Foucault, specifically the Foucauldian notion of bio-power and bio-politics, and to a lesser extent Agamben's reworking of Foucault's ideas.[9] What, then, is meant by bio-politics, and how does Butler deploy this concept? In this section, I discuss Butler's deployment of Foucault's discussion in the context of the war on terror. There are two stages to the development of Butler's argument. Whereas a substantial proportion of *Precarious Life* (2004b) deals with the fallout from the war in Afghanistan, specifically with the treatment of prisoners in Guantánamo Bay, *Frames of War* (2009a) also reflects on the Iraq war and prisoner abuse in Abu Ghraib. I begin by discussing one of her essays, 'Indefinite Detention', which is included in her book *Precarious Life*. Given the significance of this essay to the unfolding of Butler's overall argument, it is opportune to unpack her key points in detail.

The focus for Butler's discussion in *Precarious Life* is the war prison, embodied in the site of Guantánamo Bay (she reflects on Abu Ghraib in

Frames of War) and the alleged emergence of a new exercise of state sovereignty. At the heart of her analysis is her discussion of Foucault's notion of governmentality, its relationship to sovereignty, and the bio-politics of the war on terror. 'Indefinite Detention', which, as I stated, is included in *Precarious Life,* should be read against the backdrop of the treatment of prisoners taken during the military campaign in Afghanistan and their subsequent incarceration in Guantánamo Bay.[10] As is well known, the imprisonment and treatment of the detainees in Guantánamo is subject to considerable public dispute, centring in particular on the absence of due legal process and the indefinite nature of the incarceration, as well as wider concerns over the living conditions and treatment of the prisoners.[11] What animates Butler's discussion is the relationship between sovereignty and governmentality. This discussion illuminates further Butler's view on sovereignty, which should be read as a development of Foucault's discussion of governmentality in the context of the modern war prison. Foucault (1991) conceives of governmentality as a specifically modern form of power which epitomizes, in the main, the management and regulation of populations. He describes governmentality as a 'complex form of power' (102) which is targeted at populations and which operates through the apparatuses of security. Moreover, it is underpinned by specific forms of knowledge, in the main political economy, which assist the practices of governmentality. Crucially for Foucault, governmentality does not replace sovereignty. Rather, he avers that power operates in a triangular structure of sovereignty, discipline, and government. Where, though, does this account leave the state? Foucault criticizes what he considers to be a contemporary overvaluing of the state, in particular the reduction of the state to its functions on the one hand, and its portrayal of unity on the other hand. Rather, he insists, 'the state is no more than a composite reality and a mythicized abstraction' (103), less important than we tend to think, and certainly not as important as what he refers to as the 'governmentalization' of the state (103).

Butler follows Foucault's claim that governmentality does not replace sovereignty.[12] She challenges readings that offer a chronological account where sovereignty, understood as an early modern form of power, is replaced by governmentality as a late modern form of power. Rather, she insists on the simultaneous existence of sovereignty and governmentality. In her view, it is the establishment of the modern war prison which embodies the persistence of sovereignty within governmentality.

How, though, does this renewed resurgence of sovereignty occur? As Butler argues, sovereignty should not be understood as a unified power that provides legitimacy to the actions of the state, including those embodied in the law. Rather, building on Agamben, she detects an inverse relationship at play here: as she avers, sovereignty resurfaces precisely because of a lack of legitimacy and, crucially because the actions of state officials and administrators lie outside or beyond the law. Hence, sovereignty becomes 'rogue power' (*PL*, 56).[13] Central to Butler's consideration is the notion of the state of emergency that such rogue power generates. According to her, the indefinite detention implemented at Guantánamo Bay is characterized by an extra-legal and ultimately illegitimate exercise of power, which performatively established the exception as the norm, and in doing so turns it into a permanent political feature of US political life (*PL,* 67). Furthermore, such normalization of the exception attempts to construe a new form of legitimacy, which lacks accountability. The relegation of the prisoners into what she terms, again following Agamben, zones of suspended citizenship operates through the kind of sovereign power that Agamben refers to as bare life. However, contra Agamben, Butler insists that sovereign power operates differentially, following a racial and ethnic grid that distinguishes between liveable life and social death (see Chapter 2).

I want to suggest that Butler's depiction of sovereignty as the suspension of law and rogue power is more than just analysis: it functions as a critique that, in turn, prepares for an important development in her writings that departs substantially from her reductive critique of the law and of those who seek to invoke the law, which was articulated in *Excitable Speech* (1997a). In this respect, my analysis differs from Elena Loizidou's (2007). According to Loizidou, Butler 'is not interested in the *rule of law,* and to be precise she *never* has been' (87; emphasis in original); as Loizidou continues, 'she is *not* interested in upholding the rule of law' (117; emphasis in original). Admittedly, such a reading chimes with arguments presented in *Excitable Speech,* but I wonder whether it captures what, in my view, is one of the key concerns of 'Indefinite Detention': Butler's critique of the suspension of the rule of law, the production of sovereignty as an effect of this suspension, and sovereignty's resurfacing 'with the vengeance of an anachronism that refuses to die' (*PL,* 54).[14] The essay raises a further problem, though, which pertains to the quality of the state of emergency and the character of war. As Butler argues, indefinite detention constitutes an indefinite extension of extra-legal or lawless power, that is, the kind of power that is exercised by the executive branch (and in this respect it is a form of sovereign power). This use of extra-legal power, which circumvents the rule of law, the constitution, and internationally accepted treaties becomes, in Butler's view, a permanent feature of US political life, and in doing so it extend the state of emergency indefinitely. Moreover, although such power appears to be sovereign, its contemporary practices, exercised through administrative branches, are governmental. As Butler argues, '[i]t is not, literally speaking, that a sovereign power suspends the rule of law, but that the rule of law, in the act of being suspended, produces sovereignty *in its action and as its effect*' (*PL,* 66; italics in original).

Such suspension of law throws the detainees back into the state of 'bare life', but, as Butler claims, against Agamben, bare life is politically animated and differentially applied, operating through ethnic and racial frames. Thus, the deployment of 'terrorism' as an analytical lens, or the use of analogies between detainees and those who are mentally ill (and therefore need to be detained), simultaneously depoliticizes and dehumanizes those who have, willingly or unwillingly, become participants in a global conflict.[15]

To sidestep this diagnosis overlooks, in my view, the increased significance accorded to the law in *Precarious Life* (2004b) as well as in subsequent writings (see my discussion below). To elucidate this point further, it will be helpful to take a closer look at what Butler is saying. Towards the end of 'Indefinite Detention', she makes the following point:

> 'It may seem that the normative implication of my analysis is that I wish the state were bound to law in a way that does not treat the law merely as instrumental or dispensable. This is true. But I am not interested in the rule of law *per se*, however, but rather in the place of law in the articulation of an international conception of rights and obligations that limit and condition claims of state sovereignty.'
>
> (*PL*, 98; emphasis in original)

Despite her lack of interest in 'the rule of law *per se*', Butler conceives of the rule of law as a necessary enunciation and limitation of state sovereignty. Moreover, as I demonstrate further on, it is of key importance to international relations, broadly conceived. Of course, law should not be understood outside the operations of power, and, as she continues further, the modalities of power that allow for effective intervention against practices of dehumanization, especially those associated with the malpractices in the new war prison, are significant. Thus, while Butler is sensitive to what she terms arguments from the point of view of human rights, including the insistence on due process for those imprisoned and the presumption of innocence until proven guilty, she is even more insistent on what she terms arguments from the point of view of a critique of power (and I suspect that this is the point Loizidou wishes to stress): the objection to the state of emergency and the extension of lawless power that indefinite detention brings forth. In this respect, upholding the law does not become a panacea for the wider problems of precarity and global inequality, but it is one element in the broader repertoire of community-building at global level. Human rights law, furthermore, becomes part of the democratic struggle to rethink the human outside subjugating racial and ethnic frames (*PL*, 90). As she argues in *Frames of War* (2009a), 'recognition of shared precariousness introduces strong normative commitments of equality and invites a more robust universalizing of rights' (*FW*, 28–9). Butler's increased sensitivity to the significance of the law is a noteworthy and welcome development in her work, which recognizes the range and complexity of the operation of power and the potentially valuable contribution to liveable lives that the law can make. How such invocation of the law is mediated in relation to the state is less clear, though. As I argued in Chapter 3, for Butler the state remains an institution of violence, and it is around the critique of state violence that Butler envisages the formation of heterogeneous political coalitions. In fact, it is unclear to me how Butler's critique of state violence, which is heavily indebted to Benjamin's critique of the law, is compatible with her endorsement of law, due process, and legitimacy.

It is in relation to this criticism that I wish to raise a further point. As I stated previously, Butler's dismissal of the state as a legitimate site for political struggle, and the absence of a sophisticated analysis of the state has been criticized even by those otherwise sympathetic to her work. 'Indefinite Detention' does not fully consider these criticisms; rather, it evades them through a semantic shift from 'state' to 'executive branch'. This shift goes some way towards redressing the problem, but it is still some way off from a more detailed consideration of the state.

In *Frames of War* (2009a), Butler anchors freedom simultaneously outside the state and in opposition to the state. Although insisting on the important role played by law and criticizing a conception of freedom beyond or outside the law (such as is deployed in the civilising practices of the US army) she nevertheless regards the state first and foremost as a locus of violence that must be criticized. Such thinking raises several problems: first, it does not constitute a significant advance on the curtailed understanding of the state presented in earlier writings. Second (and this is an empirical point), it fails to acknowledge the significant role played by various branches of the state in the protection of freedom and those branches' refusal to participate in the military adventures of the US administration. Third, in my view it does not sufficiently think through the relationship between law, freedom, and the state. Admittedly, Butler's presentation of freedom in this essay draws on agonistic and performative conceptions that are not contingent upon the existence of state institutions and protections. In fact, her preference for associational styles of freedom, her insistence on (global) alliances and coalitions, which she tasks with formulating a critique of state violence, may not require the state. It is less clear, though, how such a conception of politics can be squared with her valuing of the law, her stress on the importance of human rights, and her stringent critique of lawless freedom (and sovereignty). Some of her most recent work on cohabitation and bi-nationalism allows for a reconsideration of these issues.

DISSONANT VOICES: SINGING THE NATION STATE

Although Butler has established herself as a thinker who is critical of the state, she keeps returning to a critical engagement with it. Furthermore, notwithstanding my reservations regarding Butler's theorization of the state and her ambivalent position vis-á-vis the state's significance as a terrain for progressive politics, her recent writings, such as her co-authored text with Gayatri Spivak, *Who Sings the Nation-State?* (2007a), as well as her reflections on Zionism in *Parting Ways* (2012a), continue to revisit the theme of the state, this time by pondering its relation to the nation. Neither of these two texts offer a significantly revised or expanded account of the state as a terrain for progressive politics, but they add to Butler's repertoire by addressing the problem of citizenship, national identity, and belonging in a world characterized by plurality, difference, and heterogeneity. This focus on citizenship connects Butler's latest work with some of her earlier discussions in *Excitable Speech* (1997a), where she criticizes the existence of so-called zones of 'partial citizenship' or 'retractable zones of citizenship' (*ES*, 103, 105; see also *AC*). There, Butler attends to the differential sexualized forms of citizenship that abject non-heterosexual life at the expense of a normalization of heterosexual citizenship. This concern with exclusion and expulsion receives substantial attention in her work on Israel-Palestine, and it is informed by her critical reading of the writings of Hannah Arendt. I address Butler's considerations on the nation in the next section; for now, I want to briefly review her assertions on the state as expressed in *Who Sings the Nation-State* from 2007 (see Butler 2007a). In this section I attend to an aspect of Butler's treatment of the state that has received much attention in her recent writings. This is her consideration of the state's structural production of a realm of exclusion or marginalization. To unravel this element of her work further, I will draw, yet again, on the writings of Hannah Arendt. Butler opens her discussion by positing the state in the context of global developments.

Who Sings the Nation-State? (2007a), a conversation between Butler and Gayatri Spivak on nation and belonging in an era of globalization, develops some of the discussions already presented in *Precarious Life* (2004b), and it pre-empts several of the concerns that surface later in *Frames of War* (2009a) and *Parting Ways* (2012a). These include the relationship between sovereignty and constitutionalism (as she now calls it) and the status of bare life under conditions of statelessness and expulsion. Central to Butler's contribution to the conversation is her analysis of the relationship between the state, the nation, and nationalism. Drawing on her reading of Arendt, Butler broadly agrees with Arendt's ([1951] 1976) structural critique of the nation state, specifically with Arendt's assertion that the nation state produces, by definition, statelessness. This is not the place to track the nuances and developments in Arendt's thinking on the topic. Rather, I want to sketch Butler's deployment of and debt to Arendtian ideas and concepts and their contribution to Butler's own work on this topic. Such debt merits particular attention, given Butler's long-standing hostility towards Arendtian ideas.[16] What, then, does Butler borrow from Arendt?

Recall that in the famous chapter of *The Origins of Totalitarianism* entitled 'The Decline of the Nation-State and the End of the Rights of Man', Arendt ([1951] 1976) assesses the disastrous consequences of the minorities treaties that were established in the wake of World War I.[17] Arendt's discussion is underpinned by her criticism of the nation state, whose insistence on homogeneity and its capacity to generate minorities and stateless populations is presented as a structural feature of the nation state itself. According to Arendt, the nation state creates forms of community that supersede the principle of a polity based upon the law, but that also and inevitably lead to conflict in light of the ethnic and communal patchwork which was characteristic of early twentieth-century Central and Eastern Europe. One aspect raised by Arendt informs Butler's discussion in particular. This is the question whether, in Butler's words, non-nationalist modes of belonging are possible (*WSNS*, 49, 50).

Butler further theorizes Arendt's ideas with her concept of dispossession. However, whereas Arendt, following Butler's reading, abandons reference to the terminology of the nation state, preferring instead terms such as 'polity' or 'federation' to stress the non-ethnic, plural, and always provisional communal ties that exist between citizens, Butler continues to pose the question of the nation by exploring the possibilities for radical resignificatory practices of the nation. Although she commences this line of inquiry by asking for the prospects for non-nationalist modes of belonging (*WSNS*, 49) and even counter-nationalist modes of belonging (*WSNS*, 59), she leaves open the prospect of the 'plurality of the nation' (*WSNS*, 58). In effect, Butler opens up the prospect of a 'nation without nationalism' (see Kristeva 1993), which accommodates the heterogeneity and plurality of its constituent parts. Helping her to illustrate such a radically resignified concept of the nation further is the *nuestro himno* movement in the United States.

Nuestro himno, translated as 'our anthem', is part of a wider movement of illegal immigrants in the United States, originating in the main from the Spanish-speaking hinterland of the US, who are fighting for access to US citizenship. This movement seeks to legalize the status of those migrants and their children who have resided in the US for many years but who are without the normal protections that come with citizenship. Part of the campaign for legal status has been fought in Congress, where the polarized nature of contemporary US politics and the emotive topic of immigration and border control has until recently prevented progress.[18] *Nuestro himno* sought to give voice to Spanish-speaking migrants by singing the US national anthem in Spanish, and thereby demonstrating the existence of a plurality of voices in the United States.[19] The singing itself caused some controversy, partly because it incorporated several verses of rap that expressed criticism of the current US immigration policy, but mainly because it was sung in a language other than English. This opposition to *nuestro himno* was articulated by the then US President George W. Bush, who claimed that the national anthem should be sung in English, and that language difference constituted part of the problem surrounding immigration (Holusha 2006).

There are two aspects that are of significance to Butler's discussion of *nuestro himno*. One is her continued insistence on translation as a political practice. As we have already seen, practices of cultural translation lie at the heart of the transversal between universality and particularity (see Chapter 4). In this respect, it is not surprising that they also feature in Butler's discussion of the nation and immigration. As she argues, 'equality is not a matter of extending or augmenting the homogeneity of the nation' (*WSNS*, 61). Rather, the nation remains a heterogeneous patchwork of groups, requiring translation to engage in dialogue with one another. The second aspect refers to the spaces where resignification and practices of cultural translation take place. Butler's emphasis on the importance of a politics in the street reinforces perceptions of her writings as privileging associational, non-state forms of political practice that chime strongly with her conception of radical democracy (see Butler 2011c).

DIASPORA, COHABITATION, AND BI-NATIONALISM

While concerns with the plight of migrant communities surfaces repeatedly in Butler's recent work, arising out of her consideration of global migration movements and state responses to diversity, her engagement with plurality takes on a particular significance in her treatment of the Israeli-Palestinian conflict. I already have alluded to several features of this latest aspect of Butler's work in the previous chapter, specifically her discussion of Zionism, religion, and public life. Here I am concerned more specifically with the question of how citizenship can be organized in multiply inhabited and contested political spaces. Butler's intersubjective account of the subject lies at the heart of her analysis of Israeli-Palestinian relations, culminating in an account of the subject as radically displaced. What, then, follows for her account of politics and specifically the state?

Although an analysis of the conflict's origins, development, and possible solutions are not my concern in this chapter, it will be helpful to provide some context. What interests me, rather, is how Butler maps possibilities for cohabitation in contested political spaces, and how these possibilities are contingent upon her radical critique of certain concepts of the nation state, national identity, and sovereignty. These possibilities are informed by Butler's engagement with the writings of Arendt, specifically Arendt's critique of Zionism, as well as by the late Edward Said's (2003) Freudian reflections on the Middle East conflict.

As already indicated in the previous chapter, a major focus in Butler's recent writings is her discussion of Israel-Palestine. As I demonstrated in Chapter 3, there are theological and ethical aspects to this discussion that also bears centrally on Butler's discussion of bi-nationalism. In many ways since the implementation of a peace process in Northern Ireland in 1998, Israel-Palestine is regarded as one of the last intractable conflicts. Like Northern Ireland, Israel-Palestine has also embarked upon a peace process, but it faltered, not least at those issues that have a direct bearing on Butler's discussion of bi-nationalism.

As is well known, the territory of Palestine came under British Mandate at the end of World War I, having been part of the Ottoman Empire since the sixteenth century. Following a series of intentional and unintentional blunders made by the British government, already existing tensions between the majority Palestinian Arab population and the small Jewish population heightened, leading to a series of crises and sporadic outbreaks of violence in the run-up to World War II. Although war and the genocide against Europe's Jews fundamentally changed the future plans for the region, there is a strong view that the roadmap for a Jewish state was already in place, not least expressed in the notorious Balfour Declaration of 1917.

At the heart of the conflict, at least in the run-up to the foundation of the state of Israel in 1948, were several issues: Jewish immigration into Palestine, the issue of land transfer from Palestinian into Jewish hands, and the rights of the indigenous, that is, the Palestinian Arab majority population. The change in demographics, accelerated by the Nazi persecution of the Jews in the 1930s and the ensuing genocidal policies and practices during the Second World War, together with increasing Palestinian frustration, led to serious violent conflict both between Palestinian Arabs and Jews and with the British. As pointed out by Milton-Edwards (2009), the shift in world power away from the European players Britain and France and towards the United States and the Soviet Union hastened the process of British withdrawal. Moreover, the nature of this withdrawal was said to be typical of British colonial policy: partition.[20]

What, then, were the main features of the partition of Palestine? Most obviously, the dividing up of territory into Jewish and Palestinian lands, leading to the foundation of Israel as a Jewish state. At one level, Israel can be described as a modern liberal democracy, with a free press, regular and fair elections, and personal liberties. These key features, however, are mediated by the theological subtext of the Israeli state, with implications for those Israeli citizens who are not Jewish, for Palestinians who fled the territory of what today is Israel, as well as for secular Jewish citizens of the state of Israel. Importantly, the self-consciously Jewish character has key implications for the configuration of Israeli citizenship. One of its features is the 'Law of Return', passed in 1950, which declares Israel as a homeland for all Jews, no matter where they live or what other cultural or historical attachments they may have. Controversially, this right to return is not extended to Palestinians who fled Palestinian territory during the violent turmoil of the immediate post-war years (or who were driven from their home by armed Jewish groups); neither does it apply to those Palestinians living in Israel today, who are not Israeli citizens even though they may be born in Israel.

How does Butler envisage forms of cohabitation that are capable of addressing competing claims? As she puts it, what kind of polity would honour a diverse range of political claims? With respect to Israel-Palestine and despite her acknowledgement of her own Jewish formation, Butler categorically refutes Zionist solutions to the problem of cohabitation. Again, Butler returns to Arendt's position (and others similar to Arendt), which opposed a two-state solution and advocated a form of federation capable of accommodating plurality and diversity. In *Parting Ways* (2012a), Butler revisits Arendt's critique of the nation state and adds to Arendt's evolving analysis of Zionism and her critique of the partition of Palestine. Butler is essentially in agreement with Arendt's critique of the nation state as articulated in *The Origins of Totalitarianism* ([1951] 1976), and she connects this critique more widely with the critique of nationalism and communitarianism. In their place, Butler stresses Arendt's emphasis on heterogeneity, plurality and unwilled proximity leading to cohabitation and, ultimately, a federated polity based on equal citizenship. Crucially, Butler delineates Arendt's critique of the nation state and her endorsement of a new polity out of a Jewish pursuit of justice, derived from the experience of the Nazi genocide. Such justice, following Butler's reading of Arendt, must apply to all and not just to Jews.

A further, mainly implicit, source of Butler's account of coalitional politics is grounded in her recent engagement with the work of Arendt. It is in *Parting Ways: Jewishness and the Critique of Zionism* that Butler develops the theme of coalition in a new direction (and my own thoughts on this are very tentative). Drawing on Arendt's coverage of the Eichmann trial, Butler develops an account of the unchosen character of inclusive and plural cohabitation. At the core of this account lies her emphasis on exile and diaspora, from which she asserts the importance of establishing an ethical relation to the other. While the focus of the discussion in *Parting Ways* lies with Butler's reading of Zionism and her critique of Israeli state violence, it is the emphasis on unchosen cohabitation—on the fact that, as Arendt states, we cannot choose with whom we inhabit the earth—that provides a further grounding for such an ethical imperative for coalitional politics.

Of further significance is Butler's reading of Arendt's critique of human rights, understood as anchored in essentially unenforceable international agreements. As Butler argues, human rights become anchored in a social ontology, where the right to have rights and the right to belong is guaranteed by humanity. Such guarantee is contingent upon human plurality, that is, upon the existence of others who guarantee my persistence; it also challenges metaphysical conceptions of bare life. As Butler argues, '[t]he rightless and stateless are maintained in conditions of political destitution, especially by forms of military power. And, even when their lives are destroyed, those deaths remain political' (*PW*, 150).

Following Butler's reading of Arendt, Arendt opposes the homogeneity of the nation state because it excludes those who do not belong to the nation. Instead, the state should protect the heterogeneity and plurality of its populations. Arendt's insistence on protecting plurality, according to Butler, is both historical, derived from the historical emergence of the nation state in the nineteenth century, and ontological, conceived as the precondition of all political life. Arendt's conclusion, Butler states, is that any attempt to eradicate plurality is potentially genocidal (*PW*, 100).

Butler offers a more detailed analysis of cohabitation in a further consideration of Arendt, this time of Arendt's coverage of the Eichmann trial

([1963b] 2006b). As is well known, one of the key charges Arendt puts to Eichmann is his participation in genocidal actions that, in Arendt's view, aim to determine who is entitled to inhabit the earth. For Arendt, unchosen-ness, including unchosen proximity, is the basis for cohabitation.

The key idea that Butler borrows from Arendt and that influences the development of her own line of thinking is plurality. Let's unpack this a little further. As Butler argues in her discussion of Arendt in *Parting Ways* (2012a) (and as she has previously outlined in *Giving an Account of Oneself* (2005)), sociality (which is implicitly linked with plurality) precedes the capacity for address, and she concludes that 'the dialogue that I am is not finally separable from the plurality that makes me possible' (*PW*, 173). If my existence and persistence is dependent upon the existence and persistence of others, including those who are unwilled, Butler concludes that it becomes an ethical obligation, not least towards my own persistence, to preserve the other. Butler anchors the obligation towards cohabitation in the precariousness of being; she concludes that 'vulnerability to destruction by others follows from all modes of political and social interdependency and constitutes a demand on all political forms' (*PW*, 174).

Of importance to my discussion is how the ethical obligation to protect plurality has implications for the positioning in relation to sovereignty. Drawing on Butler's work, I want to tentatively suggest a shift from pluralism, understood as group-based politics, towards plurality, understood as a configuration of shifting alliances and coalitions. As Butler argues, partly as a way of further developing Arendt, plurality disrupts sovereignty, dispersing it into federal forms (*PW*, 174). This claim in turn configures her further thinking on Israel-Palestine and the way she views the role of international law. Building on her reading of the Goldstone Report,[21] Butler makes a case for the relevance of international law as a law that supersedes all national law, and that, moreover, provides legal protection to those populations who are not currently protected by state law, such as refugees and the stateless.

BUTLER'S COSMOPOLITAN SENTIMENTS

In this final section, I consider how Butler's political philosophy can be located within contemporary debates on cosmopolitanism. Utilizing some of her key assertions regarding the relational and ek-static structure of the subject, I propose to read Butler's political philosophy as a variation on cosmopolitan thinking. This claim requires some justification, not least because Butler does not present a detailed exposition of her views on cosmopolitanism, neither does she speak directly to the wider debates on cosmopolitanism (see Brassett 2008, 322). Her implicit challenge to the presuppositions of the natural law tradition, which continues to exert a significant influence on modern cosmopolitan thought, also makes her an unlikely candidate for cosmopolitanism. However, following Brassett (2010), I want to suggest that Butler displays what he terms 'cosmopolitan sentiment'. Such cosmopolitan sentiment is said to emerge out of Butler's concern with the politics of vulnerability and her broader commitments to global ethics (see also McRobbie 2006). To this reading I would like to add that this politics of vulnerability is underwritten by Butler's assertions regarding the relational and ek-static structure of the subject and by her (Levinasian) claims about the obligations and responsibilities towards others. A further significant element of Butler's cosmopolitan sentiment is her allusion to the existence and the creation of global communities that transcend the legal and physical boundaries of the nation state.

To further contextualize Butler's position within cosmopolitanism, I draw on Fine's (2007) helpful distinction between 'cosmopolitan outlook' and 'cosmopolitan condition'. While the cosmopolitan outlook according to Fine constitutes an interpretive moment, a way of seeing the world, the idea of cosmopolitan condition articulates the social reality belonging to our world (134). I believe that Butler's post-9/11 writings fit both depictions: her political philosophy of the subject, her persistent call to attend to global conditions of precariousness and precarity, her consideration of war and global conditions of violence, and her attention to the geopolitical framing of civilizational temporality all make up Butler's cosmopolitan sentiment. In the remainder of this section, I want to return to a theme I already addressed earlier in this chapter. This is the significance accorded to law in Butler's recent work. I begin with a brief overview of some of the key elements of the current work produced on cosmopolitanism. What interests me particularly, though, is the way that Butler takes up the Kantian idea of law (see Kant 1993), which she radicalizes. Overall, I argue that Butler's cosmopolitanism is grounded in her idea of global responsibility and her assertion of global interdependency, leading to what I term Butler's 'ek-static' cosmopolitanism.

The idea of cosmopolitanism, as is well known, is commonly traced back to the political philosophy of antiquity, specifically to the ideas of the Cynics and the Stoics in ancient Greece and to Cicero and Seneca in ancient Rome. Notwithstanding differences between different ancient articulations of cosmopolitanism (I allude to these briefly below), their shared concern is the tension between the conventional and particularistic obligations towards the polis and the natural and universal obligations towards humankind. The idea of cosmopolitanism is best captured with the often-quoted assertion, ascribed to the Cynic Diogenes, 'I am a citizen of the world'. Yet what precisely this citizenship of the world is supposed to signify has been the subject of much debate. Although often interpreted as a call for the institutionalization of citizenship at the global level (and subsequently endorsed or rejected on the basis of this understanding), there are other ways of defining cosmopolitanism. For example, Kleingeld and Brown (2006) distinguish institutionalized forms of political cosmopolitanism from economic, cultural, and moral cosmopolitanism. Whereas economic cosmopolitanism is said to capture the idea of a global market, cultural cosmopolitanism articulates the importance of shared or universal values over and above the existence of particularistic cultural attachments. All forms of cosmopolitanism share the view that human flourishing benefits from global interaction.

Of interest to my discussion are political and moral cosmopolitanism, and I discuss both in turn. As I already have intimated, political cosmopolitanism, broadly conceived, refers to the creation of global institution with responsibility for organising collective global life. Amongst the advocates of political cosmopolitanism there is some dispute as to whether such institutions should evolve out of existing states and/or operate alongside or through existing states, or whether we should strive towards the abolition of the state system and create something akin to a world government. The United Nations system would be an example of the first kind, while the European Union comes closer to the creation of political authority that, at times, replaces the authority of national states. Regardless of the nuances and differences within political cosmopolitanism, what informs this position is the imperative that global cooperation is important and intrinsically valuable, underpinned by the idea that our obligations transcend the boundaries of national states or cultural communities. It is this latter position that connects political cosmopolitanism with moral cosmopolitanism, which stresses the ethical obligations we have towards (distant) others. Moreover, both political and moral cosmopolitanism share together with cultural cosmopolitanism the conviction of the existence of a shared humanity. In this respect, the term 'moral' cosmopolitanism is misleading insofar as both political and cultural cosmopolitanism articulate strong moral positions. This moral position, broadly conceived, consists of our obligation to help those in need, although there is some dispute as to whether this obligation increases with the proximity of others to our own lives.

Fine (2007) distinguishes between cosmopolitan democracy, which seeks to create institutions that reflect the voices of individuals on a global scale, a global civil society approach, which celebrates decentralized networks, NGOs and social movements, and a cosmopolitan law approach, which seeks to regulate relations between states and aims to back up international law with coercive practices (expressed, in different ways, by Rawls (1999) and Habermas (2001; 2006)). As Fine (2007) argues, 'new cosmopolitanism is not so much about the displacement of the national by the transnational and thence the international but rather about the 'fit' between these levels of political community. It is about the necessity of enlarging our political imagination so as to be able to break free from the fetters of nationalism politically and methodologically' (56).

At first glance, Butler's location within this taxonomy seems heavily weighted towards moral cosmopolitanism. As I have argued throughout this book, her recent work is peppered with references to interdependency, obligations, and responsibility. This moral dimension, as I have demonstrated, arises out of her claim of shared human precariousness, which for her not just implies vulnerability towards the actions of others but also entails an ethical obligation towards the creation of sustainable and liveable lives for others. Those others, as we have seen, are not necessarily bound to us by proximity, kinship, or cultural affiliation, but instead include, at least potentially, the anonymous other who may make a claim upon us. Thus, if global responsibility arises out of the ontological condition of precariousness and its unequal global distribution, it becomes heightened during war. This claim is one of the key themes of *Frames of War* (2009a), where Butler further develops her discussion set out in *Precarious Life* (2004b). Butler asks three key questions: first, what is our responsibility towards those we do not know (*FW*, 36)? What happens to the 'we' during times of war, and how can we reconsider the 'we' in global terms (*FW*, 38)?

She ponders these inherently ethical questions with reference to the notion of grievability: according to her, only those lives that are grievable are considered valuable. The condition of precarity, however, and specifically the precarity instituted by war divides the world into grievable and ungrievable lives. Moreover, those who are considered ungrievable are also conceived of as a threat to life itself, that is, as a threat to liveable lives. This differentiation maps upon the civilizational discourses that underpin the global war on terror, where Muslim populations are regarded as a threat. The discursive division into grievable and ungrievable lives is underpinned, furthermore, by a 'heightened nationalism' (*FW*, 42) that works hand in hand with war. While war is directly responsible for the destruction of those abjected populations, it also aims to destruct the vulnerability and interdependency of human life. As Butler argues with reference to the US foreign policy under the Bush administration, war and heightened nationalism shore up a sense of invincibility by insisting on the importance of securing territorial borders and boundaries. This effort, Butler argues, does not just run counter to the violation of boundaries and borders, and with it, of sovereignty that the US engages in. She also raises an important philosophical objection: as she argues, 'war seeks to deny the ongoing and irrefutable ways in which we are all subject to one another' (*FW*, 43). Thus, life persists only under conditions of interdependency, which transcends the boundaries of the national subject and the nation state.

Before I develop Butler's recent insights further, I want to attend to the debate surrounding the work of Martha C. Nussbaum, to which Butler contributed. In the lead essay of *For Love of Country: Debating the Limits of Patriotism. Martha C. Nussbaum with Respondents* (see Cohen 1996), Nussbaum (1996) maps her arguments for cosmopolitanism and against a narrowly defined nationalistic patriotism. Cosmopolitanism, as Nussbaum suggests, is not just empirically adequate in that it responds to the reality of an interdependent world with shared problems; it is, crucially, morally good in that it articulates our shared humanity and ensuing moral obligations. Arguing strongly against forms of civic education that are restricted to the dissemination of patriotic values, Nussbaum advocates instead what she terms an 'international basis for political emotion and concern' (4).

Considering Nussbaum's (1999) stinging attack on Butler in her article in *The New Republic,* it seems puzzling to see how this appeal chimes strongly with Butler's recent invocation of affective global structures and conditions of global responsibility, given the seemingly antagonistic positions represented by Butler and Nussbaum. Butler's response to Nussbaum's endorsement of cosmopolitanism elides the issue of cosmopolitanism, focussing instead on universalism and practices of cultural translation, ideas that come to occupy an increasingly important role in her work (I addressed these issues in Chapter 3). To recapitulate briefly, Butler challenges the claim, which she ascribes to Nussbaum, that the meaning of universalism can be defined in advance and subsequently adapted to the particularistic conditions of local cultures. Against Nussbaum, she argues that the very meaning of the universal is culturally (and historically) variable (Butler 1996, 45). This constitutive 'failure' to define the meaning once and for all, rather than undermining prospects for the universal, is actually the condition for its articulation, contestation, and re-articulation. Such resignification, as we have seen, requires the work of cultural translation, itself marked by Butler as a democratic practice, which will keep the concept open for future political practices.

This implicit connection between Butler's discussion of universality and her treatment of cosmopolitanism is not surprising, given that both aim at a global horizon where decisions over responsibility, action, and moral obligations are seemingly delimited from the constraints of culture and/or state. What, though, does Butler say about cosmopolitanism? I have already alluded to Butler's cosmopolitan sentiments, essentially the articulation of a global ethics developed out of the claim of precariousness. Thus, Butler pays little attention to questions of international institutional design of a cosmopolitan democracy, but she repeatedly invokes the importance of our ethical obligation towards others. Crucially, such ethical obligations include the responsibility to work within the framework of international institutions. For example, this invocation features prominently in her critique of US foreign policy towards the Middle East, specifically in her criticism of the Bush administration's disregard for an international consensus on Iraq. Cosmopolitan sentiments also infuse her discussion of the treatment of prisoners and detainees held at Guantánamo Bay and Abu Ghraib. While not arguing for a world state or world government, Butler insists on the importance of international law as the guiding tool for governmental actions. The importance she accords to international law is further underpinned in her engagement with bi-nationalism. She conjectures, with reference to the Goldstone Report (see above), whether international law should protect all populations, including citizens of nation states, as well as those without ties of citizenship, such as refugees. She also asks, 'can we think about bi-nationalism, in this regard, as basing itself on an ethos of international law that does not discriminate among the claims of the refugee, whether contained under conditions of occupation or decontained in exile?' (*PW,* 179).

The importance which Butler accords to international law lends itself to further comparisons with the work of another writer, Seyla Benhabib. As is well known, Benhabib and Butler have occupied different positions in the feminist 'theory wars' of the 1990s, and they have articulated competing positions on the female subject, agency, and feminist politics (see Butler 1995). While they both remain attached to different philosophical ideas, with Benhabib arguing within a broad Habermasian framework and Butler arguing from a broad post-structuralist position, they have both articulated overlapping positions on international politics. In a recent article, Benhabib (2009) defends the importance and value of international law, specifically human rights law, over and above claims derived from claims to sovereignty (she distinguishes here between ethno-nationalist and democratic sovereigntist claims). She criticizes claims made from a position of sovereignty because they fail to consider how cosmopolitan norms, especially universal human rights, empower local movements. Benhabib is acutely aware that cosmopolitan intents can turn, as she puts it, into 'hegemonic nightmares' (695), and she references the neo-colonial and civilizational ethos embodied in recent incitements to intervene in domestic conflicts. This caution chimes strongly with Butler's own critique of the civilizational narratives that frame the norms which, in turn, come to decide politics. Yet Benhabib (2009) (like Butler) is not willing to give up on cosmopolitan aspirations, and to further this aim she focuses on 'a *family* of global norms' (695; emphasis in original) that in her view are supported widely. These global norms, according to Benhabib, are cosmopolitan, and they are embodied in the various treaties and covenants that make up the international human rights regime. Central to her discussion is the concept of 'jurisgenerativity'. This term, which she borrows from Robert Cover (1983), refers to the ability of the law to generate normative guidelines even where these are not (yet) enshrined in formal law-making. What is so remarkable about Benhabib's argument is the way it mirrors the key assertions of Butler's claims regarding the performative power of the speech act. As Benhabib (2009) further asserts, '[t]ransnational law creates wider and deeper interdependencies among nations, pushing them farther and farther toward structures of global governance' (701).

While the emphasis on the relevance of international law to Butler's recent work is a key element of my interpretation of her writings, it is equally important to acknowledge the affective aspects of Butler's cosmopolitanism. In his analysis of the aftermath of 9/11, James Brassett (2010) refers to 'cosmopolitan sentiments' to articulate possible responses to the trauma of 9/11. Although Butler does not feature prominently in his discussion (his focus lies with the work of David Held), I want to suggest that his reference to cosmopolitan sentiments is an apt description for Butler's contribution to the wider cosmopolitan debate. As we have seen in previous chapters (see in particular Chapters 1 and 2), Butler's wider ontological commitments to the ideas of precariousness and vulnerability are also meant to initiate a dialogue on global politics above and beyond their narrow implications for a philosophy of the subject. As I outlined there, in *Precarious Life* (2004b) Butler laments the Bush administration's failure to reflect on the enabling constraints of global interdependence and the ethical obligations that arise out of them. *Frames of War* (2009a) develops this point further by reflecting on the differential global distribution of empathy and affective responses to suffering, by exposing how war and violence seek to undermine sensate responses to vulnerability, and by insisting on the development of forms of global community. As Butler argues, '[t]he recognition of shared precariousness introduces strong normative commitments of equality and invites a more robust universalizing of rights' (*FW*, 29–9).

Although Butler does not offer much in terms of precise political claims for a future global politics, she provides a sustained and convincing critique of those types of international orientation that remain anchored in conceptions of state sovereignty and that are attached to notions of boundaries and global competition. This critique of global politics is coupled with the aspiration for a global ethics that takes seriously the notion of interdependency and articulates strong claims regarding global responsibility. Interdependency and responsibility are not primarily instrumental strategies deployed by a rational self concerned with its own survival; rather, what Butler wishes to stress is how the very notion of the self is tied up with the existence of others. As we have seen, these claims are anchored in her insistence on our ethical obligations towards others, which in turn build upon her ontological assertions regarding the precariousness and vulnerability of (human) life.

As I have demonstrated, the object or target of much of Butler's critical reflections remains the state. Throughout my book, I have demonstrated that she develops critical positions in relation to state violence, including the use of torture and war and the treatment of political opponents, and with respect to the role of international law, including and in particular human rights law. And while not all of these positions are always fully spelt out or developed, they are anchored in a philosophy of the human that takes seriously global interdependence and responsibility. Significantly, what Butler's writings on these issues point to is her role as a critic and public intellectual, and it is to this aspect that I turn to in the conclusion.

NOTES

1. There are some scattered references to anarchism in some of her recent work, emerging in particular out of her reading of Benjamin, and it will be interesting to see if this is further developed in future work (see Butler 2012a).
2. For a more positive assessment see Loizidou (2007).
3. For a more recent account of the waning of sovereignty in the context of the policing of national borders see Wendy Brown (2010).
4. 'Words that wound' is also the title of one MacKinnon's books (1996). On Butler's treatment of resignification see Lloyd (2009) and Schippers (2009).

5. For a sympathetic consideration of *Excitable Speech* see Smith (2001), who further explores the linkage between language and hate speech regulation on the one hand, and socio-economic issues on the other hand.

6. For a more detailed consideration see for example Lloyd (2007) and Passavant and Dean (2001).

7. Possibly in response to some of her critics as well as building on a more sustained consideration of Foucault's notion of governmentality in *Precarious Life* (2004b), she introduces semantic changes, substituting references to 'the state' with references to 'the executive' or 'executive branch'.

8. Following Arendt, she introduces another semantic innovation with her reference to 'polity', which comes to replace references to 'the state'.

9. Although Butler's treatment of sovereignty speaks to the global condition, she does not engage with the key texts of international relations or international political theory. Perhaps because of this lack of dialogue, it is not surprising that her treatment of the topic lacks some of the detailed attention that it receives in international theory, broadly conceived. See for example Krasner (1999), whose study of sovereignty as 'organized hypocrisy' (this is also the title of his book) distinguishes between four types of sovereignty: international legal sovereignty, Westphalian sovereignty, domestic sovereignty, and interdependence sovereignty. Notwithstanding my reservations regarding Krasner's account, his distinction provides for a more subtle analysis of the workings and failures of sovereignty at national and international levels. For poststructuralist perspectives that draw on the work of Agamben and Foucault see the contributions to Edkins, Pin-Fat and Shapiro (2004).

10. One of the earlier versions of this essay was published in the journal *The Nation* under the title 'Guantánamo Limbo' (see Butler 2002b).

11. At the time of writing this chapter, the inmates held at Guantánamo prepared for Ramadan. While the US government hinted at the prospect of complying with the religious observances for those inmates on hunger strike, it would not give an absolute assurance.

12. For a detailed exposition of Butler's discussion of governmentality see Loizidou (2007).

13. See Chomsky's (2000) depiction of rogue states as those who do not consider themselves to be bound by international law.

14. Recall that in *Giving an Account of Oneself* (2005), Butler articulates the concept of ethical violence along similar lines. It is an ethos that refuses to become past and has become anachronistic, and that inserts itself into the present as violence (*GAO*, 5). Further below in the text, I attend to Butler's most recent invocation of international law in the context of her discussion of the Goldstone Report on the conflict in Gaza (see United Nations Human Rights Council 2009).

15. See Chapter 3 and the conclusion for a consideration of the term 'terrorism'.

16. In fact, I would suggest that Butler's reading of Arendt is so significant that it merits detailed attention in a separate outlet. I am currently preparing such a work.

17. On the issue of minority rights see Fink (2000).

18. On the wider issue of border control and its relationship to sovereignty see Wendy Brown (2010).

19. The song can be accessed on youTube (www.youtube.com/watch?v=Baf7nm YaTDw; accessed 22 July 2013).

20. Only two members of the newly established Security Council of the equally newly established United Nations voted against the partition of Palestine. These members were Yugoslavia, a multi-ethnic and multinational federated state, and, crucially, India, which had just undergone its own partition in the

wake of British withdrawal and had first-hand experience of the violence that accompanied its own large-scale population transfer. See Milton-Edwards (2009). For a brief reflection on India see also Butler's discussion in *Who Sings the Nation-State?* (2007a).

21. See United Nations Human Rights Council (2009) *Report of the United Nations Fact-Finding Mission on the Gaza Conflict. Human Rights in Palestine and Other Occupied Arab Territories.* (www2.ohchr.org/english/bodies/hrcouncil/docs/12session/A-HRC-12–48.pdf).

Conclusion
Critique and the Public Intellectual

[E]very critical question is initially rogue in relation to existing conventions.

(Butler 2009b)

[M]aybe one of the jobs of theory or philosophy is to elevate principles that seem impossible, or that have the status of the impossible, to stand by them and will them, even when it looks highly unlikely that they'll never be realised. But that's ok, it's a service.

(Butler 2013b)

Three aims have motivated my writing of this book: first, I wanted to elucidate Butler's contribution to a mode of political philosophising that transcends the concerns of national or state boundaries, and in doing so to assess her contribution to the emerging field of international political philosophy; second, I sought to establish the significance of Butler's contribution to public political discourse beyond the academy; and finally, I wanted to frame Butler's political philosophising within the context of the conceptual vectors of relationality, ek-stasis, and dispossession on the one hand and liveability on the other hand. As I suggested, it is prudent to read Butler's scholarly work as deeply enmeshed with the concerns of politics. Further, I argued in the introduction that this intrinsic link allows for a reading of Butler's political philosophy through the lens of existential phenomenology, addressing questions of liveability and persistence. I conclude my assessment of Butler by attending to this enmeshment between scholarly work and public engagement. The lens through which I construe this relationship is the notion of critique, which plays a key role in Butler's work, and which, I want to suggest, continues to guide her political-philosophical investigations as well as her interventions in public debate. To unravel the significance of critique, I turn to three essays: her engagement with Foucault's concept of critique (Butler 2002a; see Foucault [1994] 2000, 2002), and two later papers (Butler 2006g, 2009b).

WHAT IS CRITIQUE?

In *Excitable Speech,* Butler laments that 'we live in a time in which intellectual work is demeaned in public life, and anti-intellectualism marks a substantial part of the climate within the academy' (*ES*, 162). Although the theme of critique runs through Butler's work, I focus on three of Butler's essays (2002a, 2006g, 2009b), each of which makes critique the central aspect of its investigation and relates the practice of critique to its role in the academy. I begin with an exposition of Butler's essay (2002a) on Foucault and his concept of critique. In this essay, Butler distinguishes between the critique of a position and critique as a generalized practice that builds on the activity of questioning. Butler's aim is to assert a notion of critique with 'strong normative commitments' (214), and she contrasts this aim with a Habermasian position, which in her view remains uncritical in relation to its own normative commitments and standards. I want to suggest that it is out of this challenge to Habermas that the key objective of Butler's conception of critique emerges: this is the critique of norms and the normative standards that come to regulate lives, academic work (see below), and political practice and aspirations. Continuing her close reading of Foucault's lecture, Butler links the practice of critique with de-subjugation from the norms that come to form the subject. If norms, as I suggested in the first two chapters, simultaneously enable and constrain the subject, then critique extends the prospect for liveability by entering the subject into a critical relationship with the norms that have come to form it.

Critique, as Butler suggests, asks not merely what I can be but also what I can know. It is this context of epistemology that receives attention in a later essay, on academic freedom in the context of post-9/11 politics. Butler's essay (2006g) is a contribution to a collection of papers that explore the prospects of academic freedom; specifically, her paper responds to another contributor, Robert Post, who argues for the preservation of academic freedom within the institutional arrangement of the academy. If the essay on Foucault and critique maps the parameters of Butler's conception critique, her later essay locates critique as practice within the confines of the academy (at least on the surface). To fully appreciate the motivation of Butler's engagement, it is crucial to outline the context—the temporality—of her intervention. The context, the time, of this critique is that of an academy under pressure, where questions of academic freedom and the policing and regulation of certain subject areas, such as Middle Eastern Studies,[1] the intrusion of Christian fundamentalist approaches to teaching and research in science, or the allocation of funding and granting of tenure, are intrinsically linked to questions of power and critique. Butler is in broad agreement with Post's stress on the importance of academic freedom, even on the role that scholarly review plays in the regulation and assessment of academic work, but she objects fundamentally to the portrayal of scholarly norms as beyond contest and the connection he makes between academic freedom and the upholding of scholarly norms. Her reply to Post operates at two related levels: these are, first, the role of norms in scholarly work and their relationship to critique, and second, the role of freedom in the relationship between scholarly work and extra-mural activities.

Against Post, Butler claims that scholarly norms should not, and in fact cannot, lie beyond scholarly debate and inquiry. This emphasis on the critique of norms does not equate, though, with the abolition of norms or the questioning of the existence of norms. As Butler (2006g) argues, '[t]o question existing norms is not the same as questioning the existence of norms in general or calling for a postnormative mode of academic inquiry' (114). Thus, the contest over norms—to be precise, the contestation over which norms apply—lies at the heart of academic inquiry. In this respect, academic inquiry becomes a permanent critique that can never finally be put to rest (at least with respect to the humanities and social sciences), and that is the driving force of scholarly innovation and invention. Out of this insight Butler (2006c) links her emphasis on critique with ethics: in the context of academic work, ethics should be understood as a 'disposition' (121) that we bring to academic work. It keeps us open to the contest over norms, disputes over textual interpretation or the use of methods, or the boundaries between disciplines. Furthermore, such ethics nurture a form of humility, which, in Butler's (2006g) view, is 'conditioned by an insight into the instability and internal variance of professional norms' (123; see also Rushing 2010). Butler concludes that the protection of academic freedom is not merely an academic matter, rather it relates to universities' wider function in the provision of a public service that entails public debate and discussion, and it is in relation to this point that Butler develops her argument further.

While the dispute over the role and status of professional norms could be construed as an internal academic matter, such compartmentalization is no longer possible in a climate where public bodies and private funders stipulate, regulate, and police scholarly activities. Butler's concern regarding the watering down of academic freedom and her criticism of the regulation and policing of scholarly work by government bodies takes aim at legislation introduced in the US, such as the International Studies in Higher Education Act, which has as its objective to study, monitor, and appraise funded activities. As Butler contends, this act, operating in conjunction with the Patriot Act, has created a climate where scholarly work becomes de-legitimized, where career progression is denied, and where individuals and their work are labelled as 'terrorist' depending on their scholarly undertaking or their wider public engagement activities. One of the examples she cites refer to stipulations in the Ford Foundation's funding guidelines, which issue a ban on anyone seeking to destroy a state. Butler polemically ponders whether John Locke, Desmond Tutu, Nelson Mandela, or indeed Socrates would have qualified for funding if current criteria apply. For her, the label 'terrorist' is void of any critical reflection on context, creating instead 'a clamp on our normative aspirations for political life' (Butler 2006g, 139). As Butler concludes, academic freedom and the context in which academic freedom flourishes exceeds the boundaries of the academy and instead stretches into the wider public realm, requiring a critical reflection on norms and their formation.

In a later essay, Butler (2009b) returns to the theme of critique and the academy, this time by turning to Foucault's conception of critique, and also with reference to the work of Kant. The relationship between academic work and public engagement activities, which occupied her in the essay from 2006, continues to frame her discussion. As she stresses, the critical facets of academic work relate to questions of political dissent (Butler 2009b, 775). It is in this constellation that the academy plays a crucial role in speaking truth to power, or rather, in Butler's words, where critique becomes a form of objection to claims (in her view illegitimate) by public and governmental authorities. Thus, academic freedom is essential to freedom beyond the academy, and to elucidate her points further, Butler harnesses Kantian ideas. Although she objects to elements of Kant's thinking, specifically his dichotomy of public and private reason, she hopes to salvage Kant's thinking for today by translating Kant's language into our own.

Crucially, for Butler (2009b), critique is not 'nay-saying'. As she argues, 'the no delineates and animates a new set of positions for the subject; it is inventive' (792). Such invention, as she hopes, will produce a less governed self: in a significant aside, relegated to a footnote, Butler maps her distinction from Foucault (n12). As she argues there, self-crafting does not happen alone, it requires sociality. Thus, she encourages us to imagine critique as happening 'in the midst of social life, the very scene of being impinged upon' (789n12). This crafting in the midst of others, which emerges out of a critique of a particular mode of being governed, is essential in order to achieve recognition.

THE PUBLIC SPHERE AND POLITICS IN THE STREET

In the essay 'Is Judaism Zionism?', one of her contributions to *The Power of Religion in the Public Sphere*, Butler (2011d) professes not to be a scholar of public life. Yet, the concept of the public is significant to her discussion, and it surfaces in various manifestations, such as public life, public realm, public sphere, and public space. As I highlighted in Chapter 4, Butler links the development of the public sphere with the emergent hegemony of Protestantism and its subsequent diffusion and concealment as secularism. She returns to a consideration of the concept of the public in another recent essay, 'Bodies in Alliance and the Politics of the Street' (Butler 2011c), where she elaborates on the concept of the public space by relating it to a discussion of bodily appearance. This focus on 'the public' also occupies my final remarks, where I attend to Butler's role as a public intellectual.

The broader context of Butler's essay lies in the protest movements in the Arab world, the movements for immigrant rights, and the protest against precarization of workers (and presumably the activities of the Occupy movement). It also constitutes an opportunity for yet another engagement with the work of Hannah Arendt. Although Butler challenges what she considers as Arendt's problematic distinction between public and private realm, with its gendered subtext and the relegation of politics to the public, she builds on Arendt's performative account of the constitution for the public sphere, and she connects this account with some of her own questions concerning the political nature of marginalized groups and the concept of life. It is precisely because Butler is attentive to the important and indeed transformative actions of the 'socially dead', those without recognition, that she insists that '[t]o be outside established and legitimate political structures is still to be saturated in power relations, and this saturation is the point of departure for a theory of the political that includes dominant and subjugated forms' (Butler 2011c, 4). As she argues, furthermore, collective action emerges even from sites of abandonment, and it emerges regardless of prior legitimization. Thus, the performative nature of the collective actions of the socially dead brings into being and generates political transformation.

Three further aspects are relevant to Butler's discussion. These are (1) the formation of political coalitions or alliances, (2) the corporeal dimension of such forms of politics and its transformation of the relationship between public and private, and (3) the role played by space, or location. Although Butler fears hostility towards coalitional politics in Northern European countries, centring on the alleged tension between conceptions of (universalist) feminism and (Muslim) religious particularity (see Chapter 4), she does not detect such compartmentalization of progressive struggles in other parts of her world (she cites Istanbul and Johannesburg as counter-examples). For Butler, the paradigmatic example of 'bodies in alliance' is that of Tahrir Square in Cairo. Confronted with a repressive political regime and its institutions of repression embodied in the police and the military, the protesters encompassed a whole spectrum of Egyptian society, ranging from liberals, secularists, and Christians to the religiously conservative. Furthermore, the practice of protest and its use of space transcended the dichotomy between the public and the private. As Butler observes, the use of a square not only as a location for protest but also as a space where lives were lived, and where various bodily needs were attended to, questions the (Arendtian) distinction between public and private and the way it is overlain with gendered conceptions.

Thus, it brought to the fore the embodied nature of politics. As Butler (2011c) argues, '[f]or politics to take place, the body must appear' (3). This appearance, the essentially corporeal manifestation of politics, whether through speeches or participating in demonstrations, or by putting one's body on the line in confrontation with the police, requires attention and care to bodily needs, and she argues for the need for sustaining relationships that underpin such bodily politics:

> [T]hose most urgent and non-volitional dimensions of our lives, which include hunger and the need for shelter, medical care, and protection from violence, natural or humanly imposed, are crucial to politics. We cannot presume the enclosed and well-fed space of the Polis where all the material needs are somehow being taken care of elsewhere by beings whose gender, race or status render them ineligible for public recognition. Rather, we have to not only bring the material urgencies of the body into the square, but make those needs central to the demands of politics.
>
> (Butler 2011c, 12)

Butler remains attuned to the pressing political issues and movements of our time. It is because of this attentiveness that she has such a wide appeal beyond the academy and that she can now be regarded as a global public intellectual.[2] I wish to end my book with a quote from Butler that in my view captures how politics could be, and how lives could be lived. As she argues, 'in politics, sometimes the thing that will never happen actually starts to happen. And there have to be people who hold out for that, and who accept that they are idealists and that they are operating on principle as opposed to realpolitik. If there were no such ideals then our entire political sensibility would be corrupted by this process' (Butler 2013b).

NOTES

1. Such policing of scholarly work has come to be associated with the activities of Campus Watch (see www.campus-watch.org/).
2. While these public engagements have further enhanced her standing as a public intellectual, they have also attracted fierce criticism and indeed venomous accusations and allegations, so much so that in a recent interview (Butler 2013b), Butler announced a cancellation of her speaking engagements for a season.

Bibliography

WORKS BY JUDITH BUTLER

1986. 'Sex and Gender in Simone de Beauvoir's *Second Sex*'. *Yale French Studies* 72: 35–49.

(1987) 1999. *Subjects of Desire: Hegelian Reflections in Twentieth-Century France*. New York: Columbia University Press.

1987. 'Variations on Sex and Gender: Beauvoir, Wittig and Foucault'. In *Feminism as Critique: Essays on the Politics of Gender in Late-Capitalist Societies*, edited by Seyla Benhabib and Drucilla Cornell, 128–142. Minneapolis: University of Minnesota Press.

1988. 'Performative Acts and Gender Constitution: An Essay in Phenomenology and Feminist Theory'. *Theatre Journal* 40 (4): 519–531.

1990. *Gender Trouble: Feminism and the Subversion of Identity*. New York and London: Routledge.

1992. 'Contingent Foundations: Feminism and the Question of "Postmodernism"'. In *Feminists Theorize the Political*, edited by Judith Butler and Joan W. Scott, 3–21. New York and London: Routledge.

1993. *Bodies that Matter: On the Discursive Limits of "Sex"*. New York and London: Routledge.

1995. *Feminist Contentions: A Philosophical Exchange*. With Seyla Benhabib, Drucilla Cornell, and Nancy Fraser. New York and London: Routledge.

1996. 'Universality in Culture'. In Cohen 1996, 45–52.

1997a. *Excitable Speech: A Politics of the Performative*. New York and London: Routledge.

1997b. *The Psychic Life of Power: Theories in Subjection*. Stanford: Stanford University Press.

1997c. 'Merely Cultural'. *Social Text* Fall/Winter: 265–277.

2000a. *Antigone's Claim: Kinship between Life and Death*. New York: Columbia University Press.

2000b. *Contingency, Hegemony, Universality: Contemporary Dialogues on the Left*. With Ernesto Laclau and Slavoj Žižek. London and New York: Verso.

2000c. 'Politics, Power and Ethics: A Discussion between Judith Butler and William Connolly'. *Theory and Event* 4 (2). http://muse.jhu.edu/journals/theory_and_event/toc/tae4.2.html (accessed 17 May 2011).

2000d. 'Ethical Ambivalence'. In *The Turn to Ethics*, edited by Marjorie Garber, Beatrice Hanssen, and Rebecca L. Walkowitz, 15–28. London and New York: Routledge.

2002a. 'What is Critique? An Essay on Foucault's Virtue'. In *The Political*, edited by David Ingram, 212–225. Malden and Oxford: Blackwell.

2002b. 'Guantánamo Limbo'. *The Nation* 274 (12): 20–23.
2003a. 'No, it's not anti-semitic'. *London Review of Books* 25 (16). 21 August (accessed 4 June 2004).
2003b. 'Beauvoir on Sade: Making Sexuality into an Ethic'. In *The Cambridge Companion to Simone de Beauvoir,* edited by Claudia Card, 168–188. Cambridge: Cambridge University Press.
2004a. *Undoing Gender.* London and New York: Routledge.
2004b. *Precarious Life: The Powers of Mourning and Violence.* London and New York: Verso.
2005. *Giving an Account of Oneself.* New York: Fordham University Press.
2006a. 'Critique, Coercion, and Sacred Life in Benjamin's "Critique of Violence"'. In Vries and Sullivan 2006, 201–219.
2006b. 'Violence, Non-Violence: Sartre on Fanon'. *Graduate Faculty Philosophy Journal* 27 (1): 3–24.
2006c. 'The Desire to Live: Spinoza's *Ethics* under Pressure'. In *Politics and the Passions, 1500–1850,* edited by Victoria Kahn, Neil Saccamano, and Daniela Coli, 111–130. Princeton: Princeton University Press.
2006d. 'Afterword'. *PMLA Special Issue: The Humanities in Human Rights: Critique, Language, Politics* 121 (5): 1658–1661.
2006e. 'Afterword'. In *Bodily Citations: Religion and Judith Butler,* edited by Ellen T. Armour and Susan M. St. Ville, 276–301. New York: Columbia University Press.
2006f. 'Hegel in France'. In *The Columbia History of Twentieth-Century French Thought,* edited by Lawrence D. Kritzman, 245–250. New York: Columbia University Press.
2006g. 'Academic Norms, Contemporary Challenges: A Reply to Robert Post on Academic Freedom'. In *Academic Freedom after September 11,* edited by Beshara Doumani, 107–142. New York: Zone Books.
2007a. *Who Sings the Nation-State? Language, Politics, Belonging.* With Gayatri Spivak. Oxford and New York: Seagull Books.
2007b. 'Reply from Judith Butler to Mills and Jenkins'. *differences: A Journal of Feminist Cultural Studies* 18 (2): 180–195.
2007c. '"Serious Innovation": A Conversation with Judith Butler.' In *A Companion to Lesbian, Gay, Bisexual, Transgender and Queer Studies,* edited by George E. Haggerty and Molly McGarry, 379–388. Malden and Oxford: Blackwell.
2007d. 'I Merely Belong to Them'. *London Review of Books* 29 (9): 10 May (accessed 4 March 2008).
2008. 'Taking Another's View: Ambivalent Implications'. In *Reification: A New Look at an Old Idea,* by Axel Honneth, edited by Martin Jay, 97–119. Oxford: Oxford University Press.
2009a. *Frames of War: When is Life Grievable?* London and New York: Verso.
2009b. 'Critique, Dissent, Disciplinarity'. *Critical Inquiry* 35 (Summer): 773–795.
2009c. 'Judith Butler with Sunaura Taylor: Interdependence'. In *Examined Life: Excursions with Contemporary Thinkers,* edited by Astra Taylor, 185–213. New York and London: The New Press.
2009d. 'The Sensibility of Critique: Response to Asad and Mahmood'. In *Is Critique Secular? Blasphemy, Injury, and Free Speech,* with Talal Asad, Wendy Brown, and Saba Mahmood, 101–136. Berkeley and London: University of California Press.
2009e. 'Antigone's Claim: A Conversation with Judith Butler'. *Theory & Event* 12 (1). http://muse.jhu.edu/journals/theory_and_event/toc/tae.12.1.html (accessed 9 May 2013).
2010. 'New Scenes of Vulnerability, Agency and Plurality: An Interview with Judith Butler'. *Theory, Culture & Society* 27 (1): 130–152.

2011a. 'There Are Some Muffins There If You Want. . . . A Conversation on Queerness, Precariousness, Binationalism, and BDS'. In *What Does a Jew Want? On Binationalism and other Specters*, edited by Udi Aloni, 204–227. New York: Columbia University Press.

2011b. 'Hannah Arendt's Death Sentences'. *Comparative Literature Studies* 48 (3): 280–295.

2011c. 'Bodies in Alliance and the Politics of the Street', *Transversal: #occupy and assemble*, no. 10, http://eipcp.net/transversal/1011/butler/en (accessed 20 October 2011).

2011d. 'Is Judaism Zionism?' In *The Power of Religion in the Public Sphere*. With Jürgen Habermas, Charles Taylor, and Cornel West, 70–91. New York: Columbia University Press.

2011e. 'Confessing a Passionate State . . . <<–Judith Butler im Interview'. *Feministische Studien* 2 (November): 196–205.

2011f. 'Who owns Kafka?' *London Review of Books* 33 (5). 3 March (accessed 20 October 2011).

2012a. *Parting Ways: Jewishness and the Critique of Zionism*. New York: Columbia University Press.

2012b. 'Recognition and Critique: An Interview with Judith Butler'. *Distinktion: Scandinavian Journal of Social Theory* 13 (1): 139–144.

2012c. 'Can One Lead a Good Life in a Bad Life? Adorno Prize Lecture'. *Radical Philosophy* 176: 9–18.

2013a. *Dispossession: The Performative in the Political*. With Athena Athanasiou. Cambridge: Polity Press.

2013b. 'Willing the Impossible: An Interview with Judith Butler'. *Transformation: Where love meets social justice*,www.opendemocracy.net/transformation/ ray-filar/willing-impossible-interview-with-judith-butler (accessed 25 July 2013).

OTHER WORKS

Abu-Lughod, Lila. 2002. 'Do Muslim Women Really Need Saving? Anthropological Reflections on Cultural Relativism and its Others'. *American Anthropologist* 104 (3): 783–790.

Agamben, Giorgio. 1998. *Homo Sacer: Sovereign Power and Bare Life*. Stanford: Stanford University Press.

———. 2005. *State of Exception*. Chicago and London: University of Chicago Press.

Ali, Suki. 2008. 'Troubling Times: A Comment on Judith Butler's "Sexual Politics, Torture and Secular Time"'. *The British Journal of Sociology* 59 (1): 35–39.

Allen, Amy. 2006. 'Dependency, Subordination and Recognition: On Judith Butler's Theory of Subjection'. *Continental Philosophy Review* 38 (3–4): 199–222.

Arendt, Hannah. 1945. 'Zionism Reconsidered'. *The Menorah Journal* 33 (2): 162–196.

———. (1951) 1976. *The Origins of Totalitarianism*. Orlando: Harcourt.

———. (1963a) 2006a. *On Revolution*. London: Penguin.

———. (1963b) 2006b. *Eichmann in Jerusalem: A Report on the Banality of Evil*. London: Penguin.

———. 2007. *The Jewish Writings*, edited by Jerome Kohn and Ron H. Feldman. New York: Schocken Books.

Armour, Ellen T., and Susan M. St. Ville, eds. 2006. *Bodily Citations: Religion and Judith Butler*. New York: Columbia University Press.

Arteel, Inge. 2011. 'Judith Butler and the Catachretic Human'. In *Towards a New Literary Humanism*, edited by Andy Mousley, 77–90. Basingstoke: Palgrave Macmillan.

Asad, Talal. 2007. *On Suicide Bombing*. New York: Columbia University Press.
———. 2009. *Is Critique Secular? Blasphemy, Injury, and Free Speech*. With Wendy Brown, Judith Butler, and Saba Mahmood. Berkeley and London: University of California Press.
———. 2010. 'Thinking about Terrorism and Just War'. *Cambridge Review of International Affairs* 23 (1): 3–24.
Austin, J. L. 1962. *How to Do Things with Words*. Oxford: Oxford University Press.
Barney, Darin. 2013. 'In Defense of Judith Butler', *Huffington Post*, 28 May 2013. www.huffingtonpost.ca/darin-barney/in-defense-of-judith-butler-mcgill-b-3346589.html (accessed 6 February 2014).
BBC Northern Ireland. 2012. *The Nolan Show*. https://audioboo.fm/boos/844506-lord-maginnis-interview-in-full-first-broadcast-on-the-13th-june (accessed 12 August 2013).
Beauvoir, Simone de. (1948) 1976. *The Ethics of Ambiguity*. New York: Citadel Press.
Beckford, James A. 2008. 'Secularism and coercive freedoms'. *The British Journal of Sociology* 59 (1): 41–45.
Benhabib, Seyla, Judith Butler, Drucilla Cornell, and Nancy Fraser. 1995. *Feminist Contentions: A Philosophical Exchange*. New York and London: Routledge.
Benhabib, Seyla. 1995. 'Feminism and Postmodernism.' In *Feminist Contentions: A Philosophical Exchange*. With Judith Butler, Drucilla Cornell, and Nancy Fraser, 17–34. New York and London: Routledge.
———. 2009. 'Claiming Rights across Borders: International Human Rights and Democratic Sovereignty'. *American Political Science Review* 103 (4): 691–704.
Benjamin, Walter. 1991. '<Theologisch-Politisches Fragment>'. *Gesammelte Schriften*, Band II (1): 203–204.
———. 1999. 'Critique of Violence'. *Selected Writings Volume 1, 1913–1926*, edited by Marcus Bullock and Michael W. Jennings, 277–300. Cambridge, MA: Harvard University Press.
Bergoffen, Debra. 2003. 'February 22, 2001: Towards a Politics of the Vulnerable Body'. *Hypatia* 18 (1): 116–134.
Bhatt, Chetan. 2008. 'The Times of Movement: A Response'. *The British Journal of Sociology* 59 (1): 25–33.
Bourke, Joanna. 2011. *What it Means to Be Human: Reflections from 1791 to the Present*. London: Virago.
Brady, Anita, and Tony Schirato. 2011. *Understanding Judith Butler*. London and Thousand Oaks: Sage.
Brassett, James. 2008. 'Cosmopolitanism vs. Terrorism? Discourses of Ethical Possibility Before and After 7/7'. *Millenium: Journal of International Studies* 36 (2): 311–337.
———. 2010. 'Cosmopolitan Sentiments after 9-11? Trauma and the Politics of Vulnerability'. *Journal of Critical Globalisation Studies* 2: 12–29.
Breen, Keith. 2007. 'Violence and Power. A Critique of Hannah Arendt on the "Political"'. *Philosophy & Social Criticism* 33 (3): 343–372.
Brown, Chris. 1992. *International Relations Theory: New Normative Approaches*. Hemel Hempstead: Harvester Wheatsheaf.
———. 2002. *Sovereignty, Rights and Justice: International Political Theory Today*. Cambridge: Polity Press.
———, Terry Nardin, and Nicholas Rengger, eds. 2002. *International Relations in Political Thought: Texts from Ancient Greece to the First World War*. Cambridge: Cambridge University Press.
Brown, Wendy. 2010. *Walled States, Waning Sovereignty*. New York: Zone Books.
———. 2012. 'Civilizational Delusions: Secularism, Tolerance, Equality'. *Theory & Event* 15 (2). http://muse.jhu.edu/journals/theory_and_event/toc/tae.15.2.html (accessed 19 April 2013).

Browning, Gary. 2011. *Global Theory from Kant to Hardt and Negri*. Basingstoke: Palgrave.

Bruce, Steve. 2013. *Politics and Religion*. Cambridge: Polity Press.

Bufacchi, Vittorio. 2007. *Violence and Social Justice*. Basingstoke: Palgrave Macmillan.

——. 2009. *Violence: A Philosophical Anthology*. Basingstoke: Palgrave Macmillan.

Caney, Simon. 2005. *Justice beyond Borders: A Global Political Theory*. Oxford: Oxford University Press.

Caruth, Cathy. 2001. 'An Interview with Jean Laplanche'. http://pmc.iath.virginia.edu/text-only/issue.101/11.2caruth.txt (accessed 2 March 2008).

Carver, Terrell, and Samuel A. Chambers, eds. 2008. *Judith Butler's Precarious Politics: Critical Encounters*. London and New York: Routledge.

Cavarero, Adriana. 2000. *Relating Narratives: Storytelling and Selfhood*. London and New York: Routledge.

Chambers, Samuel A. 2007. 'Normative Violence after 9/11: Rereading the Politics of *Gender Trouble*'. *New Political Science* 29 (1): 43–60.

——, and Terrell Carver. 2008. *Judith Butler and Political Theory: Troubling Politics*. London and New York: Routledge.

Chomsky, Noam. 2000. *Rogue States: The Rule of Force in World Affairs*. London: Pluto Press.

Church of England. 2012. *A Response to the Government Equalities Office Consultation—"Equal Civil Marriage"—from the Church of England*. www.churchofengland.org/media/1475149/s-s%20marriage.pdf (accessed 15 October 2012).

Cohen, Joshua, ed. 1996. *For Love of Country: Debating the Limits of Patriotism. Martha C. Nussbaum with Respondents*. Boston: Beacon Press.

Coole, Diana. 2008. 'Butler's Phenomenological Existentialism'. In Carver and Chambers 2008, 11–27.

Cover, Robert. 1983. '*Nomos* and Narrative'. *Harvard Law Review* 97 (1): 4–68.

Daddow, Oliver. 2009. *International Relations Theory*. Los Angeles and London: Sage.

Dean, Jodie. 2008. 'Change of Address: Butler's Ethics at Sovereignty's Deadlock'. In Carver and Chambers 2008, 109–126.

Derrida, Jacques. 1991. 'Signature Event Context'. In *A Derrida Reader*, edited by Peggy Kamuf, 82–111. London and New York: Harvester Wheatsheaf.

——. 1992. 'Force of Law: The 'Mystical Foundation of Authority'. In *Deconstruction and the Possibility of Justice*, edited by Drucilla Cornell, Michael Rosenfeld, and David Gray Carlson, 3–67. New York and London: Routledge.

——. 2005. *Rogues: Two Essays on Reason*. Stanford: Stanford University Press.

Donnelly, Jack. 2007. *International Human Rights*. Boulder and Oxford: Westview.

Douzinas, Costas. 2002. 'The End(s) of Human Rights'. *Melbourne University Law Review*, 445–465.

Edkins, Jenny. 1999. *Poststructuralism & International Relations: Bringing the Political Back In*. Boulder and London: Lynne Rienner Publishers.

——, Véronique Pin-Fat, and Michael J. Shapiro, eds. 2004. *Sovereign Lives: Power in Global Politics*. New York and Abingdon: Routledge.

Elshtain, Jean. 2003. *Just War against Terror. The Burden of American Power in a Violent World*. New York: Basic Books.

English, Richard. 2009. *Terrorism: How to Respond*. Oxford: Oxford University Press.

——. 2013. *Modern War: A Very Short Introduction*. Oxford: Oxford University Press.

European Court of Human Rights. *European Convention on Human Rights*. www.echr.coe.int/Documents/Convention_ENG.pdf. Strasbourg: European Court of Human Rights.

Evans, Brad. 2011. 'The Liberal War Thesis: Introducing the Ten Key Principles of Twenty-First Century Biopolitical Warfare'. *The South Atlantic Quarterly* 110 (3): 747–756.

Fanon, Frantz. (1965) 2001. *The Wretched of the Earth*. London: Penguin.

———. (1967) 1986. *Black Skin, White Masks*. London: Pluto Press.

Fausto-Sterling, Anne. 2000. *Sexing the Body: Gender Politics and the Construction of Sexuality*. New York: Basic Books.

Ferrarese, Estelle. 2011. 'Judith Butler's "Not Particularly Postmodern Insight" of Recognition'. *Philosophy and Social Criticism* 37 (7): 759–773.

Fine, Robert. 2006. 'Cosmopolitanism and Violence: Difficulties of Judgement'. *The British Journal of Sociology* 57 (1): 49–67.

———. 2007. *Cosmopolitanism*. London and New York: Routledge.

Fink, Carole. 2000. 'Minority Rights as an International Question'. *Contemporary European History* 9 (3): 385–400.

Finlay, Christopher J. 2009. 'How to Do Things with the Word "Terrorist"'. *Review of International Studies* 35 (4): 751–774.

———. 2010. 'Legitimacy and Non-State Political Violence'. *The Journal of Political Philosophy* 18 (3): 287–312.

Forrester, Duncan B. 1988. *Theology and Politics*. Oxford: Blackwell.

Foucault, Michel. 1987. *The Use of Pleasure: The History of Sexuality, Vol. 2*. London: Penguin.

———. 1991. 'Governmentality'. In *The Foucault Effect: Studies in Governmentality, with Two Lectures by and an Interview with Michel Foucault*, edited by Graham Burchell, Colin Gordin, and Peter Miller, 87–104. London: Harvester Wheatsheaf.

———. (1994) 2000. 'What is Enlightenment?' In *Ethics, Subjectivity and Truth: Essential Works of Foucault, 1954–1984, Vol. 1*, edited by Paul Rabinow, 303–319. London: Penguin.

———. 2002. 'What is Critique?' In *The Political*, edited by David Ingram, 191–211. Malden and Oxford: Blackwell.

———. 2003. *'Society Must be Defended': Lectures at the Collège de France, 1975–76*. London: Allen Lane / Penguin Press.

Fraser, Nancy. 1995. 'From Redistribution to Recognition? Dilemmas of Justice in a "Post-Socialist" Age'. *New Left Review* 212 (July/August): 68–93.

Frazer, Elizabeth, and Kimberly Hutchings. 2007. 'Argument and Rhetoric in the Justification of Political Violence'. *European Journal of Political Theory* 6 (2): 180–199.

———. 2008. 'On Politics and Violence: Arendt contra Fanon'. *Contemporary Political Theory* 7: 90–108.

———. 2011. 'Remnants and Revenants: Politics and Violence in the Work of Agamben and Derrida'. *The British Journal of Politics and International Relations* 13 (2): 127–144.

Gilson, Erinn. 2011. 'Vulnerability, Ignorance, and Oppression'. *Hypatia* 26 (2): 308–332.

Gutterman, David S., and Sara L. Rushing (2008) 'Sovereignty and Suffering: Towards an Ethics of Grief in a Post-9/11 World'. In Carver and Chambers 2008, 127–141.

Habermas, Jurgen. 2001. *The Postnational Constellation: Political Essays*. Cambridge: Polity Press.

———. 2006. *The Divided West*. Cambridge: Polity Press.

———. 2006. 'Religion in the Public Sphere'. *European Journal of Philosophy* 14 (1): 1–25.

Ha-Buah (The Bubble). Directed by Eytan Fox. Los Angeles, CA: Strand Releasing, 2006.

Haraway, Donna J. 1989. *Primate Visions: Gender, Race, and Nature in the World of Modern Science*. New York and London: Routledge.

———. 1991. *Simians, Cyborgs, and Women: The Reinvention of Nature*. New York and London: Routledge.

Hardt, Michael. 2002. 'Sovereignty'. *Theory & Event* 5 (4). http://muse.jhu.edu/journals/theory_and_event/toc/tae5.4.html (accessed 18 January 2013).

———, and Antonio Negri. 2000. *Empire*. Cambridge, MA: Harvard University Press.

Hegel, G. W. F. 1977. *Hegel's Phenomenology of Spirit*. Oxford: Oxford University Press.

Holusha, John. 2006. 'Bush says anthem should be in English'. *The New York Times*. 28 April 2006.

Honneth, Axel. 1995. *The Struggle for Recognition: The Moral Grammar of Social Conflicts*. Oxford: Polity Press.

House of Commons Northern Ireland Grand Committee. 2008. *Risk Assessment and Management of Sex Offenders*. 17 June. www.publications.parliament.uk/pa/cm200708/cmgeneral/nigc/080617/80617s01.htm#end (accessed 15 October 2012).

Huntington, Samuel P. 1997. *The Clash of Civilizations and the Remaking of World Order*. London: Simon & Schuster.

Hutchings, Kimberly. 1999. *International Political Theory: Rethinking Ethics in a Global Era*. London & Thousand Oaks: Sage.

———. 2003. *Hegel and Feminist Philosophy*. Cambridge: Polity Press.

———. 2010. *Global Ethics: An Introduction*. Cambridge: Polity Press.

Irish Catholics Bishops' Conference. *Family and Marriage*. www.catholicbishops.ie/family (accessed 15 October 2012).

Jacobsen, Eric. 2001. 'Understanding Walter Benjamin's *Theological-Political Fragment*'. *Jewish Studies Quarterly* 8 (3): 205–247.

Jagger, Gill. 2008. *Judith Butler: Sexual Politics, Social Change and the Power of the Performative*. London and New York: Routledge.

Jenkins, Fiona. 2007. 'Toward a Nonviolent Ethics: Response to Catherine Mills'. *differences: A Journal of Feminist Cultural Studies* 18 (2), 157–179.

———. 2011. 'Souls at the Limits of the Human: Beyond Cosmopolitan Vision'. *Angelaki: Journal of the Theoretical Humanities* 16 (4): 159–172.

Joppke, Christian. 2009. *Veil: Mirror of Identity*. Cambridge: Polity Press.

Kahn, Paul W. 2011. *Political Theology: Four New Chapters on the Concept of Sovereignty*. New York: Columbia University Press.

Kaldor, Mary. 2012. *New and Old Wars. Organised Violence in a Global Era*. Cambridge: Polity Press.

Kant, Immanuel. 1993. 'Zum Ewigen Frieden: Ein Philosophischer Entwurf'. In *Schriften zur Anthropologie, Geschichtsphilosophie, Politik and Pädagogik*, 191–251. Frankfurt: Suhrkamp.

Kaufman-Osborn, Timothy. 2008a. 'Gender Trouble at Abu Ghraib?' In Carver and Chambers 2008, 204–220.

———. 2008b. '"We Are All Torturers Now": Accountability after Abu Ghraib'. *Theory & Event* 11 (2). http://muse.jhu.edu/journals/theory_and_event/toc/tae.11.2.html (accessed 20 August 2011).

Keane, John. 2004. *Violence and Democracy*. Cambridge: Cambridge University Press.

Kirby, Vicky. 2006. *Judith Butler: Live Theory*. London and New York: Continuum Press.

Kirwan, Michael. 2008. *Political Theology: A New Introduction*. London: Darton, Longman and Todd.

Kleingeld, Pauline, and Eric Brown. 2006. 'Cosmopolitanism'. *Stanford Encyclopedia of Philosophy*. http://plato.stanford.edu/entries/cosmopolitanism (accessed 20 August 2011).

Krasner, Stephen D. 1999. *Sovereignty: Organized Hypocrisy*. Princeton: Princeton University Press.

———. 2001. 'Sovereignty'. *Foreign Policy* 122: 20–29.

Kristeva, Julia. 1991. *Strangers to Ourselves*. New York: Columbia University Press.

———. 1993. *Nations without Nationalism*. New York: Columbia University Press.

———. 2002. *Intimate Revolt: The Powers and Limits of Psychoanalysis*. New York: Columbia University Press.

Lacy, Mark J. 2007. 'Responsibility and Terror: Visual Culture and Violence in the Precarious Life'. In *The Logics of Biopower and the War on Terror*, edited by Elizabeth Dauphine and Cristina Masters, 61–82. Basingstoke: Palgrave Macmillan.

Lawrence, Bruce B., and Aisha Karin, eds. 2007. *On Violence: A Reader*. Durham: Duke University Press.

Lechte, John, and Saul Newman. 2012. 'Agamben, Arendt and Human Rights: Bearing Witness to the Human'. *European Journal of Social Theory* 15 (4): 522–536.

Lemke, Thomas. 2011. *Biopolitics: An Advanced Introduction*. New York and London: New York University Press.

Levinas, Emmanuel. 1996. *Basic Philosophical Writings*. Bloomington and Indianapolis: Indiana University Press.

Lilla, Mark. 2008. *The Stillborn God: Religion, Politics, and the Modern West*. New York: Knopf.

Little, Adrian, and Moya Lloyd. 2009. *The Politics of Radical Democracy*. Edinburgh: Edinburgh University Press.

Lloyd, Moya. 2005. 'Butler, Antigone, and the State'. *Contemporary Political Theory* 4 (4): 451–468.

———. 2007. *Judith Butler: From Norms to Politics*. Cambridge: Polity Press.

———. 2008. 'Towards a Cultural Politics of Vulnerability: Precarious Lives and Ungrievable Deaths'. In Carver and Chambers 2008, 92–105.

———. 2009. 'Performing Radical Democracy'. In Little and Lloyd 2009, 33–51.

Loizidou, Elena. 2007. *Judith Butler: Ethics, Law, Politics*. Abingdon: Routledge.

———. 2008. 'Butler and Life: Law, Sovereignty, Power'. In Carver and Chambers 2008, 145–156.

MacKenzie, Julie. 2009. 'Refiguring Universalism: Martha Nussbaum and Judith Butler—An Uneasy Alliance?' *Australian Feminist Studies* 24 (61): 343–358.

MacKinnon, Catharine A. 1996. *Only Words*. Cambridge, MA: Harvard University Press.

Mahmood, Saba. 2009. 'Religious Reason and Secular Affect: An Incommensurable Divide?' In Butler 2009d, 64–100.

Markell, Patchen. 2003. *Bound by Recognition*. Princeton and Oxford: Princeton University Press.

Masters, Cristina. 2009. 'Judith Butler'. In *Critical Theorists and International Relations*, edited by Jenny Edkins and Nick Vaughn-Williams, 114–124. Abingdon and New York: Routledge.

McBride, Cilian. 2013. *Recognition*. Cambridge: Polity Press.

———, and Jonathan Seglow. 2009. 'Introduction: Recognition: Philosophy and Politics'. *European Journal of Political Theory* 8 (1): 7–12.

McIvor, David. 2012. 'Bringing Ourselves to Grief: Judith Butler and the Politics of Mourning'. *Political Theory* 20 (10): 1–28.

McNay, Lois. 2008. 'The Trouble with Recognition: Subjectivity, Suffering, and Agency'. *Sociological Theory* 26 (3): 271–296.

McRobbie, Angela. 2006. 'Vulnerability, Violence and (Cosmopolitan) Ethics: Butler's *Precarious Life*'. *The British Journal of Sociology* 57 (1): 69–86.

Mills, Catherine. 2007. 'Normative Violence, Vulnerability, and Responsibility'. *differences: A Journal of Feminist Cultural Studies* 18 (2): 133–156.

Milton-Edwards, Beverley. 2009. *The Israeli-Palestinian Conflict: A People's War*. London and New York: Routledge.

Misztal, Barbara A. 2011. *The Challenges of Vulnerability: In Search of Strategies for a Less Vulnerable Social Life*. Basingstoke: Palgrave Macmillan.

Modood, Tariq. 2008. 'A Basis for and Two Obstacles in the Way of a Multiculturalist Coalition'. *The British Journal of Sociology* 59 (1): 47–52.

Murphy, Ann V. 2011. 'Corporeal Vulnerability and the New Humanism'. *Hypatia* 26 (3): 575–590.

Neal, Andrew W. 2008. 'Goodbye War on Terror? Foucault and Butler on Discourses of Law, War and Exceptionalism'. In *Foucault on Politics, Security and War*, edited by Michael Dillon and Andrew W. Neal, 43–64. Basingstoke: Palgrave Macmillan.

Nimni, Ephraim, ed. 2003. *The Challenge of Post-Zionism: Alternatives to Israeli Fundamentalist Politics*. London and New York: Zed Books.

Norris, Pippa, and Ronald Inglehart. 2011. *Sacred and Secular: Religion and Politics Worldwide*. Cambridge: Cambridge University Press.

Nussbaum, Martha C. 1996. 'Patriotism and Cosmopolitanism'. In Cohen 1996, 2–17.

———. 1997. 'Capabilities and Human Rights'. *Fordham Law Review* 66: 273–300.

———. 1999. 'The Professor of Parody: The Hip Defeatism of Judith Butler'. *The New Republic* 22: 37–45.

———. 2011. *Creating Capabilities: The Human Development Approach*. Cambridge, MA and London: Harvard University Press.

O'Brien, Cardinal Keith. 2012. 'We Cannot Afford to Indulge This Madness'. *The Telegraph*. March 3. www.telegraph.co.uk/comment/9121424/We-cannot-afford-to-indulge-this-madness.html.

Okin, Susan Moller. 1999. *Is Multiculturalism Bad for Women? Susan Moller Okin with Respondents*, edited by Joshua Cohen, Matthew Howard, and Martha C. Nussbaum. Princeton: Princeton University Press.

O'Neill, Shane, and Caroline Walsh. 2009. 'Recognition and Redistribution in Theories of Justice beyond the State'. *European Journal of Political Theory* 8 (1): 123–135.

Ophir, Adi. 2000. 'The Identity of the Victims and the Victims of Identity: A Critique of Zionist Ideology for a Post-Zionist Age'. In *Mapping Jewish Identities*, edited by Laurence J. Silberstein, 174–200. New York: New York University Press.

Passavant, Paul A., and Jodie Dean. 2001. 'Laws and Societies'. *Constellations* 8 (3): 376–389.

Patterson, Orlando. 1982. *Slavery and Social Death: A Comparative Study*. Cambridge, MA and London: Harvard University Press.

Peterson, Christopher. 2006. 'The Return of the Body: Judith Butler's Dialectical Corporealism'. *Discourse* 28 (2–3): 153–177.

Piterberg, Gabriel. 2008. *The Returns of Zionism: Myths, Politics and Scholarship in Israel*. London and New York: Verso.

Plummer, Ken. 2001. *Documents of Life 2: An Invitation to a Critical Humanism*. London, Thousand Oaks, and New Delhi: Sage.

Presbyterian Church in Ireland. 2012. *Presbyterian Church Opposed to Marriage Changes Proposal to be Debated at Stormont*. www.presbyterianireland.org/News/Article/2012/Presbyterian-Church-Opposed-to-Marriage-Changes-Pr.

Rawls, John. 1999. *The Law of Peoples*. Cambridge, MA: Harvard University Press.

Raz-Krakotzkin, Amnon. 2011. 'Jewish Peoplehood, "Jewish Politics," and Political Responsibility: Arendt on Zionism and Partitions'. *College Literature* 38 (1): 57–74.

Reid, Julian. 2006. *The Biopolitics of the War on Terror: Life Struggles, Liberal Modernity, and the Defence of Logistical Societies*. Manchester and New York: Manchester University Press.

———. 2011. 'The Vulnerable Subject of Liberal War'. *The South Atlantic Quarterly* 110 (3): 770–779.

Rengger, Nicholas. 2000. 'Political Theory and International Relations: Promised Land or Exit from Eden?' *International Affairs* 76 (4): 755–770.

Rushing, Sara. 2010. 'Preparing for Politics: Judith Butler's Ethical Dispositions'. *Contemporary Political Theory* 9 (3): 284–303.

Said, Edward W. 2003. *Freud and the Non-European*. London and New York: Verso.

Salih, Sara. 2002. *Judith Butler*. London and New York: Routledge.

Schippers, Birgit. 2009. 'Judith Butler, Radical Democracy and Micro-politics'. In Little and Lloyd 2009, 73–91.

———. 2011. *Julia Kristeva and Feminist Thought*. Edinburgh: Edinburgh University Press.

———. 2014. 'Violence, Affect and Ethics'. In *Butler and Ethics*, edited by Moya Lloyd. Edinburgh: Edinburgh University Press.

Schmitt, Carl. (1922) 2009. *Politische Theologie: Vier Kapitel zur Lehre von der Souveränität*. Berlin: Duncker & Humblot.

Scholem, Gershom. 1964.'"Eichmann in Jersusalem": An Exchange of Letters between Gershom Scholem and Hannah Arendt'. *Encounter* 22 (January), 51–56.

———. 1971. *The Messianic Idea in Judaism and Other Essays on Jewish Spirituality*. London: George Allen and Unwin Ltd.

Schwarzmantel, John. 2010. 'Democracy and Violence: A Theoretical Overview'. *Democratization* 17 (2): 217–234.

Scott, Joan Wallach. 2007. *The Politics of the Veil*. Princeton: Princeton University Press.

Sen, Amartya. 2004. 'Elements of a Theory of Human Rights'. *Philosophy & Public Affairs* 32 (4): 315–356.

Shulman, George. 2011. 'On Vulnerability as Judith Butler's Language of Politics: From *Excitable Speech* to *Precarious Life*'. *Women's Studies Quarterly* 39 (1–2): 227–235.

Sloterdijk, Peter. 2009. '*Rules for the Human Zoo:* A Response to the *Letter on Humanism*'. *Environment and Planning D: Society and Space* 27 (1): 12–28.

Sorel, Georges. (1908) 1999. *Reflections on Violence*, edited by Jeremy Jennings. Cambridge: Cambridge University Press.

Spivak, Gayatri Chakravorty. 2008. 'More Thoughts on Cultural Translation'. *Transversal* 6. http://eipcp.net/transversal/0608/spivak/en (accessed 6 March 2013).

Steiner, George. 1984. *Antigones: How the Antigone Legend has Endured in Western Literature, Art, and Thought*. New Haven: Yale University Press.

Summers, Larry. 2002. 'Address at Morning Prayers, September 17, 2002'. Harvard College, Office of the President. www.harvard.edu/president/speeches/summers_2002/morningprayers.php (accessed 6 February 2014).

Taylor, Charles. 1994. 'The Politics of Recognition'. In *Multiculturalism: Examining the Politics of Recognition,* edited by Amy Gutmann, 25–73. Princeton: Princeton University Press.

———. 2011. 'Why We Need a Radical Redefinition of Secularism'. In Butler 2011d, 34–59.

Thiem, Annika. 2008. *Unbecoming Subjects: Judith Butler, Moral Philosophy, and Critical Responsibility*. New York: Fordham University Press.

Thompson, Simon. 2006. *The Political Theory of Recognition: A Critical Introduction*. Cambridge: Polity Press.

Tully, James. 2004. 'Recognition and Dialogue: The Emergence of a New Field'. *Critical Review of International Social and Political Philosophy* 7 (3): 84–106.

United Nations Human Rights Council. 2009. *Report of the United Nations Fact-Finding Mission on the Gaza Conflict. Human Rights in Palestine and Other Occupied Arab Territories*. www2.ohchr.org/english/bodies/hrcouncil/docs/12session/A-HRC-12-48.pdf.

Victor, Barbara. 2004. *Army of Roses: Inside the World of Palestinian Women Suicide Bombers*. London: Robinson.

Vincent, Andrew. 2004. *The Nature of Political Theory*. Oxford: Oxford University Press.

Vries, Hent de, and Lawrence E. Sullivan, eds. 2006. *Political Theologies: Public Religions in a Post-Secular World,* New York: Fordham University Press.

Walker, R. B. J. 1993. *Inside/Outside: International Relations as Political Theory.* Cambridge: Cambridge University Press.

Walzer, Michael. 2004. *Arguing about War.* New Haven and London: Yale University Press.

Watson, Janell. 2012. 'Butler's Biopolitics: Precarious Community'. *Theory and Event* 15 (2). http://muse.jhu.edu/journals/theory_and_event/toc/tae.15.2.html (accessed 19 April 2013).

Weber, Cynthia. 1998. 'Performative States'. *Millennium: Journal of International Studies* 27 (1): 77–95.

———. 2005. *International Relations Theory: A Critical Introduction.* London and New York: Routledge.

White, Stephen K. 1999. 'As the World Turns: Ontology and Politics in Judith Butler'. *Polity* 32 (2): 155–177.

———. 2000. *Sustaining Affirmation: The Strengths of Weak Ontology in Political Theory.* Princeton and Oxford: Princeton University Press.

Wolfe, Cary. 2003. *Animal Rites: American Culture, the Discourse of Species, and Posthumanist Theory.* Chicago: University of Chicago Press.

Woodhead, Linda. 2008. 'Secular Privilege, Religious Disadvantage'. *The British Journal of Sociology* 59 (1): 53–58.

Young, Iris Marion. 2003a. 'The Logic of Masculinist Protection: Reflections on the Current Security State'. *Signs: Journal of Women in Culture and Society* 29 (1): 1–25.

———. 2003b. 'Feminist Reactions to the Contemporary Security Regime'. *Hypatia* 18 (1): 223–231.

Zehfuss, Maja. 2007. 'Subjectivity and Vulnerability: On the War with Iraq'. *International Politics* 44: 58–71.

———. 2009. 'Poststructuralism'. In *The Ashgate Research Companion to Ethics and International Relations*, edited by Patrick Hayden, 97–111. Farnham: Ashgate.

Zivi, Karen. 2008. 'Rights and the Politics of Performativity'. In Carver and Chambers 2008, 157–169.

———. 2012. *Making Rights Claims: A Practice of Democratic Citizenship.* Oxford: Oxford University Press.

Žižek, Slavoj. 2008. *Violence: Six Sideways Reflections.* London: Profile Press.

Index